Southern Methodist University

Southern Methodist University

Founding and Early Years

MARY MARTHA HOSFORD THOMAS

SMU PRESS • DALLAS

Library of Congress Catalog Card Number: 74-80248
ISBN: 0-87074-138-1

Published with the Assistance of a Grant

presented through

COLOPHON

The Associates of SMU Libraries

To

my father

HEMPHILL MOFFETT HOSFORD

whose devotion, loyalty, and service

to Southern Methodist University

have remained constant

Contents

Illustrations are grouped following pages 52 and 116

Foreword

PUBLICATION OF THIS first serious—and successful—study of the first forty years of Southern Methodist University delights me, as it will all who have watched the university grow. Those who did not know SMU "back when . . ." will find answers to questions that have puzzled them. Later generations may marvel at how great an oak sprang from the little acorn.

It is neither a "loving hands" production, nor a dry-as-dust chronicle, replete with statistics and official records. Neither does it fall into the debunking category, although it does not follow the George Bancroft dictum of omitting whatever does not point toward the "onward-and-upward" developments. Rather the author follows the advice Doctor Johnson gave the man who painted his portrait, "Paint me as I am, warts and all."

Mary Martha Hosford Thomas, associate professor of history at Jacksonville State University, Alabama, has reresearched and rewritten for publication a work that she initiated as a doctoral dissertation at Emory University, SMU's sister institution.

Historians agree that institutional history is difficult and educational history is full of special problems and pitfalls. A writer personally involved with the institution may be tempted to follow the "sweetness and light" pattern or to indulge personal biases. Dr. Thomas has skillfully steered between those two traps.

By heredity and participation, she belongs to SMU. Her father registered there as a student on the opening day in 1915, was graduated at the Fourth Annual Convocation, and was an SMU professor of mathematics when she was born. After several years at the University of Arkansas, he returned to SMU and was Vice-President and Provost when she was graduated, with honors in history, in 1948. As her writing proves, these ties did not blind her but only sharpened her perception.

My own connection with the institution is longer than hers and more continuous than her father's. I entered under the first President, was graduated under the second, joined the history faculty under the third, and served under the fourth and fifth Presidents until mandatory retirement. Although I lived through most of her story, I confess that her diligence has enlightened me, corrected distorted recollections, and vivified many forgotten things.

This book, in short, explains how the institution evolved during four decades from a glittering hope into a permanent reality.

HERBERT GAMBRELL

Dallas, Texas
March, 1974

Preface

CHARTERED in 1911, Southern Methodist University formally opened its doors in 1915. This volume describes the educational situation in Texas during the early years of the twentieth century which prompted the Methodists to build a new university in Dallas. Despite the difficulties of early years, the institution was well located and was able to flourish as Dallas and Texas prospered. During its first twenty-five years the university grew from a small liberal arts college of 706 students, with a theological and music school attached, to a university of nearly 4,000 students, with law, engineering, and business schools added. There was a corresponding growth in faculty, endowment, and buildings. During these years the university was primarily a regional institution with students drawn from the immediate area and a faculty largely dominated by SMU's own graduates. By 1940 the institution was on the threshold of a new stage of development in which it would lead rather than mirror the culture of the community, and would attract students and faculty from a wider geographical area.

I am deeply indebted to many people in writing this account of SMU. Professor J. Harvey Young of Emory University patiently and constructively directed the study when it began as a Ph.D. dissertation. Many former faculty members of Southern Methodist University were generous with their time and information. Herbert Gambrell, Professor Emeritus of History, willingly answered unlimited questions and searched out correspondence and records to substantiate major and minor points. Hemphill Hosford, Provost Emeritus of the university, provided me with the original interest in the subject and was always ready to aid with his measured judgment in evaluating personalities and events. Edwin D. Mouzon, Jr., Professor Emeritus of Mathematics, and Samuel W.

Geiser, Professor Emeritus of Biology, also provided me with valuable information.

Chancellor Willis Tate allowed me to use the records in the Office of the President. Phoebe Davis, Secretary of the University, and Betty Connatser, then secretary in the President's office, extended to me every courtesy in my research. The staff of both Fondren and Bridwell libraries, especially Elizabeth Glaab of Fondren and Kate Warnick of Bridwell, were most generous with their time and assistance.

MARY MARTHA HOSFORD THOMAS

Jacksonville, Alabama
March, 1974

Southern Methodist University

CHAPTER I

Education in Texas
In the Early 1900s

THE CHARTERING of Southern Methodist University in Dallas in 1911 represented the second attempt by Texas Methodists to establish a central university supported by Methodists from the entire state. Of six colleges founded earlier, two were still operating in 1900, but neither was adequate to meet the changing needs of the twentieth century. Progressive leaders of Methodist education realized by the early 1900s that if the church was going to play a significant role in education it would need a university centrally located in a city, with broad support both from the immediate area and from the Methodist church at large. Such a university was projected in 1911, its founders imbued with dreams that it would become a great educational institution in the Southwest.

The new university was located in the rapidly growing area of North Texas and was supported by the city of Dallas, the Methodist conferences in Texas and in adjoining states, and the Methodist Episcopal Church, South, which chose to establish at SMU its only school of theology west of the Mississippi. The decision to establish the university had not been easily made, nor did its survival seem preordained. SMU could have gone the way of the earlier unsuccessful Methodist colleges, but by the twentieth century a number of external factors came into play which aided the university in its formative years.

The years prior to World War I saw two fortunate developments in higher education in Texas. During these years Texas began to offer adequate financial support to its public colleges and universities, and their phenomenal expansion created a favorable climate for private education as well. This period also saw the transition from the old-time college of the nineteenth century to the emerging university of the twentieth century. As a number of the older schools added professional, scientific, and technological courses to the curriculum and sought new knowledge through research, they ceased to be colleges and gradually achieved university status. These developments were to influence the formation and early years of Southern Methodist University.

Status of Public Education

Texas, along with the rest of the South, was slow in meeting its educational needs. Until the period of Reconstruction, Texas had virtually no free public elementary schools. The radical Republicans who came to power after the Civil War organized a "militaristic system" that was "foreign to the sentiments of the people of Texas."[1] This Reconstruction system imposed a property tax for the support of schools, made attendance compulsory, granted "autocratic powers" to the superintendent, and provided for education of black children.[2] When the Republicans were defeated in 1873, public education reverted to its chaotic antebellum conditions. But by the 1880s this reaction had run its course, and Texans began again to offer some support for free popular education. In 1883 the state constitution was amended to authorize an *ad valorem* state tax especially for school purposes. In the following year the state school law was completely rewritten in order to provide for adequate administration of the schools and for the division of the state into school districts. The chief effect of these new laws was to establish the concept that "education was no longer regarded as a public or private charity but as a necessary function of government and natural right of every child."[3] Progress was slow and was largely confined to the towns and cities. Because of the poor showing of its country schools, in 1901-2 Texas ranked no higher than twenty-eighth and as low as forty-second among the states of the nation, according to the various tests that were used to evaluate school systems.[4]

Developments were even slower in secondary education. The first high school in Texas was established in 1875, but ten years later there were only sixteen in the whole state. By the turn of the century virtually all the towns and cities possessed high schools, but not until 1911 did the legislature pass a rural high school law which provided secondary education for rural areas. As a result the period during World War I saw a tremendous increase in the number of high-school graduates.

In the field of higher education Texas had established by the early years of the twentieth century a state university, an agricultural and mechanical college, and a collection of state teachers colleges. These institutions, however, had meager beginnings and severely limited financial support. Enrollments were low, and faculty members were few and for the most part insufficiently trained and ill paid. The average bachelor's degree from some of these colleges was worth little more than a good high-school diploma. Between 1900 and 1920 the colleges and universities proliferated at a rate much greater than the growth of population and wealth. In 1900 Texas had only three state institutions of higher learning; in 1920 there were nine, and in 1925 eleven. During this period enrollment of students increased 582 percent, while the population increased only 53 percent.[5]

Efforts to establish a state university had begun as early as 1839, but it was not until 1883 that the University of Texas was opened in Austin and 1891 that its medical school in Galveston began operation. For a number of years the university received only limited financial support, but by the time of World War I it had expanded its organization so that it could truly claim university status. The institution was not, however, entirely free of political interference and invasion of academic freedom. In 1915 Governor James E. Ferguson vetoed appropriations for the university because he objected to the way in which the law school funds were used. The following year Ferguson demanded that the Board of Regents dismiss the newly chosen president of the university as well as several faculty members. The regents, supported by the ex-students association (and incidentally the faculty of the newly formed Southern Methodist University) refused to yield. This fight between Ferguson and the university was then eclipsed by a movement to impeach him.[6]

The oldest state institution of higher learning was Texas Agricultural and Mechanical College, founded in 1876 at Bryan under the authority of the famed Morrill Act.[7] In the beginning the work of the college tended to be literary rather than scientific; but because of demands by the Texas State Grange, an experimental farm was established and the study of agriculture and mechanical arts was emphasized. Like other institutions of its kind, Texas A & M was slow to define subjects that would be taught and slow to secure staffs well enough trained to do effective teaching and research. At one point, indeed, Texas A & M had a chair of chemistry, natural science, and agriculture, occupied by a doctor of divinity.[8]

The first teacher-training institution in Texas was Sam Houston Normal Institute, built at Huntsville in 1879 and founded partly with a contribution from the Peabody Fund. This fund had been set up at the end of the Civil War by George Peabody, a highly successful eastern merchant and banker, who was especially concerned with the educational needs of the South. The efforts to organize and maintain the public schools would have been seriously handicapped without this support. Barnas Sears, special agent for the fund, played a large role in developing interest in education in general and teacher training in particular in Texas. Under Sears's leadership, plans were laid for the first normal institute; a sum of $6,000 was provided by the fund's board, plus an annual subsidy for maintaining the school. In the educational confusion of the post-Reconstruction years, Sears also rendered effective aid to the cause of public education in the state. Additional state normal schools were founded at Denton, Commerce, San Marcos, and Nacogdoches, and these evolved into the state teachers colleges of the early 1920s.

In short, Texas education saw its first substantial growth during the first two decades of the twentieth century. This expansion created a favorable background for the new university that the Methodists hoped to build.

Old-Time Colleges and New Universities

The second major development in higher education which affected the founding and subsequently the early growth of SMU was the development of the newer university from the old-time college. The colleges and universities in Texas at the turn of the century bore the characteristics of the small, rural college. The concept of the newer university, which had become accepted in the North and East in the 1870s and 1880s, was just beginning to make headway in the South and in Texas by the time of World War I.[9] As a result, the founders of SMU were strongly influenced by the aims and goals of the university movement and attempted to incorporate them into their university. They were not entirely successful, however, because the university also showed characteristics of its college heritage.

The old-time college was the creature of a relatively simple, agrarian community, a community of settled ways and of ancient truths. The colleges of the nineteenth century, which covered the landscape as neighborhood schools, were primarily interested in developing character and imparting moral concepts. The schools were small, with six to a dozen teachers and one hundred to three hundred students. The prescribed curriculum of the old-time college was limited to the traditional liberal arts. The primary function of education was to get into the heads of the undergraduates as much as possible of this body of truth which was thoroughly permeated with the Christian perspective. Teaching was carried on partly by lecture, mostly by recitation, and it was literal-minded and all too frequently uninspired. So long as the curriculum was limited, no great amount of equipment was necessary; and a school in the country, where living was cheap, could attract more students than an urban college. Many a provincial American college was little more than a high-school-grade academy with an intensive program of classical studies learned by rote.[10]

These colleges responded slowly to social changes, largely because they were not knit organically into the fabric of economic life. Having college training was an advantage, but it was simply not necessary in the nineteenth century to go to college to become a doctor, a lawyer, or a teacher, much less a successful politician or businessman. Only very gradually, as society needed more highly trained people, did a more intimate relationship develop between the college and career, between school and society.

Typical of these old-time colleges were the church-supported schools which flourished briefly throughout Texas. In the nineteenth century each denomination had a dozen or more such colleges; but by the turn of the century the number had decreased, and those that remained moved to more populated areas to seek broader financial support. The Baptists, having united in a state organization, consolidated Baylor University, established in 1845, with Waco University at Waco in 1886. In 1869 the Cumberland Presbyterian church organized Trinity University at Tehuacana to take the place of two smaller colleges, and in 1902 it moved the university to Waxahachie in the heart of a rapidly growing area.[11] Texas Christian University, which was moved to Fort Worth in 1910, traced its origin from a small college founded at Thorp Springs in 1872 by two brothers who were both ministers of the Christian Disciples church. After repeated attempts to establish a permanent institution, the various Methodist conferences united in the establishment of Southwestern University at Georgetown in 1873.[12]

Southwestern University, the central university of Texas Methodism, bore all the characteristics of the old-time college. It was located in a small town twenty miles north of Austin in a thinly populated area. The 1900 catalogue described the location as ideal:

Being removed ten miles from any of the great thoroughfares of travel, the town is easily protected from contagious diseases. . . .
It is likewise free from many of the evil influences of the cities. Prohibition has been strictly enforced for a number of years.[13]

When opened for its first term in 1873, Southwestern had 33 students of college level and a faculty of three. Ten years later, under the leadership of Francis Asbury Mood, the enrollment had risen to 197 and the faculty had increased to 15.[14] All during the nineteenth century Southwestern maintained, in addition to its college program, a "Ladies' Annex" which taught music, art, and "expression," or use of the voice, and a "Fitting School" which offered work of high school level. The number of preparatory students nearly always exceeded those at the college level. The classical curriculum was required of all students, regardless of their interest, and the faculty members were responsible for a wide variety of courses without respect to their training. When Robert S. Hyer came to the university in 1882, he said "that he did not occupy a chair of a professor, but a divan, for he taught geology, chemistry, biology, and his beloved physics and any other subjects, when a teacher was needed."[15] Southwestern grew slowly; the population around Georgetown failed to increase rapidly, and the college tended to be overshadowed by the University of Texas at Austin. As a result, by 1912 there were only 31 faculty members and 374 college students.[16]

Toward the end of the nineteenth century a revolutionary turning point was reached in the history of American higher education. In the older institutions of the North and East, the age of the college had largely passed by this period and that of the university was dawning. The old-time college had all the truth it needed in revealed religion and the humanist tradition, but the new universities were permeated with a philosophy of research and inquiry. They called not simply for the preservation and transmission of knowledge, but for research to enlarge the body of knowledge. The president of Harvard, Charles W. Eliot, introduced the elective system, which swept "through the American college like a gust of fresh air"[17] and did away with many of the undesirable features of the college—its rigidity, its archaic content, its stern emphasis on discipline, and its reliance on rote learning. The new university emphasized inquiry and criticism and desired faculty and students to deepen themselves in a special field of learning. The elective principle facilitated the growth of the college into a university and helped raise American scholarship in many fields to a level equaling that of European scholarship.

The new American university followed largely the example set by the German university of a fundamental attachment to a graduate faculty of arts and sciences constituting a body of scholars who, with their students, pushed forward the frontiers of pure knowledge. As a result, the pattern the American university followed was that of a central school of arts and sciences surrounded by the professional schools not only of law, medicine, and theology, but also of teacher training, agriculture, business, fine arts, and engineering. It was this pattern which, in due course, Southern Methodist University sought to follow.

Secularization, another important hallmark of these new universities, was manifested mostly in the personnel changes that accompanied the university revolution. Unlike the presidents of old colleges, the leaders of the new education were not clergymen, but secular and scientific men with wide experience and cosmopolitan interests. The complex organization needed men of affairs who possessed administrative skill. The clergy also faded from their former preponderance on boards of trustees, replaced by bankers, merchants, industrialists, and railroad men. Although the new leaders of higher education were not consciously secular, their bent toward the practical considerations of life caused them to foster those aspects of the university which slowly eroded religious and sectarian influence in higher education. Eventually, SMU would feel this influence too, although more gradually than was true of nonreligious institutions.

The University of Texas, founded in 1883, was the first institution in the state to achieve university status. During the last years of the nineteenth century and the early years of the twentieth, the practical, technical, scientific, and professional aspects of the new higher education were emphasized there by the broadening of the curriculum and the offering of courses for immediate and practical use. In 1894 the College of Engineering was inaugurated, in 1906 the School of Education, in 1910 the Graduate School, and in 1922 the School of Business Administration.[18]

The first private institution which could claim university status was Rice Institute[19] in Houston. William Marsh Rice in his founding indenture of 1891 directed the trustees to establish an "Institute for the Advancement of Literature, Science, and Art." In academic terms this meant that the program should include instruction at the graduate and postdoctoral level, as well as research activities. In accordance with these ideas the first president stated in the opening ceremonies in 1912 that "the new institution thus aspires to university standing of the highest grade."[20] In order to achieve these ends Rice gave the institute some seven million dollars, the largest endowment in the South. Graduate work was begun in 1915 and the first Ph.D. degree was awarded by Rice Institute in 1918.

The founders of Southern Methodist University were fully familiar with this new university movement and aspired to such status for their institution. They realized that if Methodism was to play a significant role in Texas education, it would need a true university, not an old-time college.

CHAPTER II

The Methodists
And Higher Education to 1910

AGAINST THE RAPIDLY CHANGING educational background, leaders of the Methodist church began in the early years of the twentieth century to reevaluate their colleges and universities. Methodist consideration of various plans to provide quality institutions of higher education began in 1906 with an educational convention and culminated in 1910 with the formation of a commission to set up a new university. It was this 1910 commission that made the decision to build a new university in Dallas, but not until the educational leaders had undergone a period of soul-searching to find what they hoped would be the correct solution to the educational problems of the church.

Methodist Colleges and Universities to 1910

In 1900 the Methodist church in Texas operated one university, Southwestern in Georgetown, and one college, Polytechnic in Fort Worth, as well as six junior colleges and four preparatory schools.[1] These were the only schools which had survived from the more than thirty that had been established in the previous century. Southwestern was ranked a Class A institution by the church and was supposed to be the central Methodist university. It had been founded in 1873 by a prominent Methodist educator, Francis Asbury Mood, who served as its first president. Southwestern was considered the direct heir of four earlier colleges: Rutersville, established in 1840; Wesleyan College, located in San Augustine in 1844; McKenzie College, which had opened in 1841 as a school for boys near Clarksville and eventually evolved into a college; and Soule University, located in Chappell Hill in 1856. Soule University represented a slightly more ambitious attempt to organize an institution of higher education, but the Civil War caused the school to close. Mood had been originally selected to be president of Soule, with the task of re-opening the university after the Civil War. He soon realized that if the school was to be successful, it would have to be relocated near the center of the state and be supported not by just one or two Methodist conferences but by all of them in the state. These plans underlay an educational convention called in 1870 which eventually established Southwestern University at Georgetown.[2]

Despite an agreement made by the Methodist conferences at this convention that no further schools would be established to compete for funds, Polytechnic College was founded at Fort Worth in 1891 and received support from three of the five conferences. The purpose of this college was to offer training in vocational as well as academic fields in order to equip its students for useful occupations, such as working in the railroad shops of Fort Worth.[3] These ambitious plans were not realized, and the college remained smaller and less well endowed than Southwestern. In 1912 Polytechnic had a faculty of 27 and a total enrollment of 623, but of these only 210 were of college rank.[4]

The Methodist conferences in Texas had attempted to establish colleges on a financial base that was far too limited. They clearly should have been more cautious in "taking such ephemeral schools under their patronage."[5] The conferences had little understanding about how much financial backing was required to maintain a university, and they were also naïve as to what constituted an institution of learning. In other words, these early attempts to establish colleges in Texas produced institutions typical of the old-time colleges that were passing out of existence.

Despite the interest in education that the establishment of these schools indicated, not all early Methodists were fully committed to the cause of higher education. In fact, a strong prejudice against education for ministers and higher education in general was a prominent characteristic of Methodism during its early history.[6] The basic evangelical emphasis of the message of the church, together with the rapid development of membership, which caused the need for ministers to outstrip the supply, tended to discourage the formation of an educated clergy. As a result Methodism had been regarded as an enemy of learning. Methodism's greatest boast had been that she had used in her pulpits men "from the plow handles and from the forge, the colliers of Newcastle and the pioneers of the West."[7] A minister wrote in 1875, "I have been on the Whiteboro Circuit six weeks. Had 103 conversions; . . . baptized 154; . . . preached 48 times and exhortations without number. . . . Have been in Texas two years; not fully satisfied; thought of going back home this fall; but Texas will develop a young preacher faster than the 'Vanderbilt.' "[8] Prior to 1875 or 1880 American Methodism did little to encourage theological education.

While the church was in the pioneer stage, it appealed to the rank and file on the western frontier and was able to get along without educated clergymen and laymen. Vanderbilt University, established by the church in 1875 under the leadership of Bishop Holland N. McTyeire, had a Biblical Department which later became a School of Theology. But even at this date there were church leaders who believed that the way to learn to preach was to preach; and if a student took a theological course, it was likely he did so in opposition to the advice of the older men in the ministry. As Methodists rose in the middle class, however, they made middle-class demands, such as that for a college education. Therefore, by the late nineteenth century higher education was receiving wider support.

The Methodists in the South did not become united behind theological education until the controversy over the church's control of Vanderbilt. In 1914 the church lost a lawsuit to retain control of the university, and it became independent of the church. Under the leadership of Bishop Warren Candler and Bishop Edwin D. Mouzon, the church chose to sponsor two new theological schools, one east of the Mississippi at Emory University and the other west of the Mississippi at Southern Methodist University. With these two strong bishops behind theological education and the establishment of two new schools of theology, opposition to theological education rapidly dwindled.

The early years of the twentieth century saw a number of other changes take place in Texas and in Methodism which made progressive leaders in the church question more seriously the adequacy of existing educational institutions. During this period the population of the state increased considerably, as the cattleman's frontier advanced across the Great Plains and the eastern part of the state became a more thickly settled area. A new population center developed in North Texas around Dallas and Fort Worth that rivaled the older towns of Galveston, San Antonio, and Houston. The total population of the state increased from 818,549 in 1870 to 3,896,542 by 1910.[9] There was a corresponding growth in the Methodist church west of the Mississippi. In 1872 the church could claim only 144,836 members, but by 1910 this number had increased to 599,440, a total gain of some 400 percent. The number of Methodists in Texas alone had increased from 44,748 in 1872 to 276,149 in 1910.[10]

This population growth made the need for a theological school west of the Mississippi more apparent than ever. Vanderbilt University was simply too far away from the Southwest; and besides, after 1914 the church had no authority over the university. Even before this occurred, however, leaders in the church, such as Bishop Seth Ward, the first native Texan to be elected bishop, recognized this need. A short time before his death Bishop Ward said to the president of Southwestern, Robert S. Hyer, "I am not fully satisfied with conditions at Vanderbilt and if I were satisfied I think that our Church needs another theological school and I am sure it should be located in Dallas."[11] The bishop planned to begin a campaign to secure $100,000 for a theological school, but his death in 1909 put an end to these plans. A Summer School of Theology at Southwestern had been organized earlier by Bishop Ward to fill this need in part, but he realized the inadequacy of a ten-day course of study. In 1908 Southwestern had set up a two-man Department of Theology with Edwin D. Mouzon as chairman, but even with this excellent leadership the department failed to grow.

Despite the early hopes that Southwestern would grow into a real university, it was felt that the institution had no great future and that Methodism could play no major part in education unless it changed its base of operation. Georgetown had a population of approximately 3,000 and, as the catalogue had boasted, was located in an inaccessible rural area. The residents of the town had been generous, but they simply did not have the resources to support a university. The endowment was a little over $200,000,[12] which was totally inadequate; the school was forced to operate mainly on income from student fees. As a result, in a period of rising educational costs the university ran a deficit every year. The successful operation of more expensive schools, such as law, medicine, and theology, would have been extremely difficult or impossible.

Around 1905 Hyer discussed with the General Education Board of New York the possibility of the university's receiving a grant from the board. This board had been organized by John D. Rockefeller primarily to aid southern education. Wallace Buttrick, the executive secretary of the board, was not encouraging about the future of Southwestern. "You Methodists," he told Hyer, "can never build a great university here. You must move to a city before the General Board will agree to help you."[13]

From its various studies, Hyer was told, the board had come to the conclusion that a university should be located so that 50 percent of its students, as well as 50 percent of its funds for building and endowment, could come from a fifty-mile radius.[14] Only 20 percent of Southwestern's students came from a fifty-mile radius.

The Plan to Move Southwestern

The most obvious course of action for the church was to move Southwestern to Dallas in the rapidly growing area of North Texas, where Methodist membership was strongest. Of Dallas, Buttrick said, "It is the best unoccupied territory in the South. Someday someone will build a university in Dallas and you Methodists are the people who should do it."[15] Dallas was developing into a manufacturing, distributing, financial, and cultural center. The city had good railroads and interurban connections, which would enable students to travel to a university; the highly developed financial services, which qualified Dallas to be one of the twelve regional headquarters for the Federal Reserve System,[16] would aid in financing a university; and the city high schools were producing graduates capable of doing college level work. Dallas was also the location of Southwestern's medical school, which had opened in 1903. If Dallas was the proper location for a medical or theological school, it was also logical to consider it for the main campus.

The idea of moving Southwestern was quietly discussed for ten to twelve years before the issue became public or any action was taken. The editor of the *Texas Christian Advocate*, George C. Rankin, commented in 1910:

There has scarcely been a single year during the twelve that we have been editor of the paper that someone has not tried to break into these columns with an article upon the question of removing Southwestern University. But up to the beginning of this Conference year we studiously declined to permit the question to be discussed in the Advocate.[17]

If such speculation had been made public, it would have endangered the current support of Southwestern and made its future uncertain. Indeed, Hyer remarked that every time a new building was proposed for the university a question arose about the advisability of constructing further buildings on a campus that was poorly located.[18] This situation obviously posed problems for the administration of Southwestern.

Methodist education was fortunate to have Robert Stewart Hyer as president of Southwestern. Hyer had come to the university in 1882 as professor of science, after having graduated from Emory College in Oxford, Georgia. His coming to Texas may be said to mark the beginning of education in the physical sciences in the state. A decade after his arrival he began a series of experiments on X ray and ether waves which promised significant results;[19] but the demands of the presidency, which he assumed in 1898, left him little time for research. In 1904 he designed the first wireless station in Texas, which transmitted messages a mile. Hyer was primarily a scholar; and although he was for twenty-three years a college president, he regarded administrative functions as secondary to the calling of a teacher. "He was a charming conversationalist, a delightful essayist, and a singularly effective public speaker." He also had an "air of innate distinction that was heightened by his reserve and dignity."[20]

As early as 1906 Hyer was convinced that Southwestern should eventually be located in Dallas. He was doubtless impressed by the observations of Buttrick, which simply confirmed what he already knew. At the General Conference of the church held in Birmingham, Alabama, in 1906, Hyer discussed the proposition with a prominent layman of Birmingham, who promised to subscribe $25,000 to a university in Dallas. Hyer wrote, "I realized that there was a man interested in the same thing that had so long interested me and that he was willing to do something for it that I could not do."[21] In the same spring Hyer had a long and earnest conversation with H. A. Boaz, president of Polytechnic College, while they were waiting for a train after attending the inauguration of the president of the University of Texas. The two agreed to arrange a joint session of the trustees of their respective institutions to discuss moving Southwestern to North Texas. Hyer told Boaz that if either Dallas or Fort Worth would offer one hundred acres of land and $300,000 he would favor making such a move.[22] The meeting never materialized, because Hyer was persuaded by Dean C. C. Cody that such discussions would interfere with the building plans for Mood Hall, a new dormitory.

All talk of changing the location of Southwestern was kept under cover until 1909. Indeed, at a Texas Education Conference held in Dallas during April, 1906, the subject did not appear in any of the official reports, despite the avowed purpose of the conference: to consider "new conditions which compel new adjustments and new methods of procedure" to make "the educational thought within the Church . . . harmonize with that in society at large."[23] The only reference to the issue was a passionate defense of Southwestern University by John M. Barcus, a member of its board and a longtime supporter of the institution. He said:

> The wisdom of our system and the necessity for a strict adherence to it is more apparent today than ever before. Some contend that a system adopted thirty years ago does not meet the demands of Texas in the twentieth century, but stubborn facts demonstrate that such a conclusion is false. . . . What we need, therefore, is not a new system, but a faithful adherence to the one already adopted. Let us not allow any scheme, however alluring, to divert us from our original ideal.[24]

The convention did recommend the appointment of an educational commission which would supervise all schools and direct educational plans; but some conferences failed to approve this resolution, and it never went into effect. The sentiment was not yet strong enough, nor was the time ripe to make any drastic changes in the educational structure.

Another attempt was made in the fall of 1909 to establish an educational commission to study the situation, but this too was unsuccessful. Nathan Powell, minister of the church at Brenham and member of the board of Southwestern, proposed his plan for a commission to the five conferences; but only one of them approved it and appointed a commission. Powell evidently hoped to move Southwestern to Fort Worth and combine it with Polytechnic, a move which had some appeal to Boaz and Fort Worth businessmen. But Powell was not the man to succeed in this endeavor. He had not laid his groundwork carefully, and the church leaders, such as Edwin D. Mouzon and Frank Seay, were openly antagonistic to him.[25]

Meanwhile, the needs of Southwestern could not be ignored. The university had only one building for both classes and offices, inadequate space even for a small college. Hyer asked Frank Reedy, bursar of the university, to make plans for an administration and library building or at least an addition to the main building.[26] Reedy's fertile mind designed a building far beyond anything Hyer had visualized. His plan called for a large memorial rotunda with smaller rooms grouped around it to house administrative offices, a library, an auditorium, a gymnasium, a swimming pool, a bowling alley, and numerous other reception rooms and parlors.[27] The entire building would be a memorial to Bishop Seth Ward, the first native Texan elected bishop, who had died just the year before in Japan. The projected cost was $250,000. The students showed great enthusiasm for the plan and promised to raise $20,000 for the building.

At first Hyer would not accept Reedy's plan because he knew there would be fierce opposition to constructing such an elaborate building on a campus that many Methodists believed was poorly located. Hyer told Reedy:

> This scheme will disturb Methodism as it has never been disturbed in Texas. It will precipitate events that may be in the best interest of the university and Church, but it may bring both of us to an early grave and cause much bitterness.[28]

Despite these misgivings Hyer allowed the plans to be developed by a Fort Worth firm of architects and presented them to the Methodists after a laymen's conference held in Dallas in February, 1910, when they were approved by the board and enthusiastically received by the alumni, who promised to raise $100,000 for the building.[29]

It is difficult to believe Hyer was completely serious about the memorial building because of his often stated desire to move the university and because of his subsequent actions. He had long expressed his feelings privately that a great university could never be built in Georgetown; and, even while the memorial building plans were being discussed, Hyer went to Dallas to encourage the chamber of commerce to take some action before the building was constructed.[30] He was doubtless torn between two conflicting desires and was forced, because of his position, to play a dual role until the issue was brought out in the open. One contemporary observer felt that Hyer was playing a "double hand" and that while he appeared to want to build up Southwestern in Georgetown, he was secretly working to move it to Dallas.[31] After Boaz proposed to move Southwestern to Fort Worth, Hyer ceased to be ambivalent and took definite steps to move the university to Dallas.

Dr. John O. McReynolds, dean of the Southwestern medical school, commented as soon as he saw the plans that "the Memorial Hall should be erected in Dallas instead of Georgetown."[32] Boaz responded in a more definite way. He proposed that Southwestern move to Fort Worth and combine with Polytechnic College, with the city of Fort Worth providing $250,000. But only the name of Southwestern and the Ward Memorial Fund plus some of the faculty members would be brought to Fort Worth, while a Class A college would remain in Georgetown. Boaz justified this suggestion by commenting, "There is unrest and lack of unity in our educational circles in Texas. We desire to eliminate all chance of friction, to thoroughly consolidate all our interests, and to forever set at rest this problem."[33] Hyer replied that he would be willing to recommend to the board a reasonable proposal, but that this offer was not sufficiently attractive. He pointed out that "to a great university" the campus of Polytechnic "would be worth but little." "Your campus," he noted, "is already well taken up with buildings, and these were designed to meet the pressing necessities of a struggling college, and are not at all suitable for a university."[34] Hyer felt that at the least it would take $300,000 to persuade Southwestern to move, but that the timing was inopportune because of the plans for the Ward Memorial Building. After a lengthy correspondence in which each man defended the value and merit of his respective school, Boaz made a second offer of one hundred acres of land and $300,-000 for a new campus.[35]

As soon as these letters appeared in the *Texas Christian Advocate*, as well as in the secular press, Methodists from all parts of the state took sides. Some were highly critical, feeling that Boaz had brought up an issue certain to divide Methodists and weaken the schools they already had. Boaz said that he knew the step would be misjudged and misunderstood and he realized that he would be censured and abused. "But," he persevered,

having profound convictions on this question, and feeling assured that we represented a great majority of thinking men of Texas Methodism, the movement was undertaken. The cost was counted, the action deliberately taken and we were willing to endure cheerfully the fires of adverse criticisms and await the verdict of history to justify the wisdom of the course.[36]

In the exchange of letters between Hyer and Boaz, Hyer appeared to be opposed to moving Southwestern, when in reality he was only opposed to its being moved to Fort Worth:

When a tree has grown in a given place for a few years it may easily be transplanted. . . . But not so with a tree that has grown thirty-six years in the same place, has borne much fruit and is again full of blossoms, leaf, and ripening fruit. . . . Such a tree can be removed only by a great force, and the force may be used in such a way that the tree will never live again. . . . If we are to remove the old tree from Georgetown we must make very careful preparations to do it in the right way.[37]

In this last sentence, as well as in his later actions, Hyer revealed his inner thinking.

The proposition made by Boaz to move Southwestern to Fort Worth and create a Methodist educational center there aroused the interest of Dallas, which is just exactly what Hyer had hoped for. He saw his opportunity to move the university to Dallas and took positive steps in that direction. He immediately arranged a meeting in Little Rock, Arkansas, between Wallace Buttrick of the General Education Board and representatives of Dallas, Mayor S. J. Hay, Dr. John McReynolds of the medical school, and J. R. Babcock, the secretary of the Dallas Chamber of Commerce. In a private conference an agreement was worked out to attempt to establish a university upon a foundation consisting of three distinct parts, the General Education Board, the city of Dallas, and the Methodists of Texas. The city of Dallas would raise $300,000 and provide land for a campus; the Methodists in Texas would collect $500,000 from the 300,000 members in the state; and, when this had been done, the General Education Board would contribute the final $200,000 of the first one million needed to found the university.[38]

The General Conference of the Methodist Episcopal Church, South, met in May, 1910, at Asheville, North Carolina, shortly after the Little Rock meeting. Both Hyer and Boaz attended this meeting, where they consulted with a large number of the Texas delegates and leaders of the church, such as Bishop James Atkins, the Reverend John M. Moore, and the newly elected Bishop Edwin D. Mouzon.[39] A consensus was reached among the Texas Methodists that the university should be moved to Dallas and financed as outlined by Hyer. Hyer then wrote to the Dallas Chamber of Commerce indicating that if they were to make an offer of a site and $400,000[40] to the board of Southwestern, he could practically assure them that the offer would be accepted. Hyer was confident that Southwestern would be moved, and he was willing to put the weight of his influence behind a Dallas offer.[41]

When it became obvious that the sentiment of the Texas delegates favored Dallas as a location, Boaz withdrew Fort Worth's offer and for the time being worked to move Southwestern to Dallas. He had always made it clear that he felt the university should accept the best offer, whether it was from Fort Worth or Dallas.[42] Boaz must be given credit for starting the ball rolling, for originating the controversy which resulted in the establishment of Southern Methodist University. He opened up the issue for discussion and prevented the memorial building in Georgetown from being constructed, which was doubtless just exactly what Hyer hoped he would do.

Dallas had less than a month to organize the campaign to raise the $400,000. After preliminary meetings, a mass meeting of Dallas citizens was held on May 27, 1910. The entire city showed considerable enthusiasm for the university. "It was not confined to one class of people, though the local Methodists certainly did their share to make the undertaking a success. Jews and Gentiles, Protestants and Catholics, saints and sinners, all joined forces in a common cause."[43] A university was viewed as an asset in increasing the economic value and wealth, as well as the intellectual life, of the community. Immense streamers stretched across Main Street bearing the inscription, "We need $400,000 to get Southwestern. Will bring from 3,000 to 5,000 students here annually and millions of money."[44] Despite the overstatement of the benefits, "the city of Dallas had never before been so aroused over any enterprise for their city."[45] At the May 27 meeting $145,000 was subscribed in one hour and thirty minutes. The finance chairman, Horatio H. Adams, as well as Babcock, Mayor Hay, and Dr. McReynolds, was delighted and felt confident the balance could be easily raised.

In the meantime the citizens of Georgetown and some of the alumni of Southwestern became greatly alarmed at the possibility of losing the university. When Boaz first made his proposal to Hyer to move the university to Fort Worth, few people in Georgetown attached any serious significance to the proposition. They had heard such proposals in the past, and they assumed the new one would blow over. But when it became clear that the caucuses of the Texas delegation at the Asheville conference favored moving the university to Dallas, and when Dallas began taking steps in this direction, the citizens of Georgetown saw the seriousness of what portended. They sent a special committee to Dallas to attend the mass meeting of May 27 and to enter their protests against such actions. The delegation spoke at this meeting, but the "speakers and committee were treated with the most painful courtesy and stilted politeness." The *Georgetown Commercial* referred to the "sale of old Southwestern" and charged that Dallas regarded the whole affair as a business proposition. "The 'authorities' were going to sell Southwestern and Dallas simply wanted to buy it."[46] No action was taken upon their protest by the Dallas citizens, since the decision on the question of moving the university was up to the board of trustees and the annual conferences.

Dallas did manage to raise the money by June 10 and sent a committee of Adams, McReynolds, and Babcock to present its offer to the board of Southwestern. The proposal consisted of a site of fifty acres and $325,000 in valid subscriptions plus real estate contiguous to the fifty acres valued at $75,000, with the understanding that if the real estate was not regarded as the equivalent of cash, the citizens of Dallas would make good the deficit.[47] After a heated debate the board voted twenty-one to thirteen *against* accepting the Dallas offer. This decision doubtless came as a surprise to those who favored moving the university; they had simply underestimated the strength of the opposition. Because of the divided opinion both a majority and a minority report were issued. The main argument of the majority report was that the church had a binding contract with citizens of Georgetown to maintain permanently the university of Texas Methodism in Georgetown, and this contract was a valid, subsisting, and binding contract that "could not be breached either in law or morals." The entire issue, the report also added. "brings confusion into the councils of the Church, arrests the generosity of prospective donors and discourages every promising plan of progress." The minority report held that since it was impossible to build a real university in Georgetown, the offer of Dallas should be accepted. There was no reason to be bound by the actions of the founding fathers; for, it stated, "if we are so bound, then all progress is forever stopped."[48]

This division between the majority and minority members was largely one of geography. Those who opposed the move were from Georgetown, Houston, San Antonio, and other parts of South Texas. The vocal leader of this group was John M. Barcus, whose family had been attending Southwestern since 1878 and who objected vehemently to the church's violating a compact and throwing "away the foundation which ha[d] cost nearly forty years of toil and prayer and sacrifice, to begin in a new place with no assurance of success."[49] The minority of the board were largely from North Texas and included Judge M. M. Brooks, who was reelected board chairman despite his minority views, J. M. Peterson, presiding elder of the Dallas district, and, of course, Robert S. Hyer.

Hyer's position was a most difficult one. Considering his actions in trying to move the university and the subsequent vote of the board, he could have been asked to resign, but he was not. But many of his friends in Georgetown and on the Southwestern faculty turned against him, considered him a traitor to the university, and criticized him severely for his position. Hyer's daughter wrote that the "papers in Georgetown had been outspoken in denouncing [her] Father personally. They even suggested that he might be egged some night if he were out alone."[50] Nevertheless, he did not falter from his position that Texas Methodism would be far more effective with a university in Dallas. His decision took tremendous courage because he was fifty years old, not a wealthy man, and ran the risk of losing everything by choosing the wrong side. The board did instruct him to stop talking and working for the removal of the university, and he did.[51] Hereafter the active leadership fell into other hands. Once Hyer left Georgetown in June, 1911, to become president of the newly formed Southern Methodist University, he never returned there.[52]

Because the issue was so divisive, the decision of the board was not considered final, and the whole problem was thrown into the lap of the annual conferences which were scheduled to meet in the fall. Both sides organized their forces during the summer of 1910. A meeting of those who favored moving the university was held July 5, in Waco, to draft a proposal to be presented to the conferences. It was proposed that the academic and theological departments of Southwestern be transferred to Dallas with the Ward Memorial Fund, that a Class A college be maintained at Georgetown, that a woman's college replace Polytechnic, that a uniform course of study be established, and that the whole system be under the control of the annual conferences. H. A. Boaz was appointed to visit each conference and urge the adoption of the proposal.[53]

Those who opposed the move met belatedly on September 13, also in Waco, to draft their proposal. The paper decried the crisis that threatened the educational interest of Methodism and could cause it to lose what had taken forty years to build.[54] It argued against moving the institution because the church was bound legally and morally by the terms of the contract, because of the central location of Georgetown in the state, because all liquor and saloons were banned from Georgetown, and because "the seal of divine approval ha[d] been set upon the school."

The residents of Georgetown and the alumni of Southwestern who lived in South Texas were extremely noisy in their denunciation of the move. The Georgetown papers were outspoken and intemperate. The *Texas Christian Advocate* printed letters from readers on the subject which fanned the fires of controversy all during the hot Texas summer. The advocates of Southwestern felt so strongly that they threatened to sue the church if the conferences voted to move the university. C. C. Cody, dean of Southwestern, wrote, "Georgetown will have no more scruples about maintaining its legal rights, than will the Church hesitate, if necessary, to carry the Vanderbilt case to the civil courts."[55] G. W. Barcus said that "the citizens of Georgetown and hundreds of other Methodists all over Texas [would] go into court to prevent"[56] the moving of Southwestern.

By the end of the summer, the opposition to moving the university had become so strong that even if the conferences had voted in favor of the plan, the church would have been hopelessly divided and the university in Dallas would have been off to a precarious start. The move would be difficult enough without the opposition of the highly vocal residents of Georgetown. If a university in Dallas was to be a success, it would need the backing of a united church. In order to achieve this and eliminate the opposition a new approach was needed to the whole educational problem. The solution that was hit upon was to leave Southwestern in Georgetown and build a completely new central Methodist university in Dallas. Early in August this solution was discussed by Dr. McReynolds and Hyer. The Dallas Chamber of Commerce assured McReynolds, "A proposition for the establishment of a great Methodist university at Dallas, without regard to Southwestern University, meets every requirement and is entirely satisfactory to the Chamber of Commerce and to the subscribers to the fund."[57] Such a university would be equally eligible for funds from the General Education Board. Others were beginning to voice the same idea. If Southwestern does not want to be moved, leave it where it is, and, "in the language of Nehemiah, 'Let us rise up and build' a great university at Dallas."[58]

Another factor which must have influenced the decision to build a new university was the realization that Southwestern was simply not worth moving. The only gain from the move would be the name and charter of the university in addition to the Ward Memorial Fund of $76,000. There was no plan to move the entire faculty, although some would probably move in any event. The benefits of moving the university would not be worth the cost of a division within the church. On the other hand a new university would have the advantage of a fresh start toward university status without any of the encumbrances of the old-time college traditions.

The idea of a new university received favorable support from Bishop James Atkins and from H. A. Boaz. Bishop Atkins was especially interested in a solution to the controversy, since he was to preside over three of the five conferences and did not wish to have an unruly dispute on his hands. He suggested the creation of an educational commission of two clergymen and two laymen from each conference that would have plenary power to establish a university, to determine its location, and to serve as its trustees.[59] Boaz wrote out the first draft of this proposal one Sunday afternoon in September while the bishop was visiting him. After the draft was enlarged and perfected, it was presented to the conferences in the following form:

Whereas the development of the State of Texas, and the progress of the Methodist Episcopal Church South, and the educational sentiment in Texas are such that the demands for education cannot be met by the existing institutions with their present facilities. . . .

Whereas we believe that the present demand and the future growth of the Methodism of Texas and the Southwest will justify the establishment of a complete University by the Methodists of this region, THEREFORE BE IT RESOLVED: that this conference [shall establish a commission which] . . . shall have full power to consider and determine the question of the establishment of a University as above described, and to proceed to establish the same as soon as they deem wise.

This Commission shall have the power to consider and determine the location of said university. . . .

That if this Commission shall find that the establishment of such a new institution is impracticable, it is empowered and directed to take such steps for the enlargement of some existing institution or institutions as will meet the pressing and growing demands of our times.[60]

This proposal to create a commission to consider the educational needs of the church had been deliberately kept quiet. Just a few days before the meeting of the first conference, an editorial in the Georgetown paper commented:

There is grave suspicion that the Dallas politician intends to spring some surprise proposition on the Methodist conference. There have been several dark lantern meetings lately. The Methodists of Texas are still in the dark. A proposition that will not stand the light and publicity is not a fair proposition.[61]

Doubtless the advocates of the commission felt their resolution would have a better chance to succeed if it were not known in advance so no opposition to it could build up.

The commission proposal was to be one of three propositions placed before the meetings. The majority report, which advocated keeping Southwestern as the central Methodist institution, and the minority report, which favored moving the university to Dallas, were also to be considered. The educational commission was proposed as a compromise, a method of resolving this issue. It recommended that a new university should be built in a place selected by the commission but if it should not be feasible to do this, existing institutions could be expanded. It opened the way for a constructive solution to the problem without dividing the church and was accepted overwhelmingly by the conferences.

The first of the conferences to meet was the West Texas Conference, which held its sessions in Austin, October 26-31, 1910. The vote of this conference was crucial, because it would set a precedent for others and because it contained Austin and San Antonio, two pro-Southwestern strongholds. The debate on the issue lasted nearly two days and became exceedingly heated. The final vote was 104 in favor of creating the commission and 46 opposed to it. In order to appease the Southwestern sentiment the following amendment was passed:

It is hereby expressly stated that we endorse the work being done in the Southwestern University at Georgetown and instruct said commissioners to make provisions for its continuance with the present equipment and as far as practicable provide for the enlargement of the same in the future.

With this vote, success for the creation of the commission was assured.[62]

Opposition to the proposal was slight in both the Central Texas and North Texas conferences. The first of these conferences included Georgetown, but its influence was more than counterbalanced by Fort Worth, which hoped it might attract the new university. John M. Barcus of Georgetown debated with H. A. Boaz in a long and lively discussion. But the vote indicated strong approval of the commission by 175 to 20.[63] The North Texas Conference, in which Dallas was located, also heavily favored the commission by a vote of 167 to 17.[64] The Northwest Texas Conference and the Texas Conference, after relatively little debate, approved the commission unanimously.[65]

This decision obviously came as a disappointment to the advocates of Southwestern, but there was little they could do but accept it. Barcus tried to turn defeat into victory by stating that he was full of "hope and enthusiasm for the future" because "everything [was] to be left in Georgetown as it [was].[66] Barcus felt that the new university had little chance of success, and he was confident that Southwestern would continue to receive support from its alumni and the conferences.

Others were less confident of the future of Southwestern, since it would no longer be the central Methodist university and would have to share conference funds with the new institution. The greatest damage done to Southwestern, as Dean Cody saw it, was the erosion of public confidence in the institution because of the unfavorable publicity it had received. Rumors circulated that the degrees granted by the university would be degraded. Cody feared that it would be difficult to collect funds, that attendance would decrease, and that some of the faculty would resign.[67] Southwestern *was* hurt by all the talk about moving the university, but not to the extent that Cody feared.[68]

In the end the church did not forsake Southwestern. It maintained a Class A institution in Georgetown and continued contributing funds for its support. Even after the decision was made to establish SMU in Dallas, Bishop Mouzon and others were concerned about the future of Southwestern. The bishop was interested in securing for the university a new president who was a scholar and could maintain Class A standards and also one who had not opposed the new university. Eventually, C. M. Bishop was selected. Southwestern continued its existence as a small liberal arts college of the Methodist church. It did go through a trying period, but it survived and served a different need and purpose than that of the proposed full-scale university in Dallas. There was room for both types of institutions in the scheme of Methodist education.

CHAPTER III

Planning and Financing
The University

The Work of the Educational Commission

THE EDUCATIONAL COMMISSION that was elected by the five Texas conferences in the fall of 1910 began its work in January of the following year and within four months decided to build a new university, selected a site, elected officers for the institution, and began a campaign to raise the first million dollars. These decisions were not difficult to make, because the issues had been fairly well resolved the previous fall. It was widely accepted that the commission would establish a new university in Dallas with Robert S. Hyer as its president. These events came about, but not without some opposition.

When the commission convened in Austin on January 18, 1911, Bishop James Atkins was elected president. In his opening address, Bishop Atkins said that there were two fields of inquiry and action clearly marked out by the annual conferences:

> The first of these relates to the question as to whether or not the Methodist Episcopal Church, South . . . needs and is able to build and operate a university properly so called. The second has to do with the relation of our existing institutions of learning to each other and to the proposed university, to the end that a complete educational system may be established and maintained.[1]

He made it evident that he believed the church had "an absolutely immitigable obligation" to maintain a university, that there was a definite need for such an institution to serve the area west of the Mississippi where ten million people lived, and that three hundred thousand Methodists in the state of Texas should be able to raise a million dollars for endowment. There could be little doubt about the action of a commission moved by such sentiments as these.

28

However, the advocates of Southwestern made one last attempt to preserve for their university the status of the central institution of Methodism. John M. Barcus, the outspoken defender of Southwestern, again pleaded its cause; Dean C. C. Cody laid before the commission the present possessions at Georgetown and the dangers of beginning anew; and R. G. Mood, son of the founder of the institution, opposed any change in the existing educational system.[2] These last-minute pleas fell upon deaf ears.

By this time Fort Worth as well as Dallas was prepared to make an offer to the commission. William Capps, a prominent Fort Worth attorney, presented a proposition of 465 acres of land and $250,000. The Dallas proposal of 200 acres of land and $300,000 was offered by Frank McNeny, a realtor who had conducted the negotiations for the land. Both of these proposals were later increased, at least partly because Bishop Atkins told McNeny he would like to have 2,000 acres instead of 200.[3] After hearing these offers the commission voted unanimously to "build a great university" and made plans to meet in Dallas on February 2 and in Fort Worth on February 3 to inspect the two sites.

Before adjourning, the commission adopted resolutions commending the work of both Southwestern and Polytechnic and promised continued support of both schools. Plans were also made to inaugurate a campaign to raise one million dollars for endowment and to correlate all Methodist schools and colleges in the state.[4]

By February 1 the citizens of Dallas had increased their original offer and added two additional areas for consideration. The best Dallas proposal was for an area adjacent to Highland Park, a new residential site north of Dallas, and now included 300 acres of land and $300,000 in cash. Two other sites were considered: 300 acres in Oak Cliff and 50 acres in East Dallas offered by a prominent Methodist layman, R. S. Munger.[5] Dr. John O. McReynolds, dean of Southwestern's medical school who headed the citizens committee, conducted the commissioners to the various locations and entertained them during the day.

The next day the commissioners traveled by interurban to Fort Worth, where they received a tremendous welcome. The businesses of the city closed between nine and ten o'clock, and the employees lined the streets waving American flags to welcome the commission. Twenty-five leading citizens were waiting in twenty-five automobiles, and each commissioner was thus individually chauffeured to inspect the various locations.[6] As this parade of cars passed each public school, the children stood out front to greet the delegation.[7] At the banquet that evening Robert S. Hyer said, "I know the real meaning of the Fort Worth spirit now. I came into contact with it today for the first time. I was dazed, almost fascinated."[8]

Not only was Fort Worth's reception of the commission more spectacular and enthusiastic than that of Dallas, but its offers were considerably larger. Fort Worth also made three proposals. The first was 100 acres of land south of Hemphill Street, half interest in 1,100 acres, and $300,000 in cash. The second offer was $500,000 in cash, 100 acres of land, and half interest in 1,500 acres, all located near Southwestern Baptist Theological Seminary. The last offer, probably the best, was in Arlington Heights and comprised 100 acres, a third interest in 1,500 acres, and $400,000 in cash.[9]

The Fort Worth newspapers failed to mention, however, that no money had actually been pledged and that citizens desiring to attract the new university expected to obtain the cash from the sale of land.[10] This system had serious drawbacks, because the land would have to be developed before it could be offered for sale. It also assumed there would be a market for it. All of this would take time and money and would delay the opening of the university indefinitely. On the other hand, Dallas's offer of $300,000 was based upon more tangible assets. Citizens had actually conducted a campaign in May, 1910, and had subscribed over $300,000, some in cash, most, doubtless, in pledges, but nevertheless, more likely to be collected and available than the "cash" offers of Fort Worth.

Despite this discrepancy, the Dallas people were extremely worried that they might lose the university they had assumed was theirs. Frank McNeny convinced Dr. McReynolds and H. H. Adams, who had been chairman of the original committee to raise the cash, that Dallas would simply have to offer more land. McNeny favored asking W. W. Caruth, who owned 7,000 acres north of the proposed campus, for an additional donation. When Caruth came down to the office of the Methodist Publishing House, where the commissioners were meeting, he was taken into the office of William C. Everett, manager of the publishing house, to meet with McReynolds, Adams, Hyer, and Bishop Atkins. Caruth promised a half interest in 725 acres of land in order to secure the university for Dallas.[11]

The additional offer, presented to the commission by Dr. McReynolds, increased Dallas's land offer from 300 acres to 662½ acres. Immediately the Fort Worth people, led by H. A. Boaz, strongly objected to this addition to the original offer, because the bids were supposed to have closed at ten o'clock the night before. Boaz was so persistent that Bishop Atkins finally said, "Dr. Boaz, sit down and stay down."[12] The bishop then ruled that Fort Worth could submit an additional bid also and the bids would remain open until two o'clock that afternoon. The Fort Worth advocates felt they had been dealt with unfairly, but they made no additional offers; they had gone their full length the first time.[13] One of the Fort Worth papers published a cartoon which showed Dallas and Fort Worth at a game of poker in which Dallas could view Fort Worth's hand through a mirror named the "Methodist Commission."[14] Bishop Atkins explained that he had wanted the church to have the choice of the best possible offers.

The commissioners considered these offers for two days before reaching a decision. They figured and refigured what the various proposals were really worth. At one point Boaz erected a blackboard on which he estimated Dallas's best offer as $1,130,250 and Fort Worth's as $1,700,000. Other commissioners objected to his method of arriving at these figures.[15] According to Dr. McReynolds, Bishop Atkins took a rosy view of Texas land investments and encouraged commissioners to favor Fort Worth.[16] However, a majority of the commissioners, including James Kilgore and J. W. Blanton, were opposed to the church's being involved in a holding company for real estate which would be operated by the university and the Fort Worth committee.[17] This drawback of the Fort Worth offer was an important factor. But perhaps fundamental to the decision was the fact that Dallas was heavily favored from the beginning. Wallace Buttrick's statement about Dallas's being the best unoccupied territory was repeated again and again. In any case, the vote in favor of Dallas's Highland Park vicinity offer was fourteen to four.[18] The commissioners chose wisely. The site was six miles from downtown Dallas in a sea of grass with few trees and no houses in sight. It took vision to see this as an ideal location, but in a relatively few years Dallas was to grow up to and beyond the campus.

At the third session of the commission held April 13-14, 1911, Robert S. Hyer was elected president of the yet unnamed university by "a rising vote that was unanimous and enthusiastic."[19] Since Hyer had long been working for just such an institution and was the leading Methodist educator in the state, his election as president came as no surprise.[20]

H. A. Boaz was chosen to be vice-president,[21] with the primary function of raising money for the institution. Boaz had made a name for himself by rescuing a small struggling church from debt and by raising money for a congregation that needed a new building. His first task was to organize a campaign for a million dollars. Boaz was hesitant to leave the presidency at Polytechnic College, because the college had a debt which he feared would be hard to liquidate. However, Hyer "almost demanded the election of Boaz to help him in harmonizing the different elements in the Texas educational problems."[22] The special talents of both were needed in this endeavor. Hyer, a reserved scientist of unusual academic understanding, needed Boaz, who was a man of action, a capable speaker, and an institutional financier. Despite the need each had for the other, neither was to be entirely happy in the collaboration.

The commission elected Frank Reedy bursar of the university.[23] Reedy had come to Southwestern in 1909 with the idea of starting to college at the age of thirty-six, but Hyer persuaded him that he would be worth more to the university in the office than in the student body. As a result Reedy became "Bursar, Registrar, Business Manager, Advertising Agent, Secretary, Collecting Agent, Promotion Director, Bookkeeper, etc., etc."[24] With his warm, outgoing personality and cordial manner he was well suited to public relations work. His job for the new university was not only to keep the records but also to advertise and promote the institution.

A name for the university was not immediately or easily found. Bishop Atkins strongly urged that *Texas Wesleyan University* be adopted. In fact on two occasions he made hour-long speeches on the subject. The commission would have liked to oblige the bishop, because he had given much of his time and effort in traveling from North Carolina for the meetings. Indeed, at one point the name was actually adopted; but the following day the commissioners rescinded their action.[25] There were a number of objections. The name "had fallen with a thud on Dallas ears" when it was publicized; the students of TWU would be known as "tightwads," and the term *Wesleyan* had simply been used too often in the Methodist colleges of the East and North. After several other unsatisfactory suggestions, such as *Southland University, Trans-Mississippi University,* and *Central University,* the name of *Southern Methodist University* was chosen by a narrow margin.[26] It was a logical choice, indicating the church affiliation of the university, yet at the same time appealing to a wider area than the state of Texas.

The final piece of business at this meeting was an attempt to bring all the schools of Texas Methodism into "one harmonious system" and under the control of one board of trustees. The head of the system was to be Southern Methodist University. Southwestern University would become Southwestern College, which would be more in keeping with its true status; but it would remain Class A in rank. Polytechnic College would be changed into the Woman's College of Texas Methodism as soon as SMU opened.[27] This closely knit system never came into being, nor would it have been harmonious if it had. Southwestern refused to change its name and desired to keep its own board. Polytechnic did become a woman's college in 1915, but it too had its own board after that date. The idea of operating all the schools as a unit was shortly dropped and never considered again.

In a casual, almost offhand way, the commission recommended that Southwestern's medical school be given to the newly organized Southern Methodist University.[28] On the surface it might appear that this would be an easy way for SMU to acquire its first professional school. However, this gift was a liability rather than an asset. The guiding spirit of the medical school, which had been organized in 1903, was Dr. John O. McReynolds. The school did not have a salaried staff; all of the thirty-two faculty members were practicing physicians. Its only source of income was its fees, which in 1909 were $7,150. It was only nominally connected with Southwestern University, largely to protect the trustees from liability. The famed Flexner Report on medical education published in 1910 was highly critical of the medical school:

> The school possesses a new building, externally attractive but wretchedly kept. It contains a disorderly and incomplete chemical laboratory, a small amount of new physiological apparatus, a single laboratory fairly well equipped for pathology and bacteriology, and an ordinary dissecting room. There is a "reading room" with nothing to read. The lecture rooms are bare, except for chairs; in a corner of one of them is an abused manikin.[29]

The report closed by saying that the school was without resources, without ideals, without facilities, and that the state was badly overcrowded with just the kind of doctor that the school was engaged in producing. Nevertheless, the Methodists continued for another five years to try to make the school operational.

Finally, in June, 1915, the long overdue decision was made when the board voted to "suspend operations for one year." The medical school never again opened; and after the building was sold to the State Dental

College for $18,000, the Methodists could put their full energies behind their new university.

Ownership and Control of SMU

The ownership and control of Southern Methodist University went through a series of changes before the university formally opened. The first charter, filed April 17, 1911, listed the five Texas conferences as the sole owners of the university and named a board of trustees from these conferences.[30] These trustees were then confirmed at the conference sessions of 1911, and the board was organized March 29, 1912. The immediate affairs of the university then passed into the hands of the trustees.[31]

By the following year four additional conferences desired to join in support of the new Methodist university. As a result the charter was amended to include the German Mission, the East Oklahoma, the West Oklahoma, and the New Mexico conferences.[32] These conferences had early expressed a desire to support a Methodist university in North Texas. In fact, one of the reasons for locating the university in Dallas was that it could receive support from the entire Southwest, which would broaden its financial base.

In May, 1914, the Supreme Court of Tennessee decided that the church no longer had any rights in Vanderbilt University. This decision was the result of a prolonged battle between a strong-minded president, James H. Kirkland, and an equally strong-minded bishop, E. E. Hoss, who had tried to enforce control by the church over the university. These rights had long lain dormant; and the revival of insistence upon them constituted a threat to the freedom and independence of the university, as Kirkland saw it. The church brought suit and lost.[33] This left the church without a school of theology.

At the General Conference of the church in 1914, the church took steps to remedy the situation. An educational commission was created with authority to establish and provide maintenance and endowment for two schools of theology, one east of the Mississippi and one west of the Mississippi. The report specifically recommended Southern Methodist University to the commission.[34] The following summer the commission met in Dallas and acted upon the recommendation, making Southern Methodist one of the two connectional institutions for the church at large. The other selected was Emory College, which was fortunate to receive a million dollars from Asa Candler and $500,000 from the city of Atlanta.[35] Eventually, after the report of this commission was officially adopted at the General Conference in May, 1918, Southern Methodist University was supported by conferences in Texas, Oklahoma, Arkansas, Louisiana, Missouri, and New Mexico.[36] With this action the support of the church for the theology school was put on firmer ground, and the theology school's status in the eyes of the church increased.

The loss of Vanderbilt to the church was closely connected with the establishment of Emory University, but contrary to popular belief it had little to do with the selection of Southern Methodist as the connectional institution for the church west of the Mississippi. As has been shown,[37] the Methodists in the Southwest and especially in Texas felt the need for a school of theology long before the controversy at Vanderbilt was resolved by a court decision. Since Methodism had grown so rapidly in Texas, the need for increased theological educational facilities was evident. Indeed, this need was one of the factors behind the establishment of SMU. It is probable that an informal understanding was reached between the church leaders and the backers of SMU at the General Conference in 1910 to the effect that a university established in North Texas would be chosen as the location for the church's official school of theology.[38] Given the decision that the church would have two schools of theology, there was no doubt that SMU would be selected. There simply was no other possible choice. SMU was the only Methodist university in the Southwest.

In 1939 when the two branches of the Methodist church were reunited and the breach caused by the division over slavery in 1844 was finally closed, SMU was made the property of the South Central Jurisdiction of the Methodist church. Since then all the annual conferences in this area have had members on its Board of Trustees and participate in its ownership and control.[39]

Financing the University

The administrative staff of the newly created university moved into offices in the Methodist Publishing House on Commerce Street lent to them by the manager, William C. Everett. The affairs of the university were conducted from there until 1914, when the first building on the campus was near enough to completion for use.[40] The first tasks facing the team of Hyer, Boaz, and Reedy were to lay plans for the buildings and campus and, at the same time, to begin a campaign to raise a million dollars.

Before a money-raising campaign could be effective, however, specific plans for buildings needed to be made and presented to the Methodists. This job fell to President Hyer, who had received plats of campuses and arrangements of buildings from several universities.[41] The *Advocate* wrote a prominent article about Hyer's consulting with David Starr Jordan of Stanford University and Pratt Judson of the University of Chicago.[42] These two relatively new universities had been founded by generous benefactors with huge sums of money. Leland Stanford had given his university $20 million, and John D. Rockefeller ultimately made the University of Chicago beneficiary of $30 million.[43] Hyer and Southern Methodist University did not fit into the same category as Chicago or Stanford. Instead of one enormously wealthy benefactor, SMU had to rely on the Methodists of Texas and the citizens of Dallas, who contributed money in relatively small amounts. Nevertheless, President Hyer designed a campus and buildings on a grand scale that would cost the kind of money Chicago and Stanford had. His goal was to build a "great university," not just another little Methodist college. His dreams were bigger than his resources and nearly brought the university to disaster. But in the end his goal prevailed; and the institution could truly claim university status by the 1960s, although perhaps not quite in the way Hyer had visualized.

The scope of Hyer's dreams is most clearly evident in his plans for the buildings and campus. These plans, made during the summer of 1911 and designed by a Chicago firm of architects, provided for some thirty buildings spread over the 133-acre campus.[44] Hyer was determined the university would not just grow but would have a definite plan of development. He wrote:

I had given some considerable thought to the general plans for this great university, . . . for I realized that it would be very unfortunate to do anything out there until we had arranged for a harmonious group of buildings, properly related to each other, not only in architectural design, but in all mere matter of location, so as to make the condition of their accessibility by the student body as near ideal as possible.[45]

He planned for two approaches to the university on wide boulevards with shade trees. The site for the main building was on a slight rise from which one could see the buildings of downtown Dallas. Grouped around this center building on one side would be a science building and a language building, on the other side the library and a building for law and theology. The engineering building would be grouped with the powerhouse and work house farther away, near one of the entrances where the athletic field, stadium, baseball diamond, and football gridiron were to be situated. This was indeed a far-reaching design for a new university that planned to spend half a million on buildings.

The remarkable feature about this plan is not that it was visionary but that the university developed very much as President Hyer wished. With relatively few changes, the buildings are grouped as he designed them, and the architectural style he proposed has been consistently followed. Today the buildings present the "harmonious" appearance of the Georgian architecture with red brick and white columns that Hyer desired. It took considerable vision to see that the huge field of Johnson grass without a house in sight and relatively few trees could develop into a campus of some fifty white-trimmed red brick buildings with shaded walks.

By the end of the summer of 1911 definite plans for four buildings were announced. An administration and classroom building would be built with the $300,000 from the city and named Dallas Hall. It was planned to be "a magnificent fireproof structure and of such architectural beauty as to be worthy of the crowning feature of the campus."[46] The other buildings projected at that time were two dormitories, one for men and one for women, a science building, and a powerhouse for light and heat. The plans for the science building were dropped almost immediately, and later one of the dormitories was abandoned. In the end there was money only for Dallas Hall, one dormitory, and a temporary powerhouse. Just before the university opened, three inexpensive dormitories for men were hastily constructed.[47]

An integral part of the financing of the university was a gift from the General Education Board. The board made a contract with the university in early November, 1911, that it would contribute $200,000 toward the first million, provided the university could raise $800,000. In other words, for every four dollars the Methodists raised, the board would contribute one dollar. The $300,000 promised by the city of Dallas would be acceptable toward the $800,000. The money had to be collected by June 30, 1913, eighteen months from the date of the contract, and was payable in not more than five equal annual installments beginning November 1, 1912, and ending July 31, 1917. The university would not be eligible for the board money if it had any debts outstanding. Of the million dollars, only half might be used for buildings and the other half must be reserved for endowment. None of the money donated by the board could be used for theological education; all had to be used exclusively for the arts and sciences college.[48]

Earlier Hyer had hoped to receive $300,000 from the board, but when Buttrick learned that the money from Dallas was not in cash but in subscription form, he was much less willing to be generous with the new university. The board refused to sign a contract with SMU until the subscriptions from Dallas were negotiable notes and at least one payment had been made.[49] This evidently had been accomplished by November.

The primary efforts of the university leaders were directed toward raising this money by June, 1913. This task fell upon the shoulders of H. A. Boaz, whose talents lay largely in this direction. He headed up a well-organized campaign among the Texas Methodists. The annual conferences of fall, 1911, assigned L. S. Barton and J. T. McClure to aid Boaz as full-time salaried financial commissioners.[50] They were assisted from time to time by J. D. Young, W. W. Watts, and W. B. Wilson. Each district had a non-salaried commissioner who worked with the individual ministers to secure pledges from the laymen. Boaz wrote of the campaign:

It was my custom to solicit funds for ten days out of two weeks and I usually delivered an address at night, explaining the program of the Church in founding the University in Dallas. Four days out of the two weeks were allowed for coming home to make reports and make preparations for the next trip. What a time that was! God had endowed me with the gift of securing funds where others failed. . . . It was a joy to do such work for the Kingdom, but very exhausting and exacting.[51]

These efforts appeared to pay off when the first financial report of the university in June, 1912, listed as "signed endowment subscriptions" $524,313.55.[52] During the months of April and May an intensive push was made to collect all possible pledges by the deadline set by the General Education Board. At the university board meeting on June 30, 1913, President Hyer announced that:

After paying all expenses of a protracted and vigorous campaign, the university is in possession of subscriptions which fully meet the conditions laid down by the General Board as to the liberality that must be manifested by the Methodists of Texas in the founding of their university. This announcement will cause great rejoicing throughout all Methodism.[53]

The university officials estimated that the total amount subscribed to the university was approximately $750,000.[54] However, in retrospect, Boaz put the sum at nearer $700,000.[55] Whatever the exact figure was, it appeared that sufficient money had been collected to enable the university to receive the $200,000 from the General Education Board. An editorial in the *Advocate* stated:

Every element of doubt concerning its founding is eliminated, and it is only a question of time when the splendid administration building now looming up on the campus just north of the city, will have grouped around it dormitories and other needful buildings for a successful opening in September, 1914.[56]

These optimistic statements proved to be premature. It was one thing to have notes and subscriptions, but it was another thing to collect them in time to make payments on the construction of buildings or even in time to satisfy the General Education Board. In fact, it proved to be impossible. Even in 1912 when the financial report optimistically listed over a half million dollars in subscriptions, the actual cash in the bank was only $36,955. Despite the small amount of cash, the contract was let for Dallas Hall for $212,902. At the same time President Hyer wrote a letter to the citizens of Dallas asking if they could favor SMU officials with advance payment of subscriptions before time for the university to open.[57] This plea must not have been successful; the following February President Hyer was authorized to borrow $100,000,[58] probably to meet the demands of the contractor of Dallas Hall for cash. It was also evident by this time that the $500,000 allotted for buildings would not be adequate and another $150,000 would be needed for Dallas Hall, two dormitories, and a powerhouse.[59]

Worst of all, the officers of the General Education Board would not accept as valid all the subscriptions the university claimed. The board regarded as good only $446,159 worth of notes and subscriptions; and as a result it paid the university not the $200,000 it expected but only $111,539.85, which it received July 20, 1914, a year after the campaign closed.[60] This money made up the bulk of the university's first endowment of $146,758, as of 1915.[61]

The net result of this campaign to raise a million dollars fell short of its goal and accounts for the economic distress of 1919 and 1920 which eventually brought about the resignation of President Hyer. The citizens of Dallas came far nearer meeting their pledges than did the Methodists of Texas. Dallas paid SMU $272,000 of its $300,000 pledge,[62] an extremely high collection rate. The financial statements of the university show that it eventually regarded as uncollectable approximately $500,000 of the $750,000 subscribed by the Methodists.[63] In 1916 the audit lists $257,834 as the total of doubtful subscriptions, and in 1921 there was another $239,236 written off.[64] As a result, the university began operation with approximately $633,540, including the money from the Methodists, Dallas, and the General Education Board, which was considerably less than the one million goal. It was impossible to launch a university of the scope envisioned by President Hyer with this limited financial backing.

One of the major difficulties of the financial campaign was that the Methodists attempted to raise a relatively large amount of money from individual congregations throughout the state. This meant that the appeal was made primarily to the small-town or rural Methodist who had little money. Texas as a whole had accumulated little capital in 1911, as compared with a decade later. The money for SMU was pledged in small amounts over a long period of time. The largest pledges were for $25,-000, but there were only three of these. Vice-president Boaz estimated that the university needed ten donations of this amount.[65] It was extremely easy to default on small, long-term pledges, as experience was to show.

Furthermore, it was difficult to communicate to small-town or rural Texas the vision of a "great university" that President Hyer possessed. To most of these people, who did not have even a high-school education, the concept of supporting a university in Dallas seemed visionary. Many Methodists were called upon also to support a junior college or preparatory school that was within their own conference. Such a school was tangible and a reality to these people, whereas Southern Methodist University was far away and existed only on paper. Yet it was upon these people that the university had to rely for support. Later, in 1920, when the university conducted its financial campaign, it relied not on thousands of small pledges from congregations all over the state but on a few wealthy Methodists who contributed much larger amounts. However, in 1911 this would have been an impossibility.

The cost of collecting the small subscriptions was excessively high. The Key Memorial Fund (one of several theological funds) had $12,341 subscribed. Of this sum only $6,830 was ever collected, but the cost of this collection was $3,806, making the net cash realized $3,024.[66] One of the reports of the financial commissioners indicated that between August 1, 1913, and February 14, 1914, seven commissioners collected $16,-859.05 in subscriptions at a cost of $7,606.34.[67] An operation of this kind is clearly uneconomic. Shortly after this period the commissioners were recalled from the field and collections ceased for a time.

This move was necessary because of a severe depression in Texas and the nation as a whole in 1914. An industrial depression in 1913-1914 was followed by the outbreak of the First World War. The failure of the European market in 1914 not only brought severe losses to cotton farmers but also upset the national balance of trade. In Texas most cotton sold for eight cents or less a pound, the lowest price in a decade.[68] In a desperate effort to sustain the market, public-spirited citizens in many communities launched the "buy-a-bale" movement, appealing to people to purchase at least one bale to be held off the glutted market.

This situation seriously affected the university's campaign for funds. Several commissioners reported "that their labors were unsatisfactory, and . . . indicated that they could not expect to remain upon the payroll of the University unless conditions changed."[69] The depression disappeared as soon as war orders from the Allies began to be placed in the United States, but it had dealt a crippling blow to the collections of subscriptions.

The severe financial situation of the university was not immediately obvious to the general public and perhaps not even to the university officials, largely because of the method of bookkeeping. The financial reports of the university listed as assets all of the pledges and subscriptions that were made, so that the university appeared to be in good shape on paper, especially when the land values were thrown in. The total pledges and subscriptions were also used for publicity purposes, with the result that the *Texas Christian Advocate* and other promotional media wrote glowing reports of the financial campaign.[70] However, by late 1914 and 1915 it was becoming evident that the money was simply not being collected and the university would have difficulty in opening as scheduled in 1915. An article in the *Advocate* stated: "Collections are far from what we would like for them to be, but they are much further from being a failure . . . . The people must understand that the University must have funds at once."[71] In an open letter entitled "Methodism Expects Every Man to Do His Duty," Bishop Mouzon said in January, 1915, that the university needed $250,000 to open in the fall. He listed (in a more accurate fashion than elsewhere) past due notes at a total of $150,000 with $200,000 worth of notes due by fall. The actual collections during the previous six months had totaled only $16,000. Since only one Methodist in twenty in Texas had contributed to SMU, the bishop pleaded for support similar to that shown by Dallas.[72] But even the relatively strong language of his letter failed to bring results.

Every year since the university had been chartered, optimistic statements about the date of the opening had been issued. After the commission had located the university and selected the administration in 1911, it set the opening date as the following fall.[73] Hyer was slightly more realistic and suggested the fall of 1913 as the opening. But as soon as the administration officials began the job of planning for the university, they realized that it would take far longer. In his report to the Board in June, 1913, Hyer said: "Under the most favorable circumstances the university can scarcely develop so rapidly as public sentiment will demand. To become a real university, it must continue for a number of years to conduct as successful a campaign for funds as has been the one now closing."[74] Despite the pressure from the public for an early opening date, Hyer and Boaz tried to make it clear that they were not building a "fresh water college" but "a great university" which simply took more time and money and effort to start. Boaz wrote:

> Great enterprises necessarily move slowly at first. . . . We must remember that we are building a university—not a single building, not a schoolhouse, . . . but a number of large buildings that not only must accommodate a great many people, but must have arrangements peculiar to the needs of a great Methodist University.[75]

The buildings that were being constructed were not light, cheap, temporary affairs but were built to last and serve the needs of a permanent and growing university.

For a time, university officials thought that classes could begin in the fall of 1914. But by the first of that year it was clear that Texas was in a depression, the pledges were not being collected, and the two buildings under construction could not be completed.[76] Again a plea was made to the Methodists for payment on the subscriptions. In order to relieve some of the pressure to open the university, President Hyer announced that in the fall of 1914 a limited number of freshmen might enroll at the medical school and take their first year science courses with the medical students. In this way, they could secure a year of college training.[77] Under this questionable arrangement fourteen students entered SMU the year before it actually opened. Two of them graduated four years later in 1918.

Postponing the opening of the university created a vicious circle which was difficult to break. The failure of the university to open was a detriment to the collection of pledges. Subscribers were reluctant to continue payments when little seemed to be happening as a result of earlier payments. Of course, the fewer pledges that were collected, the less likely it was that the university would open. Finally, in 1915, the university officials decided to break this impasse and open the university that fall. This was accomplished only with the greatest effort.

Dallas Hall and one dormitory were completed, but not furnished. The men had no place to live, and the buildings did not yet have heat, lights, or water. President Hyer estimated it would take $250,000 to get the university operational. For a time it was proposed to allow the men to live in rooms in Highland Park and Dallas; but since there were so few houses nearby, it was decided to build three inexpensive brick veneer dormitories for them.[78] By borrowing additional funds from the Dallas banks, using the subscriptions as securities,[79] the administration managed to get the dormitories constructed; all buildings were furnished; heat, lights, and water became realities; and the physical plant was at last ready to receive students.

CHAPTER IV

The Formative Years,
1915-1920

DESPITE THE BLEAK financial outlook for Southern Methodist, the academic plans for organizing "a great university" continued. President Hyer definitely remained steadfast in his desire to build a true university,[1] not just another small Methodist college. But universities are made, not born; and it was half a century before SMU would achieve university status. The only tangible evidences of the hoped-for university in these early years were the imposing structure of Dallas Hall and the obviously superior ability of Robert Stewart Hyer. What the Methodists really established in 1915 was a small liberal arts college with a theological seminary and a music school attached to it.

Some institutions were actually founded as universities, such as the Johns Hopkins University, Clark University, and most spectacularly the University of Chicago. Other universities, like Harvard, Yale, and Columbia, were created on the base of older liberal arts colleges. But SMU fit neither of these categories. It obviously did not have the resources to become a full-scale university immediately, nor did it have a long history as a liberal arts college. Like most all new institutions, the course it had to follow was to build first the liberal arts base and to add afterward graduate work for advanced degrees. Frederick A. P. Barnard, president of Columbia, once described the three stages in the evolution of a university. The first period, he said, is that of the college. The second is dominated by the adding of professional schools. The final period is that of the true university, when a comprehensive program of graduate studies is developed.[2] This is the evolution that SMU followed. The liberal arts college was the central one at the founding, and gradually the professional schools were added: theology and music from the beginning, law and engineering in 1925, and business administration in 1941.[3] Even though

44

graduate work was offered, it was not emphasized until after the Second World War; and not until the 1960s were the first Ph.D. degree programs offered.

Academic Organization of the University

During the first five years, therefore, the university consisted of three colleges: the College of Liberal Arts, the School of Theology, and the School of Music. The College of Liberal Arts offered courses in the sciences and mathematics, foreign languages, English, philosophy, and history. The only degree that was granted was the B.A.; the B.S. degree was not awarded until 1920.[4] The curriculum emphasized the traditional cultural values and was distinctly classical in tone and spirit. It was patterned after the curriculum of the older colleges in the North and East, which by then was the traditional course of study, infiltrated by the sciences and modified by the elective principle. The arts college at SMU has always been the academic center of the university with the greatest enrollment and the largest number of faculty.

Within the framework of the arts college until 1920 was the graduate school. A master of arts degree was offered the first year, but obviously the quantity and quality of such work was severely limited. The catalogue requirements were vague. Evidently a master's degree was offered in all fields, but in actual practice this would have been an impossibility. Even under limited circumstances, though, thirty-two M.A. degrees were awarded during the first five years. In 1920 a separate graduate school was created with its own chairman, who became a dean in 1926.[5]

The second major school was that of theology, a logical development since the need for a theological school was one of the motivating factors behind the founding of SMU. Edwin D. Mouzon, resident bishop, served as dean and organized the first faculty and curriculum.[6] The school was designed primarily as a graduate school offering the B.D. degree, which required a three-year course. Students with two years of college work could take a two-year course and receive a B.A. degree. However, older men with no college work could be admitted on an individual basis and receive a certificate rather than a degree after three years of study. For the first few years there was a large number in these last two categories and relatively few divinity graduates. Between 1915 and 1920 only twenty-four B.D. degrees were granted. This number gradually increased.[7]

The School of Music, the third college established, offered a bachelor's degree in music. Students had to meet the same entrance requirements as those in the liberal arts college and also take much of their work there. In the first five years only two degrees were granted. Most of the music students were special students who received individual instruction with no degree. The faculty of the music school were all trained in conservatories and had no academic degrees. Most of them were not actually paid a salary but received a percentage of the fees from their students.[8] Having the School of Music appealed to the new university because it attracted women students and had the advantage of paying its own way.

Curriculum of the Arts College

The first bulletin for SMU was prepared during the summer of 1915 by President Hyer with the assistance of John H. McGinnis of the English department and Frank Seay of the theological faculty.[9] These three put together a small pamphlet containing a preliminary announcement of the entrance requirements, course descriptions, and graduation requirements. This announcement was tentative in nature and underwent considerable modification and revision during the first years.

The admission policy adopted by this new university was a generous one, designed to attract as many students as possible. A student was required to have fourteen units of high school credits but was not required to have a diploma. After the entrance requirements were stabilized, they included three years of English, two and a half of mathematics, two of history, and three years of one language or two years of two languages. Only two units of vocational work were accepted. These requirements constituted the traditional classical program taught by virtually all high schools. SMU also established a conditional admission policy, to aid students who did not have the entrance requirements but were capable of doing college work. The first year twenty-nine students were admitted in this fashion. These special admissions continued until 1922. Not until 1929 was an entering student required to present a high school diploma, although most early students probably did; and not until 1940 was the quality of the high school record judged as a basis for admission.[10]

The curriculum of these early years was patterned after that of the older colleges and universities. By 1915 these institutions had undergone profound changes by fragmenting the traditional large blocks of subject matter into smaller and more precise areas of study. Natural philosophy proliferated into physics, chemistry, biology, and geology. Moral philosophy subdivided into political science, economics, sociology, and anthropology. And the studies of belles lettres became the study of poetry, drama, and the novel.[11] The romance languages were added to the classical Greek and Latin studies.

With this proliferation of courses students could no longer cover all fields of knowledge in one four-year course. It was to manage this problem that Charles William Eliot of Harvard had introduced his famous elective system toward the end of the nineteenth century. To Eliot this system was simply a part of that expanding freedom of spirit that the new university represented. It left the student free in large measure to determine his course of study. The elective system allowed universities to develop departments of knowledge and enlarge areas of scholarly interest. It was, in short, the instrument that enabled colleges to become universities.

A great number of the colleges followed Harvard's lead, but the smaller liberal arts colleges hung back. These schools incorporated into their courses certain aspects of this more flexible program. Modifications of the program included making only a half to a third of the curriculum elective, the use of the major-minor system, and the use of the group system. This last system was organized to put all subject matter into certain broad groups and required the student to take most of his work in one group.[12] Some institutions used one or two of these modifications. SMU was to use all three.

By 1918 SMU had established requirements for graduation with the B.A. degree which remained constant, with a few minor exceptions, until 1940. Each student was required to have eighteen term hours[13] of English, which included a year of composition and a year of literature. Because of its Christian orientation, the university required each graduate to take a course in the Bible. The foreign language requirement was particularly stiff. It specified eighteen term hours above the elementary level. This requirement assumed that the students had taken two years of a language in high school and would study it for two more in college. If a student began at the elementary level in college, he would need to have three years of a language for graduation. The amount of mathematics a student was required to take varied from three to nine hours depending upon his entrance credits. Nine term hours in each of two sciences were required, and at least one of the sciences had to include laboratory work. The requirement was the same for the social sciences, nine term hours in each of two departments. In 1921 two years of physical education were added to the requirements. These standard requirements totaled 75 to 79 term hours, almost half of the total 180 hours needed for graduation.[14]

The choice a student had was further circumscribed by the group system. By 1918 four different groupings had evolved: the English group, which included art, English, general literature, English Bible, music, and public speaking; the foreign language group, which consisted of French, German, Greek, Latin, and Spanish; the science group, which contained biology, chemistry, geology, mathematics, and physics; and the social science group, composed of economics, sociology, education, history, political science, home economics, and philosophy. Students were not allowed to take more than forty-five term hours in one department, nor more than ninety term hours in one group. In addition, students selected a major department from within one of the divisions. The requirements for a major varied from department to department and from year to year, but the usual requirement was from thirty-six to forty-five term hours for a major.

The intention of these graduation requirements was to insure that all students would possess a common core of knowledge in the required subjects. These subjects were considered indispensable to an educated person. Beyond this point a student might choose what interested him most, provided he did not take all his other work in one department or one division. The requirements were intended to be a balance between the rigid old-time college curriculum, where every student took the same subjects, and Eliot's elective system, which allowed a student to take whatever he chose. The compromise was a common one adopted by many colleges and universities. Evidently the leaders of SMU took the pattern for granted and did not feel they needed to justify or explain it. There is no statement of purpose or aims in the catalogue until 1934. However, President Hyer had indirectly suggested that such a curriculum was his goal.[15]

The elective system was responsible for the speedy development of subject matter specialization and departmentalization. Gone was the old-time college professor who was a jack-of-all-trades, expected to teach anything and everything. The newer professor tended to become a subject matter specialist. Entirely new fields of study pushed their way forward and were recognized by the college curriculum. Several examples of this development can be seen in the curriculum of SMU. When the university opened, the department of history included economics, political science, and even sociology for a short time. However, by 1919 each of these subject areas had been separated into different departments each taught by a faculty member trained in that specific field. Psychology was not offered until 1919, at which time it was combined with philosophy. These two subject areas were not separated until 1930. Comparative literature was part of the English department until 1919, when a separate department with a faculty of its own was created.

Not only were new subject areas added, but the older ones were expanded, thus revealing their exploration in a more intensive way. For example, four courses in botany were added to the biology department by 1919. Geography was an addition to the geology department in 1924 and remained part of that department until the mid forties. During these early years the English department increased its offerings with four advanced courses, one of which was Recent English and American Poetry. Advanced courses in both Spanish and French literature were added. The history department increased its predominantly American history courses by two new offerings in European history.[16] The emergence of these new courses of study as well as the broadening of the older ones enlarged considerably the intellectual horizons of Southern Methodist University.

The elective system also made possible the broadening of the American college curriculum in still other ways. Vocational and utilitarian courses were finding their way into the program and claiming equal status with the older liberal arts subjects. SMU viewed these courses with an uneasy eye and was unsure where to put them. Education was part of the arts college from the beginning, but home economics was set off to one side like a stepchild along with art and public speaking. By 1920, however, a new college was created for these new utilitarian subjects that did not fit into the traditional program.

This new College of Applied Arts and Sciences contained five departments: commerce, education, home economics, applied art, and journalism. The motivating factor behind this college was the creation of a department of commerce designed to serve the needs of the Dallas business community. The business leaders of the city encouraged its growth, and the first classes were actually held downtown for the convenience of the commercial students.[17] The early courses offered were business administration, accounting, advertising and selling, finance, and insurance. This department grew into a full-blown business school by 1941. The other departments were included in the college because of their vocational nature. Applied art meant interior decoration and commercial art.[18] The education department had been a part of the College of Liberal Arts since the university opened; but when it was transferred to the new college, its course offerings nearly doubled. The home economics department, which had moved once before, seemed a logical addition to the College of Applied Arts and Sciences, as did the first journalism department.

All of the course offerings of these departments were vocational in nature and designed to train students in areas that were practical and marketable. SMU's innovations reflected the national educational trend. No longer was education viewed as a course of study designed to create a Christian gentleman who pursued knowledge for its own sake. Now its fundamental purpose was to train people in areas that were useful and necessary to society.

With the erection of this new college, SMU offered the B.S. degree for the first time. The requirements for this degree were similar to those for a B.A., except that the students did their major work in either of two new fields, commerce or education. These new fields, now defined as groups, were added to the original four. Commerce now included accounting, banking and finance, commerce, and marketing; and education contained the fields of education, physical education, home economics, and journalism. A student was given the option of taking a B.S. degree in science or mathematics rather than the B.A. degree. The one significant difference between the two degrees was the language requirement. Candidates for the B.S. needed only one year of foreign language as opposed to two years for a B.A. degree. The College of Applied Arts and Sciences lasted only a little more than a year. Vocational subjects were not strong enough to warrant a separate college. In 1922 the college was combined with the College of Liberal Arts to create a College of Arts and Sciences which contained the vocational subjects as departments. This was a far more logical combination and one that was destined to last.

The Early Faculty and Students

The selection of the faculty for Southern Methodist University lay entirely in the hands of President Hyer. The educational commission that founded the university had expressed the hope that professionally trained men and women with Ph.D. degrees should be chosen if possible.[19] With this goal Hyer heartily concurred. He worked diligently at the task of selecting the first faculty, traveling around the country and interviewing various candidates. He systematically kept a file on all prospective faculty members and entered their names in a small black notebook, but saw fit to make relatively few comments.[20] Hyer evidently set his goals high. He listed over 150 names, among them men who later achieved distinction, such as Frank Aydelotte, who became president of Swarth-more College (and incidentally introduced the honors program), and Goodrich C. White, who was later chosen to head Emory University. Quite obviously, men of this caliber were unlikely to accept a teaching position at a projected Methodist university in the Southwest. Neither was Hyer in a position to raid the faculties of the older universities as William Rainey Harper had done for the University of Chicago. In the end, Hyer was forced to select men and women who were for the most part products of the region and its institutions, primarily Southwestern University or Polytechnic College. This strong local or regional influence was to be expected in an embryo university whose reputation was yet to be earned.

When the university opened, the College of Liberal Arts had a full-time faculty of fifteen, but it was without a dean. John H. Keen, who had been appointed to the position from the University of Texas, was unable to assume his duties until the following year because of a serious illness. As a result, he had no voice in selecting the faculty, constructing the curriculum, or formulating a program for the college. These functions were performed by President Hyer, with the assistance of R. A. Hearon of the history department.[21] When Keen did arrive in the following year, his strong leadership was felt in the organization of the college.[22] However, Keen remained only until the spring of 1918, when he left to take a position with the federal government.

No permanent dean was immediately chosen, but John Preston Comer was asked to serve as acting dean until 1919. Comer, a graduate of Trinity University who had a master's degree from Columbia, taught history and economics until 1923, when he left SMU. Later he received the Ph.D. degree in political science from Columbia. However, during his brief deanship, Comer had no responsibilities for any matters beyond routine administration. President Hyer continued to perform most of the functions of a dean until his retirement, not a difficult task because the institution was small.[23]

In the fall of 1919 before his retirement in 1920, President Hyer appointed Albert Shipp Pegues (M.A., Wofford, 1895) as dean of the college. Pegues had been a long-time professor of English at South-western; but during his two years at SMU, he hardly became acquainted with the institution. It was not until 1922 with the appointment of Elzy Dee Jennings that the college had a dean of long tenure. Jennings had received the B.A. and M.A. degrees in education from the University of

Texas in 1913, and in 1924 the Ph.D. from the same institution. He remained dean of the College of Arts and Sciences until his death in 1938. During these years Jennings was conscientious about the performance of his duties, but he offered little in the way of academic leadership to the faculty. Any proposals for academic planning originated with the faculty and involved little on Jennings's part beyond "standardizing" the course offerings or compromising conflicting departmental interests.[24] The College of Arts and Sciences did not have strong leadership until after the Second World War.

When the university opened, each of the twelve departments had only one member, with the exception of English and history. The English department was easily the strongest department on campus, partly because all students were required to take English and partly because of the caliber of the faculty and students. The first chairman was. Olin D. Wannamaker (M.A., Harvard, 1902), who came to SMU from Alabama Polytechnic Institute (now Auburn University); but he remained only until 1918.[25]

The two other members of this department stayed much longer, and hence their influence was far greater. One of these was John H. McGinnis, the first faculty member to arrive, who remained with the university for thirty-nine years until his retirement in 1954. McGinnis had taught at Southwestern when Hyer was president there. He had received the B.A. degree from Missouri Valley College in 1904 and the M.A. from Columbia University in 1915. He was an excellent teacher who made students either hate or love him, but they all learned from him. He made them aware of the value of good writing and clear thinking. He served as editor of the *Southwest Review*,[26] the literary journal published by SMU, and of the book page of the *Dallas Morning News*. McGinnis's technique was

to raise questions rather than answer them; to subtly convince students and others that they wanted to find answers . . . and to demonstrate to themselves that the answer to every question opens up a galaxy of new questions that need answering . . . . No university could survive a faculty made up exclusively of McGinnises, but any region which has not at least one McGinnis is indeed the poorer for it.[27]

The other influential member of the English department was Jay Hubbell, who was asked to join the faculty in October, 1915, after the large enrollment made it obvious another teacher was needed. McGinnis had known Hubbell at Columbia and suggested his name to Hyer.[28]

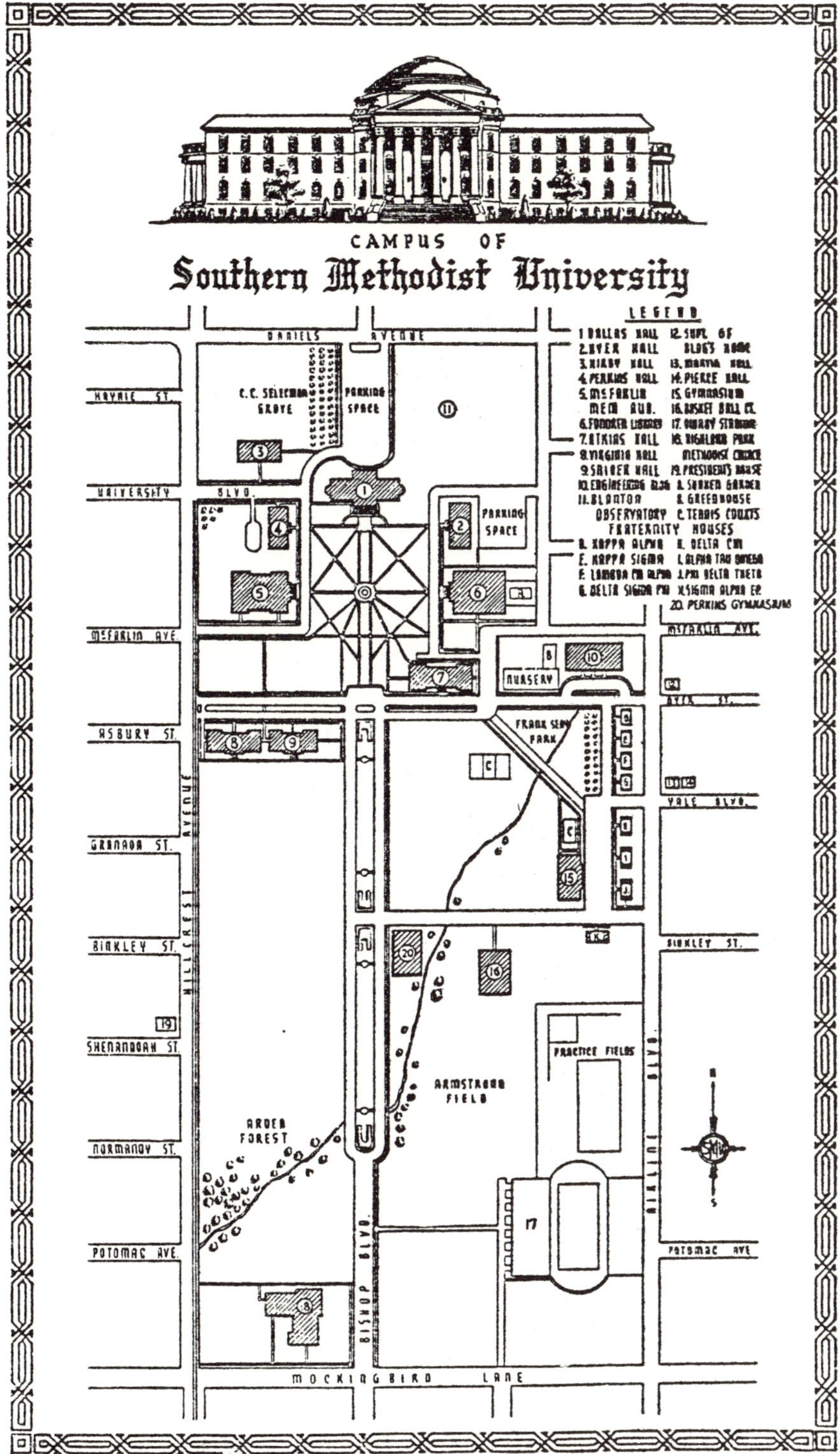

Map of the SMU campus as it was in the 1940s.

Members of the Methodist Educational Commission which located SMU at Dallas tour proposed sites, February 1, 1911.

H. H. Adams, representing the City of Dallas, presenting $300,000 in cash and pledges to the Methodist Educational Commission for the location of SMU in Dallas, February 3, 1911. Upper row, left to right: R. S. Hyer, Dallas; H. A. Boaz, Fort Worth; Hon. W. L. Dean, Huntsville; Hon. Thos. F. Turner, Amarillo; Horace Bishop, Hillsboro; Rev. J. G. Putnam, Stamford. Second row: Col. C. C. Walsh, San Angelo; John A. Rice, Fort Worth; Rev. L. B. Elrod, Marshall; Judge M. M. Brooks, Dallas; Rev. Thos. Gregory, Uvalde; J. W. Blanton, Gainesville; J. K. Parr, Hillsboro; Rev. H. M. Peterson, Dallas. Bottom row: Mr. Adams; Hon. J. W. Robbins, Austin; Gov. George T. Jester, Corsicana; Bishop James Atkins; Rev. O. S. Thomas, Greenville; Judge John C. Box, Jacksonville; Rev. George C. Slover, Clarendon.

Campus about 1915, with Dallas Hall and the Woman's Building, later Atkins Hall, rising from a "sea of grass."

Dallas Hall and Atkins Hall after the landscaping of Bishop Boulevard.

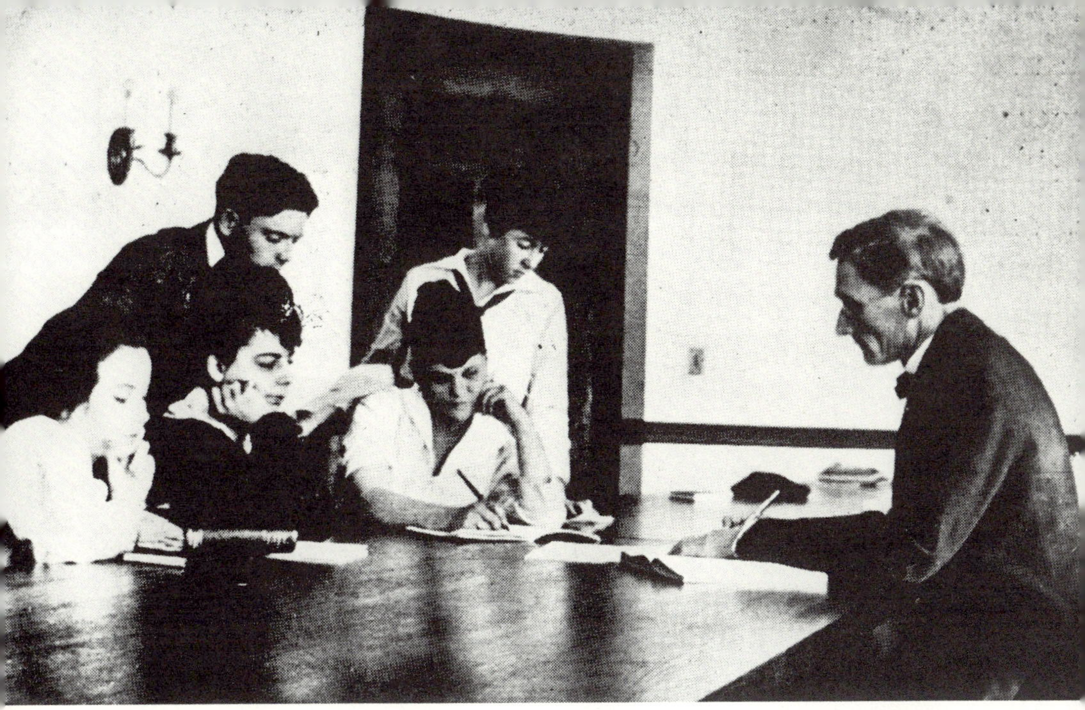

Professor R. A. Hearon registering some of the first students at SMU in the fall of 1915.

Frank Reedy, Bursar of SMU, and "Dad" Johnson, motorman, with "the Dinkey," which ran between SMU and Knox Street during the university's early years.

SMU's first football team. Front row, left to right: End Roy Parks, Center and Captain J. A. Barton, Halfback A. Brice "Mike" Cole. Middle row: Tackle Irl W. Brown, Guard L. Homer Thomas, Fullback J. F. Collins, Tackle K. P. Lester, End A. Lyle May. Back row: Manager Jack Kennedy, Halfback B. C. Glenn, Quarterback C. W. "Billy" Neal, Coach Ray Morrison.

The Arden Club in 1916.

Bishop Edwin D. Mouzon, member of SMU's first Board of Trustees, organizer and first dean of the School of Theology.

John S. McIntosh, Professor of Classical Languages from 1915 until his death in 1945. As chairman of the athletic committee during those years, he upheld high standards and in a time of controversy retained the confidence and respect of the faculty.

Jay B. Hubbell, Professor of English from 1915 to 1927 and head of the English department from 1918 to 1927; the first editor at SMU of the *Southwest Review* (1924-27); organizer of The Makers, poetry group whose widely noted contests brought the publication in 1924 of *Prairie Pegasus*.

John H. McGinnis, Professor of English, the first faculty member to arrive at SMU in 1915, who became a legend and an inspiration to generations of students. He served as editor of the *Southwest Review* from 1927 to 1943 and was the prime mover in the establishment in 1937 of the SMU Press.

Charles F. Zeek, Professor of French, member of the original SMU faculty.

Ellis W. Shuler, Professor of Geology, member of the original faculty; chairman and then first dean of the Graduate School.

Frank Seay, Professor of Greek and New Testament, member of the original faculty.

Robert S. Hyer, first President of SMU, who held that office from 1911 to 1920.

Four SMU Presidents. From left to right: Charles C. Selecman, 1923-38; Hiram A. Boaz, 1920-22; Umphrey Lee, 1939-54; Willis M. Tate, 1954-72.

The "Martha Sumner University," (name taken from Charles Ferguson's satirical novel), c. 1931. On stairs, left to right: Samuel Wood Geiser, Umphrey Lee, Samuel D. Myres, Jr. Standing: Elmer Scott, Gaynell Hawkins, Herbert Gambrell, John Lee Brooks, William F. Hauhart, I. K. Stephens, Frank Rader, Sam Acheson. Seated: C. M. Bishop, May Whitsett, Ernest E. Leisy, Mayne Longnecker, F. D. Smith.

Stanley Patterson, Superintendent of Buildings and Grounds, 1919-57; Instructor in Mechanical Engineering, 1940-57.

Samuel A. Myatt, member of original faculty; Professor of Spanish until 1945.

Harvie Branscomb, Professor of New Testament in the university's early years.

Robert W. Goodloe, Professor of Church History, who served from 1920 to 1957.

Henry Nash Smith, member of the English and Comparative Literature faculty from 1927 to 1941. During his entire tenure at SMU he served with John H. McGinnis as an editor of the *Southwest Review*.

Hubbell became chairman of the department in 1918 when Wannamaker resigned and remained in that position until 1927 when he went to Duke University. Hubbell had a B.A. from the University of Richmond (1905), an M.A. from Harvard (1908), and a Ph.D. degree from Columbia (1922). He was a scholar who helped make American literature respectable at a time when it was not fully appreciated. Hubbell was solely responsible for the acquisition of the *Southwest Review*, served as its editor for three years, and even had hopes of establishing a review devoted to American literature.[29] After he went to Duke, he did found *American Literature,* and published several substantial works in the field of American literature which earned him a national reputation.

Aside from his work with the *Review*, Hubbell also encouraged the writing of poetry. Even from this struggling university in the raw Southwest, Hubbell was able to see the national increase of interest in poetry. He brought to the campus such poets as Carl Sandburg, Robert Frost, Vachel Lindsay, Witter Bynner, and Harriet Monroe, who brought SMU in contact with the national literary scene. Hubbell organized a poetry club, The Makers, which consisted of a small group of students who met informally to write and read poetry. This club sponsored a poetry contest annually from 1922 until 1927. Prizes were offered for the best poems, and entries were received from all over the United States. Each year some sixty to seventy colleges and universities participated in this contest. Hubbell was able to attract an impressive group of judges, such prominent poets as Sandburg, Monroe, Bynner, Sara Teasdale, John Hall Wheelock, and Louis Untermeyer. In 1924 a collection of the best prize poems was published as *Prairie Pegasus.* Sandburg wrote to Hubbell that he "would not be surprised at any sort of work of genius that might issue from [this] group; the feel is there; it has the rebel yell, the lone wolf howl, and the yellow rose of Texas in it."[30]

The most substantial contribution to these poetry contests was made by George Bond, a student of both Hubbell and McGinnis. In the 1922 contest Bond entered "Sketches of the Texas Prairie," which won first place in all three of the categories. These prizes were an honor for Bond and SMU. Judges who selected Bond's poems included Bynner, John Erskine, William Rose Benét, John Hall Wheelock, and Robert Adger Law.[31] Bond also worked with Hubbell on the *Review* and was editor of the *Campus.* He left SMU in 1927 to work with a publishing company in New York, but returned during the 1930s, earned his doctorate (Michigan, 1948), and became a contributing member of the SMU faculty.

Hubbell and McGinnis attracted other capable students during these years, such as Ima Honaker Herron and John Lee Brooks. Herron graduated in 1921, and, after teaching at a small college, returned to SMU in 1927. She earned the Ph.D. degree at Duke (1935) and later published two books: *The Small Town in American Literature* (1936) and *The Small Town in American Drama* (1969). Brooks also graduated in 1921 and, after teaching several years at SMU, received his doctorate from Harvard (1934). He was coeditor with John Bowyer of *The Victorian Age* (1938), with John O. Beaty et al. of *Facts and Ideas* (1939), and with Ima Herron, John Bowyer, and George Bond of *Better College English* (1950). Both of these scholars are representative of a large group of SMU students who earned Ph.D. degrees elsewhere and returned to spend productive careers at their alma mater.

Another excellent student from the early twenties who later played a prominent role was Henry Nash Smith. Slightly younger than Herron and Brooks, having graduated from SMU in 1925, he earned both the M.A. (1929) and Ph.D. degrees (1940) at Harvard. He began teaching at SMU in 1927 and remained until 1941. After leaving the university Smith established himself as an authority on Mark Twain and is the author of *Virgin Land: The American West as Symbol and Myth* (1950) and other books. Smith worked closely with McGinnis on the *Southwest Review.*

The activities of Hubbell and McGinnis and the caliber of their students were difficult to duplicate in other departments. History and economics were combined into one department when the university opened and consisted of two men, one a veteran schoolmaster and the other a recent graduate of Trinity University. The veteran was R. A. Hearon, who had formerly taught at Polytechnic College. His B.A. degree was from Peabody (1906) and his M.A. from Wisconsin (1913). He was "a tall, thin, Savonarola-like man who had come up academically the hard way." Despite, or perhaps because of, his lack of experience in a well-established liberal arts college, "he became a chief advocate of high standards and rigid enforcement of academic regulation in the college faculty." Because of his age and experience, he was often asked to assume additional administrative chores and as a result wielded considerable influence among the faculty. He remained at SMU until his death in 1928.[32]

John Wynne Barton, the other member of the department, had a master's degree (1914) from Columbia. He remained only until 1917, but returned in 1919 for a brief period. At this time he became dean of the short-lived College of Applied Arts and Sciences. After the resignation of the second president of SMU, H. A. Boaz, Barton was chosen to succeed him but declined in order to become publishing agent of the church at Nashville. Later he became president of Ward Belmont College.[33]

In 1919 Clyde Eagleton, a Rhodes Scholar, and Joseph David Doty, who was elected a Rhodes Scholar in December of that year, joined the history faculty. Eagleton, who had an M.A. from Princeton (1914), came to SMU from the University of Louisville but remained only until 1923. He later earned a Ph.D. degree at Columbia (1928) and became an authority in international law at New York University.[34] Doty was a product of SMU, having received the B.A. in 1916 and the M.A. in 1917. He joined the faculty in 1919 and remained until 1927, except for three years at Oxford (1920-23). He was a brilliant teacher; but he offended President Charles C. Selecman, the third president, and was not allowed to return after completing his doctorate at the University of Pennsylvania.[35]

Herbert Gambrell, who was a student of Hearon, Eagleton, and Doty, received the B.A. (1921) and the M.A. (1924) from the university. Gambrell began teaching in 1921 and remained on the faculty until his retirement in 1964. In addition to his duties at SMU, he was director of the Texas Hall of State and director of the Dallas Historical Society. He became an authority on Texas history with the publication of *Mirabeau Bonaparte Lamar* (1934) and *Anson Jones* (1947). He received the doctor's degree from the University of Texas in 1946. Gambrell was always active, articulate, and a faculty member who served on countless committees. With his light touch and ever ready story, he spoke with a voice his colleagues respected.[36]

During these early years the science and mathematics departments were all small, each department consisting of only one member. The biology courses were taught by Frederick N. Duncan, who had a B.A. (1900) and M.A. (1901) from Indiana and a Ph.D. from Clark (1906). Just prior to coming to SMU, he had been doing postdoctoral work in genetics at Columbia. He is remembered as "a well-trained, gentle scientist who loved his subject and his students."[37] Duncan remained at SMU until 1924, when he went to the California Institute of Technology.

Chemistry was taught by John Henry Reedy, younger brother of Frank Reedy, the bursar. John Reedy had also taught under Hyer at

Southwestern but had left to study for his doctorate at Yale, which he received just before coming to SMU. He remained at the university three years before going to the University of Illinois in 1918. E. O. Heuse followed Reedy as chairman of chemistry and remained in that position until 1949. Heuse had received the B.A. (1900) and B.S. and M.A. (1906) from Hanover College, Indiana, and the M.S. (1907) and Ph.D. (1914) from the University of Illinois. He had taught at several small institutions, including Upper Iowa University and Monmouth College, before coming to SMU. Heuse always operated his department on a meager budget, asking little in the way of equipment or personnel. These self-effacing and self-denying traits did not enable him to build up a strong department. As a result, the chemistry department never had the resources of the other sciences and appeared to be a stepchild of the university.[38]

Ellis W. Shuler was the chairman and sole member of the geology department. He came to SMU in 1915, having just completed his doctorate at Harvard. His strong Methodist background was reinforced with a B.A. (1903) from Emory and Henry and a M.A. (1907) from Vanderbilt. From 1908 to 1913 he had taught at Polytechnic College. In 1922 he was appointed chairman of SMU's graduate committee, and in 1926 he was made dean. At the same time he retained his place as head of the geology department. He began with literally nothing in the way of equipment, library, or laboratory. By the time he retired in 1953, the university had a library adequate for research, extensive facilities for laboratory work, and a five-man staff.[39] One of Shuler's most promising students was Edwin Jay Foscue, who graduated in 1922. Foscue earned an M.A. the following year from Chicago and a Ph.D. (1927) from Clark. He began teaching at SMU in 1923 and remained until his retirement in 1965.

President Hyer himself taught all the physics courses for the first four years in addition to his presidential duties. In 1919 John Daniel Boon joined the department. Boon had only a B.S. degree (1901) from Granbury College, Texas, but he had done advanced work at Chicago and Wisconsin. Prior to coming to SMU he taught for fourteen years at Polytechnic College. In addition to physics, he was interested in geology and astronomy.[40] He was, in short, reminiscent of the old-time college teacher who lacked training in a field of specialty.

All the mathematics was taught by Edward H. Jones, who was slightly older than most of the first faculty members and who had been teaching at Daniel Baker College, a small Presbyterian school in Brownwood, Texas. His bachelor's degree was from Texas (1908) and his master's degree from Harvard (1910). He was a modest, quiet man who made friends and held them, but he was of limited influence on the faculty.[41] Jones remained on the faculty until his retirement in 1933. Two men later to have wide influence in the development of the university who were students of Jones during the early period were Hemphill Hosford and Edwin D. Mouzon, Jr. Hosford entered SMU in 1915 as a freshman and, when he graduated four years later, began teaching. He continued on the faculty until 1929 except for four years during which he earned a Ph.D. degree at Illinois (1926).[42] Mouzon was the son of the bishop who was closely associated with the university from its inception. He graduated in 1920 and taught at SMU until he went to the University of Illinois, where he received a doctor's degree in 1929. He then returned to SMU and in 1933, when Jones retired, was made chairman of the department. Mouzon also was an influential member and, later, chairman of the athletic committee before he retired in 1966.

Beginning the first year, SMU offered five foreign languages: Greek, Latin, French, German, and Spanish. Both Latin and Greek were taught by John S. McIntosh, who had a bachelor's degree (1899) and a master's degree (1902) from Cornell College, Iowa. He had received the Ph.D. from the University of Chicago (1909). Just prior to coming to SMU, McIntosh was teaching at Upper Iowa University. His classes at SMU were small; yet he always had some capable students who were majoring in the classics in a day in which the subject was declining in popularity.[43] McIntosh served as chairman of the athletic committee from 1915 until his death in 1945. He held the position during the athletic crisis of 1922-1923, which will be discussed later. During all the controversies over athletics he had the confidence and respect of the faculty.[44]

C. F. Zeek was the sole member of the French department. He was a graduate of Tulane (B.A., 1907), a Rhodes Scholar (1910-1913), and had received the Docteur de l'Université from Grenoble (1914). Immediately prior to coming to SMU, he taught for one year at the University of Wisconsin. Zeek almost did not secure the position at SMU. But the man who had earlier been selected to fill it attempted to assassinate J. Pierpont Morgan and was killed while trying to escape. Zeek heard about the turn of events from R. A. Hearn, who was also at Wisconsin from 1914 to 1915, and applied for the position. Years later Zeek wrote:

It was quite an experience arriving at a university that was starting from scratch. There were two [permanent] buildings . . . but no library and hardly any books. In French there was not even a French dictionary.[45]

Zeek, a teacher of unusual ability and an asset to the faculty, remained until 1937, when he went to Vanderbilt University.

German was taught by A. D. Schuessler, who had a B.A. degree from Central Wesleyan College, Missouri (1906), M.A. from Northwestern (1907), and a Ph.D. from Michigan (1916). Before coming to SMU, he taught at Upper Iowa University and Missouri State Teachers College. Schuessler was the schoolmaster type who gave his students a firm foundation in German. When German became unpopular during the First World War, he ceased teaching temporarily and between 1920 and 1924 was the secretary-treasurer of the university. From 1926 until his death in 1944 he was the chairman of the Campus Beautification Committee. During this period Schuessler transformed the campus from a treeless sea of Johnson grass into a well-shaded campus with hundreds of trees and shrubs.

S. A. Myatt taught Spanish. He had received both the B.A. (1896) and M.A. (1899) degrees from Vanderbilt and had taught Latin for several years at Polytechnic College and Texas Christian University before joining the SMU faculty. He too appears to have resembled the old-time college teacher whose interests were broad but whose training was not deep. He remained at the university until he retired in 1942. One of Myatt's promising students was John A. Cook, who graduated in 1921 and immediately joined the faculty. He later (1940) earned a Ph.D. degree at the University of Texas and followed Myatt as chairman, a position which he held until 1963.

The lone member of the speech department was Mary McCord who received a B.A. from Peabody College (1894) and an M.O. (1917) from the National School of Oratory. Under her leadership the speech department grew from an appendage of the arts college in 1915 offering courses in "expression" for a fee to a recognized department in 1920 offering enough work for a major. Miss McCord also worked with the theological students, teaching them how to speak.[46]

Mary McCord was responsible for forming a drama group, the Arden Club, which is still in existence. President Hyer asked her to present a play for the first commencement in 1916. With no actors, no stage, no scenery, no equipment, Miss McCord was forced to improvise. She put on a production of *As You Like It* in a small grove of trees later called the Forest of Arden. The play was a tremendous success, and the cast achieved a unity and camaraderie out of which the Arden Club was formed. Later, plays were presented on the steps of Dallas Hall, which made a more effective setting.[47]

Another woman whose force was felt at the university during these early years was Dorothy Amann. Miss Amann began her career at SMU in 1913 as President Hyer's secretary. When the university opened, she was made librarian and served as head librarian until 1949. Dorothy Amann was a leader among women for her day. She had desired to become a doctor but was able only to work for the *Southwestern Medical Journal*. She was reading law when Frank Reedy, the bursar, asked her to come to Dallas. During those early years in the library she had little money to work with, but she used her meager resources wisely. She was an intelligent, capable person who guided the growth of the library.[48]

The faculty of the School of Theology was selected by Bishop Edwin D. Mouzon, who had been asked to serve as its first dean. He was assisted by William Daniel Bradfield, a prominent minister and member of the Board of Trustees, who later was editor of the *Advocate* and still later became a member of the theological faculty.[49]

The chairman of the faculty was Ivan Lee Holt, who held a B.A. from Vanderbilt (1904) and a doctorate in Old Testament from Chicago (1909). At the time that Holt was asked to come to SMU he was serving a church in Cape Girardeau, Missouri, which he hesitated to leave; but he was persuaded to do so by the personality and dedication of President Hyer. In addition to teaching, Holt served as university chaplain and conducted the daily compulsory services. He remained with the university only until 1918, when he returned to the ministry. After the second president of SMU resigned, Holt was asked to become president; but he declined the offer. He served on the Board of Trustees of the university and in 1938 was elected bishop.[50]

The most thorough scholar of the theological faculty was Frank Seay, who taught Greek and New Testament. He held a B.D. degree (1902) from Vanderbilt and had studied at Chicago, Harvard, the University of Berlin, and Oxford, but declined to take a doctor's degree. Seay had been teaching at Georgetown six years before coming to Dallas. There was every promise that he would develop into an outstanding New Testament scholar, because by 1919 he had already published two books. However, in 1920 at the age of thirty-nine he died in a flu epidemic.[51]

To fill the vacancy for the remainder of the year Harvie Branscomb, who was teaching in the department of philosophy, was asked to teach

New Testament. Branscomb had a B.A. degree (1914) from Birmingham-Southern; he had been a Rhodes Scholar (1914-17), and he was to earn a Ph.D. (1924) at Columbia. He joined the SMU faculty in 1919 and remained until 1925. He was active during the athletic controversies of 1922-1923.[52]

A permanent dean for the School of Theology was found in 1916. Hoyt M. Dobbs, a graduate of Vanderbilt, was elected and served until 1920. In 1922 he was elected bishop.[53] Paul B. Kern succeeded Dobbs as dean in 1920 and served until 1926. He had been on the original faculty teaching English Bible in the Arts College and homiletics in the School of Theology. He was a graduate of Vanderbilt (B.A., 1902, and B.D., 1905) and in 1930 was also elected bishop.

The senior member of the theological faculty was James Kilgore. His degrees were from Southwestern (B.A., 1889, and M.A., 1890). He had served as a minister in the Texas Conference for twenty years and was also on the educational commission that had established SMU. When the second president of SMU was elected bishop, Kilgore served as acting president (1922-23), and later he served as acting dean (1926-33). He also served on the Board of Trustees from 1915 until 1936 and, as a member of both the faculty and the board, played an influential role in the life of the university.

The music faculty was small during the early years. The first dean of the school was Harold von Mickwitz, who served two years before returning to the Bush Conservatory in Chicago. At that time Paul van Katwijk, a Dutchman, became dean and continued in that position until 1949. He retired in 1956. During all these years he was the driving force behind the school. Both Harold Hart Todd and his wife taught piano. Todd organized a Men's Glee Club and a Woman's Choral Club and took them on tours around the state. Mrs. J. H. Cassidy taught organ at her house a few blocks from the campus.[54]

The first faculty was quite naturally a young group of men and women. Their average age was thirty-five.[55] President Hyer, at age fifty-five, was by far the oldest. The first arts faculty consisted of fifteen members with the rank of assistant professor or above; and of these, six held doctor's degrees (40 percent) while nine held master's degrees (60 percent). In addition there were five instructors who held only bachelor's degrees. This relatively high percentage of doctor's degrees was not maintained. By 1920 it had dropped to 25 percent.[56] Harvie Branscomb described the faculty during these early years:

As one came to know the faculty, however, a number of them, one could see, were first-rate in ability, though the older ones had been drawn mostly from Texas schools and colleges and were provincial in outlook. Alongside the academic elders were a number of would-be scholars picked up in various places. The faculty was not an accomplished one, but it had the virtues of integrity and simplicity. . . . The instruction we gave was not profound— the academic elders had codified knowledge in their respective fields at an early date . . . and we younger ones only knew enough to keep one day ahead of the class.[57]

This new faculty met for the first time September 7, 1915. A few of them had arrived earlier during the summer. John McGinnis and Frank Seay had been on hand for several weeks aiding with the preliminary planning. Ellis Shuler arrived toward the end of August with "almost four tons of geological material,"[58] which he donated to the university. But aside from these, the rest of the faculty arrived just before the opening date. Few of them knew each other and no one, of course, had any precedents to use as guides except their experiences at previous institutions. Some tentative decisions had been reached with regard to entrance requirements, courses offered, and graduation requirements; but these were to be revised several times before they achieved any stability. Rules and regulations regarding student discipline and conduct were apparently made as the need arose. During the first few weeks in September the faculty met daily at nine o'clock[59] and discussed the schedule of classes, the course of study, and the entrance requirements. Since these were fundamental questions that should have been discussed early, not the week before registration, it is surprising that students managed to get registered and that classes ever got underway.

President Hyer had anticipated about 300 students the first term. When more than that registered the first day, the faculty was amazed, even a little alarmed.[60] Before the year was over, 706 students had been enrolled, a number exceeded only by the opening enrollment at the University of Chicago.[61] Such a quantity of students caused chaos in a new and unorganized institution without precedents to guide it. The greatest job was that of classifying and organizing the students. Some came as freshmen from unaffiliated schools and failed to pass the entrance examination. Others came as transfers from various institutions (mostly Southwestern or Polytechnic) and presented credits that needed to be evaluated. This proved to be a laborious task for a faculty not completely familiar with local educational conditions.[62] Registration was so difficult that the opening of classes was delayed for several days.

After the classes got underway, the faculty met weekly instead of daily, and finally members were able to keep the university in operation with semimonthly meetings. The theological faculty attended these meetings along with the arts faculty. Together they made the decisions for the whole university. The members of the music faculty were never present. Whether they were not considered part of the academic faculty or whether they chose not to attend, the records do not make clear. These general faculty meetings continued until 1918, when the faculty was reorganized.[63] At this point it was decided to have only one general faculty meeting a month. Each of the three faculties organized itself separately and arranged its own monthly meeting. A correlation committee was appointed to decide which faculty should consider which problems.

SMU and World War I

The university had been in session not quite two full academic years when the United States entered the First World War on April 6, 1917. Prior to this time the European conflict seemed far away and totally unrelated to a young Methodist college in the Southwest. The students and faculty, like most American citizens, felt the fighting in Europe was little of America's concern. However, as soon as war was declared, a great feeling of patriotism swept through the students and many felt they should answer the first call to arms.[64]

Before the armistice was signed, the academic life of this infant institution was disrupted by the loss of both faculty members and students to the armed forces. Enrollment fell 30 percent during 1917-1918.[65] This situation required readjustment in personnel and also a reduction in the number of teachers because of the decreased income. The deficit rose from $33,000 in 1917 to $40,000 in 1918.[66] This situation dealt a hard blow to a struggling institution already beset with financial problems.

President Hyer made it clear that the university was fully behind President Wilson and the war effort. But he also stressed that the best way students could serve their country was to remain in school until called for duty. He said to the students in chapel shortly after the declaration of war:

Our country cannot be efficiently served by voluntary enlistments. The world's business today is war. Let us enter in a business-like way. Anything short of compulsory service would be playing at war when other nations are consecrating every possible energy to the preservation of their national life.[67]

Hyer's goal, after the declaration of war, was to support the patriotic spirit heartily and sympathetically but also to attempt to channel it in a direction that would make it possible for the university to continue its regular classroom work without undue interruption.[68]

Even before the actual declaration of war, a group of students voluntarily formed themselves into a unit for marching drill. They were directed by other students who had had some previous training either in the national guard or in a military preparatory school. They had no uniforms, guns, or other equipment, solely a desire "to do their bit for their country."[69] Before the school year was over, the university employed the services of Major Conner, who had charge of the cadets in one of the Dallas High Schools, to direct the drills. In this way the university was successful in keeping the school operating. However, all seniors who left for military service were given credit for their courses and allowed to graduate provided they were doing passing work.[70] Only about thirty students enlisted, whereas it had appeared earlier that the entrance of the United States into the war would virtually empty the college classrooms.[71]

For the school year beginning in 1917 President Hyer had more definite plans. He proposed that military science be formally introduced into the university as part of the prescribed work for all men. He felt that the course should consist not only of instruction in drilling and manual of arms but should be accompanied by classes and lectures on military science. He also recognized the need for the study of mathematics, modern languages, mechanics, and electricity. Hyer asked the War Department to send him a trained officer for this purpose, but unfortunately three hundred other colleges and universities wanted military officers also.[72] The United States simply did not have surplus officers to send to colleges at this point. Hyer then turned to the Canadian government and secured the services of Captain E. H. Saer, a wounded artillery officer who was unable to serve on active duty.

Captain Saer was a dashing figure on the campus in the fall of 1917. All the boys respected him and the girls were charmed by his "beautifully tailored uniform . . . brightly polished leather puttees, Sam Brown belt, and officer's cap [worn at] just the correct angle."[73] However, this experiment in a department of military science was not entirely successful. Despite the fact that all men were required to take military drill, many of them failed to take it seriously. After the first drill the *Campus* described the action: "Attempted battalion drills that were executed by some well meaning commanders resulted in a perfect rout. . . . Several men reported late to drill. This must not be repeated." The drills were not held if the weather was too cold or rainy. In addition to these drills there was a two-hour elective course taught by Captain Saer. By the spring term the students presented the faculty with a petition requesting that the compulsory military drill be discontinued. The program had ceased to be "successful and profitable" due to the lack of adequate equipment.[74] The faculty complied with this request.

By the fall of 1918 the War Department was prepared; and it established in colleges the Student Army Training Corps, which was designed to give men under twenty-one years of age some army training while they were still in college. An S.A.T.C. (sometimes referred to as Safe At The College) unit was organized at SMU with three hundred men who were actually under army discipline, wore uniforms, and received pay. Rankin Hall and North Hall, two men's dormitories, were converted into barracks by replacing the beds with army cots, tearing out the clothes closets, and taking off the doors.[75] At the same time a War Aims course was inaugurated. It consisted of three parts: history and ethical study of war, governmental study, and study of immediate causes of war and the United States's part in it.[76] These programs came to an abrupt end with the armistice in November. By early December the S.A.T.C. was demobilized (doubtless the closets were rebuilt and the doors put back in the men's dorms), and by the spring of 1919 most campuses had returned to normal.

The faculty of SMU was also disrupted by the war. Several of the younger men went into the army, such as Zeek of the French department and Paul W. Terry, who taught education. Two members of the English department, Wannamaker and Hubbell, left for Y.M.C.A. work.[77] John Wynne Barton, who taught economics, went to work for the War Risk Insurance Commission. And Dean Keen of the arts college left briefly in the spring of 1917 to work for the Justice Department with the Secret Service. The board agreed to "lend" him to the government with half pay. He returned to SMU for the 1917-18 session but left permanently at the end of that year.[78] These changes in the faculty disrupted classroom instruction and made necessary numerous adjustments in teaching assignments.

When the war period was over, SMU showed the marks of these troubled years, as did every other institution. The financial condition of the university had been shaky from the beginning, but the strains of these war years with decreased attendance precipitated the financial difficulties of 1919-1920.

Student Life in the Early Years

The system of government and discipline of college students which was adopted by Southern Methodist University was the traditional paternalistic one with elaborate rules for control. It was a system which regarded college education as far more than an intellectual enterprise. The college assumed responsibility for the moral as well as the intellectual development of the students. This "collegiate way of living" stressed the housing of students in closely supervised dormitories, compulsory attendance at religious exercises, and the enforcement of discipline *in loco parentis*. There was no doubt in the minds of the Methodist leaders or the faculty that this was the kind of control that SMU should exercise. The parents of the students expected this, and the condition of the times demanded it.

The roots of this type of discipline and control go back to the old English system of colleges which was transplanted to this country and took root in the colonial colleges. These schools had a deep concern for saving the student's soul and overseeing his moral life. Character training was just as important as intellectual training. According to this system college students were regarded as immature adolescents, requiring guidance at every turn. Student misconduct outside of class, or even academic failure in class, was regarded as reflecting on the university, not on the individual. This attitude was in direct contrast to that at the continental universities, where the students were regarded as responsible adults, so that an intellectual, impersonal atmosphere prevailed. At these institutions the students made their own arrangements for board and room and were responsible for their own moral growth, while the universities assumed responsibility merely for their intellectual training. It is difficult to imagine two more different outlooks.

Southern Methodist was thoroughly permeated with paternalism, especially with regard to the women students. All women, except those with close relatives in the city, had to live in the dormitory. The Women's Building was a handsome structure, one of the two permanent buildings on the campus. Every night except Saturday the students were expected to be in their rooms by eleven o'clock. On Saturday they were allowed to remain out until half past eleven. Quiet hours were to be observed every evening from eight o'clock when the study bell rang until half past seven the following morning and during two hours on Sunday afternoon. Women were forbidden to leave the campus without a chaperon, forbidden to ride in automobiles on country highways, or to sit in a parked car after dark. An automatic sentence of confinement to the campus for one week was levied against a girl who danced. Smoking was so unlikely that there were not even rules against it during the first few years.[79]

Mrs. Hyer, the wife of the president, was in charge of the Women's Building, and she supervised all the students as closely as she would her own daughters. She was a cultured lady of the old southern type whose demeanor demanded ladylike behavior. The Hyers had an apartment in the dormitory, and all the women students, some of the faculty, and the Hyer family ate in the dining room. At the sound of the bell the students would file down the steps and remain standing until President Hyer said grace.[80]

The Hyers continued to live in the women's building until 1919, when the president built a home across the street from the campus. The earlier arrangement had posed some difficulties. In the fall of the second year Hyer was questioned by the board because he and his family seemed to be provided with room and board at no cost. Hyer made it clear that his contract provided for these privileges. This episode led to a change. Henceforth, all the "managers, employees, and occupants of both dormitories were charged the scheduled prices for both room and board."[81]

An important aspect of the traditional college life was compulsory chapel. Even by the second decade of the twentieth century, many colleges and universities still adhered to this rule. These included Yale, Princeton, and even such public institutions as the University of Georgia. This concept was on its way out. It had been abolished by Harvard, Johns Hopkins, Cornell, and the University of Wisconsin, although not without a struggle.[82] But it was to remain a prominent feature of church-supported schools. It was not until 1940 that compulsory chapel was abolished at SMU.

Chapel services at SMU were held every day at ten o'clock and lasted for twenty minutes. The services were conducted by the chaplain—Ivan Lee Holt until 1918, then Paul Kern. Students were assigned seats: freshmen in the front, then sophomores, juniors, and seniors in due order. Each row had a monitor who checked any vacant seats and reported absences. "If a student missed chapel he must turn in an excuse; the only acceptable excuses," wrote a former student, "were illness, absence from the city, battle, murder, or sudden death."[83] If a student missed chapel, the dean would have a talk with him. If the absence continued, the student's parents would be informed. If he still did not mend his ways, he would be asked to withdraw.[84] However, there is no record that this ever occurred. The students were also expected to attend a church service every Sunday. In order to accommodate the students, a church was organized on the campus early in 1916. A. Frank Smith was the first minister of this Highland Park Methodist Church.[85] It was obviously more difficult to enforce this church-going rule, and by 1920 the regulation was abandoned. As further indication of the influence of the church, every student was required to have a course in the Bible to graduate.

Absence from class was regarded more seriously than absence from chapel. For the first couple of years a student could be suspended if he missed a class more than six times in a term. Later this rule was changed to read one-tenth of the class sessions.[86] The first term the university opened, a senior was expelled for exceeding six unexcused absences. A few weeks later another student even apologized to the faculty for leaving school, but he was not allowed to return until the following term.[87] Thus, the university played to the hilt the role of a parent in regulating what the students could and could not do.

However, this was not the only force at work within the American university. Even in the closing years of the nineteenth century, the concept of treating students as adults and expecting them to use self-discipline was gaining headway at Harvard under Charles William Eliot. Other reformers of the period, Barnard of Columbia, White of Cornell, and Harper of Chicago, aimed for a similar goal.[88] The idea of expecting students to exert a mature sense of responsibility permeated even this small Methodist college in the Southwest.

This concept was expressed in the various movements for self-government, which assumed three principal forms on American university campuses. First was the establishment of student committees to maintain order in the dorms. Second, groups of student advisors were formed to consult with the faculty on various matters. And last was the actual delegation of responsibility for disciplinary control to the students.[89] The first two of these approaches were put into effect during the early years of SMU, but the last was not implemented. Both the men's and women's dormitories set up committees to enforce the various rules and regulations. The Women's Governing Board attacked unladylike behavior and lack of decorum, but the men were left far freer to write their own rules.[90]

The students who met with the faculty to consult on various matters were the officers of the Student Association. This was an organization of all students which had "general oversight on all matters pertaining to student conduct and student elections."[91] This group was basically responsible for all student activities and organizations and had authority to control these, within the rules set down by the university. The officers frequently appeared before the faculty to discuss such matters as appropriations for the yearbook, length of trips for the Glee Club, and the number of extracurricular activities in which a student might participate. Student groups, however, were never delegated any real responsibility for disciplinary control of students. This authority rested first with the discipline committee, but in the last analysis, with the faculty who had to vote on the suspension, dismissal, or expulsion of a student.[92]

A special form of the new concept of self-discipline and responsibility among American college students was represented by what came to be called the honor system. This plan took deeper roots in the universities south of the Mason-Dixon line. The honor system was introduced at one of the early faculty meetings the first year SMU opened[93] and remained in effect until 1929. It was administered by the students themselves. Two members elected from each class had the responsibility for enforcing this system. If a student was accused of violating the honor system, he was brought before an honor council. This system worked only so long as the students informed the council of violations. But the continued vitality of the idea that it is not honorable to inform on a fellow classmate made the system unworkable. This was the situation that developed in the late twenties and caused the honor system to cease functioning effectively.[94]

During these early years the students who attended SMU came primarily from Dallas and the surrounding area. Approximately 70 percent of the students lived within a hundred miles of Dallas. By 1925 this figure had risen to nearly 80 percent.[95] These figures bore out the expectation of President Hyer and Wallace Buttrick of the General Education Board that a university would flourish only if it were in an urban area from which it could draw its student body. SMU was distinctly a regional institution, a characteristic that did not begin to diminish until after World War II.

The students were an unsophisticated but eager group, drawn largely from Dallas and the surrounding area in North Texas. They came to SMU "expecting anything but the routine they had known" and were bursting with energy, anxious for experience. The first few generations of students possessed an unusually large number of able young people, a "scattered leadership of high talent," as shown by the wit and ability which was demonstrated in the campus newspaper, the student assemblies, and the classrooms.[96] Perhaps the spirit existed for a few years because the university, the students, and a large portion of the faculty were all young together. Patterns had to be formed, precedents set, a task at which all worked together.[97]

An observant, articulate student of these first years perceived this characteristic. The university community which existed on the northern edge of Dallas was like a big family. All its members were new, most were young, and everyone felt the spirit of adventure of a new university. Flora Lowrey wrote of the relationship between the faculty and students:

> There was a rapport between the first faculty and the first student body, our relationship was informal. There were no snack bars, no place to drink a cup of coffee together, but we talked together through paths (there were no walks), talked together in the parlor, discussed issues in the classrooms and offices. We all had the same goals. We were establishing a university, setting precedents, and laying a foundation. The spirit of endeavor was high, and we worked together in perfect accord.[98]

Paul van Katwijk, the second dean of the music school, described these early years as ones of "almost idyllic simplicity and freshness," which were filled "with joys of new cultural enterprise."[99] Even allowing for the romantic glow that ensuing years can throw over events passed, one concludes that a certain espirit de corps must have marked the faculty and students then.

At least a couple of factors aided this feeling of unity. One was the geographic isolation of the campus from the city of Dallas. Highland Park had very few homes which were close to the campus, and University Park possessed even fewer. Since the academic community was small and isolated, it developed a cohesion of its own. Another factor which brought the group together was true propinquity: all the classes were held in one building, Dallas Hall. Everyone saw everyone else daily. All gathered together daily (or at least were supposed to) for chapel. Herbert Gambrell wrote later of this unity in spirit:

> It all seemed pretty grand, that university under a single roof. Of course, fumes from the chemistry laboratory and hamburger grill in the basement had a way of rising and penetrating; and the sounds of piano's lungs and brass instruments at work on the third floor floated downward. Odors from the cooking laboratory beneath the library made hungry students drool and

some complained that the embalming fluid in which biology specimens were preserved was unpleasant to smell in adjacent rooms. But it all seemed right and proper to us pioneers.

Not many of us knew anything about higher education except what we had observed in Dallas Hall. We just naturally supposed that these were things that made college different from high school.[100]

CHAPTER V

A Series of Crises,
1919-1925

DESPITE THE OUTWARD SIGNS of vigor and health that the university
possessed with an active student body increasing in size every year and a
group of young, reasonably capable faculty members, Southern Methodist
was by 1919 in severe financial troubles. For a time it appeared the school
might even be forced to close. This was the most serious problem. However, these years saw in addition two other controversies: one between the
faculty and the board over the control of athletics, the other between the
forces of fundamentalism and modernism within the Methodist church
which resulted in the forced resignation of two faculty members. By 1925
the financial basis of the university had improved considerably, but the
two other disputes left a residue of bitter feelings among the board, administration, and faculty.

Financial Problems

The financial support of the university had been inadequate from the
very beginning. The situation failed to improve after the university began
operating; in fact it became worse. The lack of students and decreased
income brought about by the First World War caused further financial
hardships. The crisis came to a head in 1920 when President Hyer was
asked to resign to make way for a new man who, it was hoped, could
solve the financial problems. This new president was H. A. Boaz.

The board expressed its confidence in the ability of Boaz to rescue
the university from these financial straits. He did not disappoint them.
Within a year the debt was reduced and a new campaign for the "Second
Million" had begun. Again the university turned to the General Education Board and for the second time received a conditional grant. This
time, however, SMU was able to meet the conditions laid down by the

71

board and received the full amount offered. The result was that by 1924 the university had received a third of a million dollars from the General Education Board, had raised and actually collected over a million itself, and was completely free of any debts or mortgages.

Such a great accomplishment was not the work of Boaz alone. He was president only two years, during which time the groundwork was laid. In 1922 he was elected a Bishop of the Methodist Episcopal Church, South. After an interim of nearly a year, a new president was finally found, Charles Claude Selecman. It was he who carried the financial campaign to a successful conclusion. By the mid 1920s the university was on a far more stable basis and could look to the future with a measure of confidence.

President Hyer had attempted to deal with the growing financial crises, but his great talent as a college president was not in the role of a promoter or fund raiser. He was well aware of his lack of talent in this direction and always attempted to assign such duties to someone else. At the time he was elected president of SMU, he was insistent that H. A. Boaz serve as vice-president with the primary duty of raising money. Boaz served in this capacity for two years during the initial campaign to raise a million dollars. When the campaign was over in 1913 and it appeared that the university had raised enough money to meet the conditions of the General Education Board, Boaz resigned and returned to the presidency of Polytechnic to aid that college in its transformation into the Woman's College of Texas Methodism.[1] The post of vice-president and financial officer remained vacant until 1915, when Casper S. Wright, a Methodist minister, was selected for that position. He was designated as an adviser to the president for financial matters and was to be the university's chief fund raiser.[2] But unfortunately Wright was no more successful in collecting the promised money from the Methodists than anyone else. He served as vice-president until 1917, when he resigned. The post was not filled until 1919, when Horace M. Whaling, Jr., of the School of Theology was selected.[3]

Shortly before the university opened in 1915, the liabilities of the institution were $261,767. At this same time the endowment was $146,-758, of which $111,539 had come from the General Education Board.[4] By the following year the liabilities had nearly doubled, rising to $414,-379. This increase represented the money that the university had to borrow in order to open and begin operating. The sum included the cost of building the three hastily constructed brick veneer dormitories for men, furnishing the buildings, and constructing the steam plant. The endowment had happily risen, to $212,147, but the amount was still so small that the income produced from it was insignificant. The net loss for operating the university proper the first year was $22,955.[5]

The university continued to operate with a deficit every year. In 1917 the deficit had risen to $33,000, and by 1918 it was $37,000; in 1919 it was slightly smaller, $34,000. With annual deficits the total indebtedness of the university rose throughout the period. In 1917 it was $339,122, by 1919 it had risen to $358,697, and when Hyer resigned it was $362,-802.[6]

During these years the university was trying to operate on the income it received from tuition and fees. But as Hyer pointed out in his letter of resignation, "Higher education costs more than its selling price, and the cost is rapidly increasing." He stated further that in 1915 the average cost per student in the 574 colleges and universities in the United States had been $294. During this year SMU had only $170 per student from its income, far below the national average.[7] In order to have an adequate income a university needed a substantial amount of productive endowment. This is always the problem of the private college. During these early years the university tried to operate with support that was provisional and temporary in nature. Its financial problems continued until more permanent support was found in the early twenties.

By the spring of 1919 a crisis faced the university. The Visiting Committee of the Methodist Church reported:

Our present financial condition is little short of desperate. The banks which hold our notes have every inclination to be kind, but they are becoming increasingly uneasy concerning the securities which they hold against our note. . . . The institution is leading, financially, a hand-to-mouth existence which is in a real degree perilous. Frequent financial emergencies are met by the local supporters of the University, either by actual cash donations or by advancing personal collateral to secure loans. . . . We urge that some practical, intelligent plan be adopted at once to secure an adequate and dignified support for the immediate needs of the university.[8]

Twice within the past two years the university officials had been called upon to improvise in order to pay the salaries of the teachers. In 1918 Hyer himself lent the university $10,000 of his personal funds for this purpose,[9] and in June, 1919, a similar crisis occurred. On this occasion $40,000 was needed or the university would not be able to open its doors in the fall. Hyer called together twenty leading businessmen in Dallas who were interested in the university to discuss the latest financial crisis. He asked them to sign a note in order to borrow the money from the Security National Bank. Those present hesitated to obligate themselves for such a large amount but did finally agree that each of them would sign an individual note for $2,000. These notes were paid off in the spring of 1921.[10]

As early as the spring of 1919 the members of the Board of Trustees were sufficiently dissatisfied with the leadership Hyer was providing that they seriously considered asking him to resign. One proposal put forth by R. H. Shuttles was to ask Bishop John M. Moore to be chancellor. The idea evidently was to increase the status of the head of the university in order to make the raising of money easier. Bishop Moore was not at all interested in the proposition.[11] Bishop Mouzon also encouraged him to decline the offer, because he could not be both a bishop and the head of a university.

As soon as word of this move became known, the faculty rushed to Hyer's defense. All those who were full professors signed a letter to the board expressing their confidence in Hyer and asking that no changes be made. They wrote:

> We hold the President in the highest esteem as regards those matters which are really vital to the success of the enterprise in which we are jointly engaged. He has conceived and steadily held in mind the true ideal for a university. . . . In largeness of conception, and in rightness of estimate as to the fundamentals of an institution of higher learning, he has proven preeminently wise, and is a leader among educators in the South. The entire faculty are his earnest supporters, and covet for the institution his continued direction and leadership.[12]

The faculty of the School of Theology also supported the action of the arts college.

This quieted the criticism of Hyer, but only briefly. The financial situation remained as grave as ever, and the board slowly became convinced that the only way to improve it was to replace the leadership of the university. The choice of the executive committee fell quite naturally upon H. A. Boaz. He had long been associated with education in Texas and had the reputation of being a promoter and a fund raiser. By this time Boaz had left Fort Worth and moved to Louisville, Kentucky, where he was the secretary of the Board of Church Extension. He was invited to meet with the members of the executive committee, Joseph E. Cockrell, W. D. Bradfield, R. H. Shuttles, and Bishop Mouzon, who offered

him the presidency of the sorely troubled university. Boaz was not in-
clined to accept this difficult task, but Shuttles told him unless he accepted the presidency and got SMU out of debt, the university would have
to close. The institution had borrowed all the money it could, and without
money it could not operate.[13] Bishop Mouzon expressed the same sentiments to Boaz in a letter: "We must have better business management or
nothing but ruin is before us."[14]

Shortly after this meeting Bishop Mouzon was in Louisville on other
business and further urged Boaz to accept the presidency. Boaz agreed
upon certain conditions. Whereupon Bishop Mouzon wired Judge Cockrell that Boaz had accepted. However, the telegram that Cockrell received
read (in the days of Prohibition): "*Booze* is available. Call the Board
at once."[15] The good Methodists were duly shocked.

The arrangements between Boaz and the university included several
points. Boaz was to receive a salary of $6,000 a year ($1,000 more than
Hyer) and to be provided with a "suitable" house (Hyer had to provide
his own). In return, Boaz would be expected to raise a million dollars
for the university. Boaz also expressed as a condition of his acceptance
that his election be unanimous and that it meet with Hyer's approval.[16]

The truth of the matter is that Hyer had very little to say about it.
He was asked by W. D. Bradfield, as a representative of the board, to
resign. He evidently had not anticipated this action. His daughter wrote:

> I remember most vividly that cold, rainy afternoon when Mother and I
> were in the little garage house; Father came in with a strange look on his
> face, sat down, gripped the arms of the chair, and said in a strange voice:
> "I have been asked to resign the presidency."[17]

This was a blow to him, but he behaved in his usual quiet, dignified
manner. His letter of resignation to the board is a poignant, beautifully
written document.

Naturally enough, he did all he could to defend the record of his
administration. He pointed out that his own personal efforts had always
been directed toward the academic side of university work, and he felt
he had accepted the presidency with this understanding. The promoting
and raising of money was simply not his area of responsibility. The
nature of the presidency had changed, he noted:

> For a number of years there has been a growing feeling that a college
> president must be a diplomatist in politics or a promoter in finance; the
> president of a state institution should be the former, the president of a private

institution should be the latter; while the president of a church institution must be both. . . .

. . . We have tried financial agents and vice-presidents, and now to the one who in the judgment of the Board is capable of relieving our present stress and of providing adequate funds for future growth I gladly yield all of the honors that properly belong to the presidency of the university.[18]

Hyer was given the title of President Emeritus. He retained the professorship of physics at his presidential salary and continued teaching at the university until his death in 1929.

Robert S. Hyer would have made an excellent president of a small, adequately financed liberal arts college. He was at his best in his relationship with the faculty and in administering academic matters. He was a scholar and a teacher who possessed rare academic insight. By his own admission he was not a public relations expert or a fund raiser. Nor was he ever convinced that this should be a function of the presidency.

His only previous academic experience had been at Southwestern, where administration was pretty much of a one-man affair. In addition to his duties as president, Hyer had acted as chief disciplinarian, kept the academic records of the college, taken charge of the routine business details, as well as taught classes in various fields of science. It was not until the end of his administration that C. C. Cody became dean and not until 1909 that Frank Reedy was hired as bursar. Operating a little college like Southwestern was possible with relatively little administration.

With a few exceptions Hyer tried to administer Southern Methodist in the same manner. His indispensible right-hand man was still Frank Reedy, who did anything and everything President Hyer wanted. Three out of the five years he was president after the university opened, Hyer performed the tasks of dean as well as president. For a shorter period there was no vice-president at all. All during his tenure in office he taught physics and was chairman of that department. It is no wonder that he did not find time to be a fund raiser (even if he had had the inclination).

In short, his conception of the presidency of Southern Methodist University was the same as it had been of Southwestern. But by 1920 even a university the size of SMU required more in the way of administration. It required a president who was not so much a scholar or teacher as a businessman and promoter, one who could seek out new sources of revenue and not wait for them to appear on the doorstep of the university. These new universities were of necessity highly organized institutions unlike the colleges of an earlier day.

The board was aware that Hyer was trying to do everything himself and instructed him in June, 1919, to give up the teaching of physics "in order that he might give his time more exclusively to executive and administrative interests of the university."[19] Bishop Mouzon also indicated disapproval of Hyer's desire to make someone else the financial agent for the university while he held himself aloof from that chore.[20]

Despite these differences, Hyer served the university well. He had the respect and admiration of the faculty, which the following two presidents, who were far better fund raisers, did not always have. He had a vision of a great Methodist university in Dallas. Toward this goal he worked diligently for years. He designed the campus and buildings on a grand scale; he selected capable members of the first faculty; he organized the schools and departments; and he set high standards of scholarship. This kind of leadership is absolutely indispensable to a new institution.

The situation that Boaz faced when he began his administration was made more difficult by the nation-wide depression that followed the First World War. This depression brought a decline in farm prices that saw little recovery even after prosperity returned in 1922. All educational institutions were highly vulnerable to the economic conditions of the nation. To help relieve the distress of the colleges, John D. Rockefeller gave the General Education Board a special gift. Even before his resignation, Hyer had contacted the board and received a promise that SMU would be included in the list of institutions that would be given aid.[21] Boaz, Hyer, and Bishop John M. Moore went to New York to make the final arrangements with Wallace Buttrick, who was still executive secretary.[22]

The agreement that was made in 1920 provided that the board would grant to SMU a third of a million dollars for endowment, the income from which was to be used in raising teachers' salaries. This gift was conditional upon the university's raising another two-thirds of a million, which also had to be used for endowment, and upon the university's being free of debt. For additional assistance, the board would grant to the university $16,667 annually for two years while the money was being raised.[23] This sum equaled 5 percent of the grant, which meant the university was receiving as much money as if the grant had already been awarded and invested at 5 percent. Boaz promptly raised all salaries 15 percent for 1920-21 and 10 percent for the following year.[24] This increase in salaries was a morale builder and aided in the acceptance of the new administration.

The university was also in need of immediate cash to pay current bills amounting to $50,000. Boaz secured $100,000 by selling fifty lots north of the campus to a small group of wealthy Methodists in Wichita Falls: W. B. Hamilton, J. J. Perkins, and Norris Martin.[25] Later additional land was sold, and the proceeds were used to reduce the debt from $362,802 in 1920 to $123,000 in 1922.[26] These lands had been given to the university when it located in Dallas.

The campaign began immediately for the $666,666 which the university had to raise to meet the conditions of the General Education Board. Boaz devoted most of his time to this project and was aided by bishops Mouzon, Moore, and Ainsworth, as well as by Dallas presiding elder W. J. Johnson. Toward the end of the campaign J. D. Young, who had assisted with the 1912 campaign, worked strenuously in Dallas by organizing dinners for solicitors and creating rivalry among them. The plan was effective, and by November, 1920, pledges of an adequate amount had been secured.[27]

This time, however, the stumbling block that held up the qualification for the grant was not so much the inability to turn pledges into cash as the failure of the university to liquidate its debt and, most of all, the failure to provide itself with an adequate system of accounting. The General Education Board indicated that it could not pay the $333,333 until a new system had been set up. In February, 1922, the board sent H. J. Thorkelson to perform this service. And, indeed, it was a service, although the university probably did not regard it as such at the time. One of the creative roles played by the General Education Board and similar agencies was in establishing uniform accounting systems in colleges and universities.

The report issued by Thorkelson in May, 1922, was highly critical of the old system of bookkeeping and suggested certain corrections. Thorkelson found that the audits from 1916 through 1921

betray[ed] from the beginning, a lack of understanding of the meaning of endowment, the fundamental difference between an institution conducted for pecuniary profit and an educational institution, the effect which the terms of a gift have on its accounting classification, and a failure to appreciate the necessity of keeping inviolate such gifts as were made for endowment.[28]

In other words, endowment money must be kept separate and must never be put in the general fund, as the university had done on a number of occasions because of great financial pressures. The report also deplored the listing of subscriptions and notes on the credit side, whereas only cash, securities, and gifts of real estate should be so counted. Thorkelson ended by terming the financial picture "not particularly bright, although by no means hopeless." He pointed out that the enrollment, which was rapidly increasing, indicated the need for the institution and that SMU's location in a growing, active community with a large population afforded the university every chance for success. The most pressing need was for money to meet the current debt and then a larger endowment to meet SMU's growing obligation to the public.

These defects in the accounting system had not gone completely unnoticed by university officials. The Visiting Committee of the Methodist Church had noted in 1920 that certain funds which had been collected for building or endowment purposes had gone into the general fund. President Boaz had observed that money which had been assessed and collected for the School of Theology had been consumed in the general budget.[29] While he was president, Boaz attempted to institute some better financial practices, such as making out a budget for the coming year. There is no record that this was ever done and the budget formally presented to the board before 1920. It was also Boaz who finally threw out $239,236 of doubtful notes from the campaign back in 1911-1913.[30] In short, he was moving in the direction of a modern system of accounting.

Not only did the General Education Board require the university to systemize its books, but it required that any money which had been diverted from endowment or building funds since the university began operation be restored to its proper category. Thorkelson figured out how much the university had collected for each of these funds and discovered that neither of them contained the proper amount. The university had to restore $181,047 to the original endowment fund and $42,736 to the building fund. Moreover, it appeared to Thorkelson that the university had never even qualified for the original grant the board had given the university. All of this refiguring of the finances meant that now the university had to raise more money than originally thought necessary to qualify for the new grant. Now they needed to collect not only $666,666 and pay off the current debt, but also had to raise an additional $223,783 to restore the endowment and building funds.[31]

The magnitude of the task was enormous, but another intensive campaign was undertaken with Bishop John M. Moore acting as chairman. By the following year the remarkable feat of meeting the General

Education Board's terms had been accomplished.[32] This meant that by the spring of 1924 the university had raised in cash or stock $1,101,599, which included the $666,666 required by the General Education Board, the $223,783 needed to reimburse the endowment and the building funds, and $211,150 for payment of the debt. Considering the tremendous difficulty that the university had had in raising even half that amount during the earlier campaign, this accomplishment was indeed a step forward. For the first time the university was out of debt and had an endowment of $1,523,213. The total plant assets were valued at $1,546,-635.[33] The future looked brighter than it had at any other time.

Several factors made possible the success of this campaign as compared with the earlier one when the university was seeking its original money. In the first place, money was pledged and collected in considerably larger amounts than it had been earlier. During the first campaign there were only three pledges of $25,000, and these were the largest. The bulk of the money was collectd in $25, $50, or $100 notes and paid over a long period of time. During the 1920 campaign, in contrast, gifts were for much larger amounts and were paid either immediately or within a two or three year period. For example, S. I. Munger of Dallas pledged $100,000, and both J. J. Perkins and W. B. Hamilton of Wichita Falls gave $50,000 each. There were two gifts of $25,000 each, two of $15,000, four of $10,000, and thirteen at $5,000.[34] In contrast with the many uncollectable pledges of the first campaign, the collection rate for the second was virtually 100 percent.

The larger contributions were made possible by an increased accumulation of capital in Texas and especially in Dallas. Oil has been, of course, Texas's greatest mineral resource. The famous Spindletop oil field was drilled in Beaumont in 1901 and substantially increased oil production in the state. The discovery of oil at Ranger in 1917 was a matter of world-wide importance, for it added to the oil supplies of the United States and her allies during World War I. It was largely from this field that J. J. Perkins made his money. Perkins aided the university in these early years, and he was to become one of the great benefactors as his wealth increased. Oil production in Texas increased at a phenomenal rate during the twenties and thirties. By 1940 the state was producing 36 percent of all the nation's oil and 23 percent of all the oil in the world.[35] Southern Methodist was to benefit directly from Methodists who became wealthy in this period and from the overall prosperity in general.

The bulk of the support for the university came from the citizens of

Dallas, as it had in the earlier campaign. President Boaz said in 1921:

The city of Dallas is to be commended most highly for the ready and liberal response it has made to the calls of your university. The Chamber of Commerce gave its hearty support to the financial campaign. Individual citizens of wealth and influence who are not members of our Church were active and cordial in their support.[36]

By 1924 it was even more obvious that the great majority of the contributions came from Dallas. Over 70 percent of the money collected came from the local area.[37] An impressive number of business firms contributed substantial sums.

Thus, by the mid 1920s the people of Dallas began to take pride in the university. They sent their children to it in increasing numbers. During this period approximately 50 percent of the students came from Dallas.[38] As early as 1905 Wallace Buttrick had described Dallas as the best unoccupied territory for a university. Events were to prove Buttrick correct many times over. Dallas was a growing urban area, both in wealth and population, and the university was able to grow along with it.

Several other factors aided the financial condition in the early 1920s. At the same time that SMU was conducting its own campaign, the church initiated a Christian Education Movement which was designed to collect $33 million for the ninety-one Methodist colleges and universities owned and operated by the Methodist Epispocal church, South. This campaign got underway slowly and came nowhere near the goal, but by 1924 SMU had received $373,385 from this source. This figure represented only 12 percent of the total asking, but it was gratefully received.[39]

Other revenues were becoming available to the university now that it had achieved something of a reputation. In 1922 the institution was astounded to learn that Col. L. A. Pires, who had never even been on the campus, had willed the university approximately half a million dollars.[40] The E. A. Lilly Estate contributed $50,000 to the university in the form of an annuity plan. The interest from the fund was to be used in educating the Lilly children; then it was to be used to endow a professorship.[41] This annuity idea proved to be a popular one which was used by other donors. A School of Citizenship was established by Ora Nixon Arnold with a gift of $120,000.[42]

Originally the university had relied on the Methodist churches throughout the state to support the institution. But they had simply not been able to produce the kind of money a university needed. The conference assessments throughout these early years were low. For example,

the university received only $24,000 for both the School of Theology
and the arts college in 1917-1918. The sum was increased to $56,000
the following year.[43] This was a fairly reliable source of income; but when
it came to large sums of money for buildings and endowments, the university had to rely on individuals of wealth throughout the state. These
wealthy benefactors rather than the church itself sustained the university.

The two years during which Boaz was president were tumultuous,
troubled times. While his main efforts were directed toward solving the
financial crises, he was also besieged by such diverse problems as heresy
and football. Because of his brief tenure, Boaz never became intimately
concerned with the academic affairs of the university. These were left
largely in the hands of A. S. Pegues, dean of the College of Arts, and
Paul B. Kern, dean of the School of Theology. Boaz described the situation in his annual report:

During much of the session now closing I have been absent from my
office by reason of the financial campaign. Since these campaigns have been
concluded I am hoping to devote my entire time and all my energies to the
internal affairs of the university for the next session. By this means I hope to
get in closer touch with the faculty and student body and make my influence
felt for more good in the internal affairs of the university. A great and
effectual door is here open before me.[44]

President Boaz's idea of how to become closer to the students and the
faculty was to uplift the religious life of the university by a revival. He
secured the cooperation of the faculty and students in planning and organizing a "Week of Adjustments," during which speakers were brought
to the campus and additional church services and discussion groups were
held. To President Boaz's mind, it was a period during which anyone who
was "out of adjustment" with himself, his fellow man, or God could
seek a remedy.[45] In order to bring this about Boaz spoke twice a day
during this week; and to cap the climax, Sherwood Eddy, one of the
famous revivalists of the day, conducted the closing services. Administrative opinion conceded the week a success:

Practically the entire student body not already in the knowledge of the
Son of God was swept into the Kingdom. Remarkable demonstrations of
divine power were seen in the conversion of strong young men and women.
Perhaps 300 were reclaimed from a life of religious indifference, about one
hundred professed faith in Christ and the entire faculty and student body
was greatly strengthened in the religious life.[46]

It may be safely concluded from President Boaz's deeds and words that he was not primarily concerned with the university as an educational institution. Instead, he thought of it in terms of its ability to provide the proper Christian atmosphere and adequate religious training. He was entirely innocent of ideas on education or the function of a true university. Indeed, these were of little interest to him. He was first a Methodist minister intent upon spreading the kingdom of God. Secondly, his talents lay in the area of fund raising and the promotion of causes. This accounts for lack of interest in the academic aspects of the university. Perhaps if he had remained as president for a longer period, he would have developed some concern for educational policy. But his election to the episcopacy cut off such growth.

Boaz's greatest service to the university lay in the belief he inspired in others that he could solve the financial problems and the rapport that he had with the business community of Dallas. The image of the university in the eyes of Dallas acquired a brighter luster. Boaz was in the presidency just long enough to claim the honor of saving the university,[47] but not long enough to have felt the consequences of any of his policies. As can now be seen, his successes were accomplished at the price of considerable smoldering internal friction.

A successor to President Boaz was not immediately found. In fact, the university was without a president from May, 1922, until March, 1923. The nominating committee appointed by the board consisted of Joseph E. Cockrell, R. Hall Shuttles, S. B. Perkins, Bishop John M. Moore, and Cullom Booth.[48] It was almost immediately apparent that the selection of a president would take a long time, because by September the committee had no nominee.

One of the prominent contenders for the presidency was Charles C. Selecman, the forceful and articulate minister of the First Methodist Church in Dallas. Since Selecman was obviously talented and capable, a "boom for him for president" was started by some of the Methodists in Dallas. Both Shuttles and Perkins favored him, but Booth, who was a prominent minister from Waco, was less than enthusiastic.[49] The major objection to Selecman was that he did not have even a B.A. degree. Booth felt that "at this juncture . . . a school man of proven ability" was needed as well as "a layman who would make the building of a great university the supreme task of his life with no episcopal ambitions to divert him."[50] Whether the previous experience with Boaz or knowledge of Selecman's desires prompted this reference to episcopal ambitions it is impossible to determine, but it would apply in either case.

Finally on October 11, 1922, the board elected John Wynne Barton president.[51] According to H. M. Whaling, Jr., the vice-president, Barton was a compromise candidate, the only name upon which the board could agree.[52] He had been a member of the original faculty and had left at the time of the First World War to work for the War Risk Insurance Corporation. He returned to the university briefly in 1920 to become dean of the newly organized College of Applied Arts and Sciences. At the time he was elected president, he was serving as the publishing agent for the church in Nashville.[53]

The board obviously failed to ask Barton if he would allow his name to be considered, because Barton was completely surprised by his election. He wrote to Judge Cockrell:

I can hardly express to you how powerful my surprise was to receive your telegram last night. I had thought that my name would not even be mentioned and I can hardly see how I can accept. I shall write you more fully when the letter referred to in your telegram is received.[54]

After considering the matter for several weeks, Barton declined the presidency. He had assumed his duties with the publishing house only a few months earlier, was just beginning a major reorganization, and felt he could not leave. It is entirely possible that if the offer had come a few years later, he would have been pleased to accept it. In 1933 he became president of Ward Belmont College in Nashville, where he remained until his death in 1936.

At the same time that Barton was selected president, the board realized that some provision would have to be made for an acting president, since it was assumed that Barton, even if he accepted, would not begin the duties until the following June. James Kilgore of the theological faculty was chosen to fill this position.[55] He was a logical choice, because he was one of the senior faculty members who had long been active in the educational work of the church. From all indications, he was not being considered for the presidency on a permanent basis.

To aid Acting President Kilgore, Bishop John M. Moore was asked to serve as counselor to the administration with a desk and a salary. He was also invited to live in the president's house until the coming of a permanent president. Earlier the bishop had been informally asked to serve as chancellor; but he had declined the honor, indicating he would serve in any other capacity he could.[56]

The second choice for the presidency apparently was Ivan Lee Holt, who had been on the original theological faculty and had been the first chaplain. Holt had remained with the university only until 1918, when he left to take the pastorate of St. John's Methodist Church in St. Louis. The board must have profited by the experience with Barton, because Judge Cockrell wrote Holt and asked him if he would allow his name to be considered. Holt replied that he was unable to leave his work in St. Louis at that time and declined the offer.[57]

Not until March 31, 1923, did the board agree upon the election of Charles Claude Selecman as the third president of Southern Methodist University. By this date other possibilities had been exhausted, and the board returned to one of the first names suggested. Evidently the nominating committee did not present any names in nomination. The board simply voted and when the ballots were counted, it was found Selecman had a majority of the votes.[58]

The choice of Selecman for the presidency was achieved reluctantly and with little enthusiasm because of his lack of formal academic education and of any experience in university affairs. He had attended Central College in Fayette, Missouri, but had never graduated. He had earned his reputation as a forceful minister and strong preacher by his twenty-six years in various pastorates which included St. Louis, New Orleans, Los Angeles, and Dallas.[59] His support came from the Dallas Methodists, but the faculty probably viewed his election with skepticism.

Athletic Controversy

During the interval between presidents, a power vacuum existed. Both the faculty and the executive committee of the board attempted to fill this vacuum and exercise the power that belonged to the presidency. The result was a tug of war between these two groups that erupted in a dispute over the control of athletics or, more specifically, whether SMU football recruiting was conducted according to the rules of the Southwest Conference. This dispute was the manifestation of the deeper issue of who would run the university, the faculty and the administration or the executive committee of the board. The laymen on the board, notably chairman Joseph E. Cockrell and Hall Shuttles, felt the university should be run by the businessmen of Dallas, not by the faculty and president. The faculty and administration, naturally enough, disagreed with this idea.

The background of the athletic controversy goes back to the Boaz administration. Southern Methodist did not possess a winning football team in the early years, which troubled no one greatly. But by 1920 some of the businessmen in Dallas put pressure upon the university to build up a team that could at least make a respectable showing.[60] President Boaz described his efforts to assemble a winning football team:

Since the University was on a sound financial basis and the spiritual atmosphere on the campus had been greatly improved, and since the faculty was doing most excellent work in the classroom it seemed to me that we ought to lay some emphasis on securing a winning football team. . . . Ray Morrison was secured as head coach. His task was to assemble and train a winning team if that could be done. Our vice president, Dr. H. M. Whaling, was to assist him in any way he could. In keeping with the practice of other universities, scouts were looking for good players and the usual inducements offered to them in order to have them registered in S.M.U.[61]

By the fall of 1921 a freshman football team composed of these recruits and some transfer students had been assembled. Since neither was eligible to play under the rules of the Southwest Conference, these players trained all year in order to be ready for the 1922 season. The *Campus* followed the activities of this freshman team as closely as it did those of the varsity team.[62] The freshman team set a record during the year which made it clear that SMU would provide some competition in the conference the following year.

During the spring of 1922 voices of criticism were heard from both the faculty and the students about this new policy. The faculty were unhappy with the emphasis placed upon football and were critical of spending money to build up a winning football team when the university had little money to run its academic program.[63] The students spoofed the administration's policy in the April Fool edition of the *Dinkey*[64] so severely that the board thought it reflected on the character and the motives of President Boaz and demanded an apology.[65] The students signed an apology but did not make any retractions regarding the substance of their comments.

The situation which developed at SMU regarding the subsidizing of football players was not unique. Other colleges and universities were doing the same thing. In an effort to keep football on an amateur basis, the Southwest Conference established in May, 1922, a new series of rules which were designed to prevent a college or university from offering financial inducements to athletes. These rules prohibited campaigning for athletes either by correspondence or personal solicitation. No athlete was to be paid for work that he did not perform. No scholarship was to be granted for athletic ability only. Training tables could be maintained but only for those athletes who could afford them.[66] These were drastic rules: almost every action taken by SMU to build up its team was now declared illegal.[67] The president of the Southwest Conference was J. S. McIntosh of the SMU faculty, a man who had long fought to uphold high standards and who continued to believe firmly in faculty control of athletics.

In the fall of 1922 the team which had been carefully groomed the year before was now ready to perform. This season turned out to be the best that the university had ever had. SMU played nine games, won five of them, lost three, and tied one. The year before, the SMU Mustangs had played only six games and lost five of them.[68]

Clearly the system of recruiting players produced a better football team. All its endeavors, however, backfired on the university when in December, 1922, the Southwest Conference proposed a resolution charging that SMU had violated the rules of the conference and should be suspended. The resolution maintained that the faculty was not in control of athletics and that some of the football players were ineligible to play under the conference rules. Some athletes were not full-time students but were registered as adult specials. Others were transfer students who lacked the required credit. These athletes had also been subsidized to an extent not allowed by the conference. Some were paid as high as $1.75 an hour for services they did not perform, and cash loans were made to others without requiring them to sign notes. The investigating committee recommended that SMU be suspended from the conference until the faculty gained control of athletics, and the questionable athletics were declared ineligible. This resolution failed to pass, four delegates voting in its favor and three against it. SMU escaped being suspended because the required two-thirds majority fell one vote short; the vote which saved SMU was that of its own representative.[69]

The action of the conference was based upon an investigation conducted the previous spring by a conference committee in which these numerous irregularities were found. Officials of the university reflected various attitudes toward the charges. Ray Morrison, the coach, denied they were true and insisted that the whole controversy was a political attack against the administration. The vice-president, H. M. Whaling, Jr., acknowledged that the shortcomings had existed but maintained they had been corrected. Harvie Branscomb, a member of the athletic committee, believed that the faculty had gained a measure of control but was not receiving full cooperation. He asked that the faults be pointed out and assured the conference they would be corrected.[70] These reactions illuminated the divisions within the university.

Even though the university had not been suspended, it needed to take some action to clear up these accusations. The conference authorities informed the university that it would be under suspicion until its faculty had made a thorough investigation and assured the conference that the faculty controlled athletics.[71] The executive committee of the board stated that it "felt deeply the disgrace of the charges and attendant publicity" and asked the athletic committee to prepare a report on the charges and "clear the university of the odium attached to them."[72] This the athletic committee did, but it did not whitewash the university as seemingly the board desired.

The athletic committee at this time was made up of E. H. Jones, chairman, Ray Morrison, Clyde Eagleton, Harvie Branscomb, and J. P. Comer. After the investigation was held, a majority of the committee decided "that certain officials of the university ha[d] adopted a definite policy of favoritism toward athletics."[73] The vote of the committee was three to two; Eagleton, Branscomb, and Comer were the majority, and Jones and Morrison the minority. The full report was presented to a general faculty meeting where it was upheld by a vote of forty-four to twenty-one. Those who voted with the majority included Acting President James Kilgore, Dean E. D. Jennings, and Dean Paul B. Kern. Among those who did not favor the majority report were Vice-President Whaling and Secretary-Treasurer A. D. Schuessler.[74]

The majority report upheld virtually all the charges that were leveled at the university by the Southwest Conference. SMU had continued giving scholarships to athletes after they had been declared illegal by the conference, under the guise of student activity scholarships. On occasion some of the athletes failed to make high enough grades to maintain these scholarships and lost them. However, as soon as an athlete's grades improved, the scholarship was restored with money that was found for him from outside sources. Certain athletes charged their books to the business manager of athletics, who then turned the bill over to the university for payment. Loans were made to athletes upon the unsupported order of the athletics business manager. Campus jobs were created which could not possibly have entailed any real work. The committee felt that beyond a doubt athletes received favors that no other students would have received. It singled out three players as the major recipients of these favors—E. M. Smith, Glen Huff, and Eugene Bedford—and declared them ineligible to play.[75]

The executive committee of the board requested the athletic committee to present its report to the board first.[76] The athletic committee disregarded this request by giving the report to the faculty first, since it felt it was responsible to them, not to the board. This action infuriated the executive committee. Shuttles presented a scorching indictment of the athletic committee to the board. He stated that he regarded such action as contemptuous of the board and felt the findings were a reflection on the Boaz administration. He further felt that the members of the committee who constituted a majority had been elected by a put-up job and that the athletic committee had no right to criticize or interfere with affairs that belonged specifically to the trustees. Shuttles made it clear that he regarded loyalty to the university as an absolute necessity. This statement was tabled after a two-hour discussion.[77]

To emphasize his point further, Shuttles resigned from the board. He explained:

Believing that SMU should be run and officered by business men while faculty of the university believed that the affairs of the school should be handled by churchmen and the faculty, I was forced to tender my resignation some two weeks ago.[78]

However, Shuttles's resignation was not accepted, and he remained on the board.

Bishop Mouzon described Shuttles as an able businessman and a great friend of the university, but the bishop objected when Shuttles wanted to run the university as he did his wholesale jewelry business.[79] Indeed, it seemed not to occur to Shuttles that there was any difference between a business and a university. The faculty and the administration did not share Shuttles's views and found in the control of athletics a way to make their point.

The faculty had a strong case. According to the rules of the Southwest Conference, the faculty was to have control of the athletic program. The executive committee recommended in July, 1922, that this control be delegated to the faculty, and this was approved by the board in October.[80] Here was a matter over which the faculty members had full authority, and under the leadership of Branscomb, Comer, and Eagleton they intended to use it. Bishop Mouzon upheld the faculty in this view as he made clear in a letter to Selecman. The bishop wrote:

It is to be hoped that you will save the university from the complete dominance of a group of laymen who have sought to take over the entire control of the institution. If the president and the faculty are not to manage the internal affairs of the university, the church will soon make itself heard from.[81]

Chairman Cockrell, though, agreed with Shuttles. He even denied that it was the intention of the board to give the faculty control of athletics, and they certainly were not to have control of all university affairs. "If this were the case," he wrote, "we would soon have no university."[82] In this case, however, the board dared not overrule the athletic committee and declare the football players eligible, because SMU would then be suspended from the conference and it would be clear to all that there was no faculty control of athletics.

The board did try to counteract the report of the athletic committee. H. M. Whaling, Jr., wrote a long article denying that the university had shown favoritism. He tried to answer the faculty report point by point but in doing so shed more heat than light on the subject. His comments contained innuendos and accusations aimed at the athletic committee. He said in conclusion:

The majority of the Faculty Athletic Committee seems to construe everything in a way to humiliate SMU and to injure the two men declared ineligible. I get the notion that the majority are always groveling before the Southwest Conference. We have our duties in that conference and we will discharge them like a gentleman. But a group that treated SMU as four members of that body treated our school in December, cannot expect us to sacrifice any of our students just to prove they were right.[83]

Another attempt to present the board's view was contained in an eighty-four page book, supposedly written by Cockrell, entitled *A Review of the Athletic Situation and the Case of Huff and Smith*. The subtitle added that it was "addressed to the Friends and Enemies of Southern Methodist University within and without."[84] Cockrell ordered twenty-five hundred copies so that each student could have one, and Shuttles ordered an additional five hundred copies. The book is full of ridicule and sarcasm and is most concerned with attacking the "enemies of the university within," whom it fails to mention by name. These "enemies" doubtless included John H. McGinnis, J. P. Comer, and Clyde Eagleton. These three had been mentioned at the board meeting as being "disloyal" to the university,[85] and the book's comments are clear enough to permit identification of these faculty members.[86] This publication only intensified the tension already existing between faculty and board.

An editorial in the campus paper put the whole affair in perspective:

It would be impossible to meet the intense ridicule of the pamplet [*A Review of the Athletic Situation*] without employment of similar methods—something which this student paper has neither the right nor the desire to do. . . . The majority report and subsequently the overwhelming endorsement of the faculty established one thing: the system was unwholesome to the best interest of collegiate sport and out of harmony with conference regulation.[87]

When Selecman was elected president, the board passed a resolution which was designed to close this whole affair. It was couched in far more moderate language than Cockrell's book and attempted to end the episode on a conciliatory tone. In essence the resolution declared that the board had confidence in the honesty, sincerity, and integrity of the athletic committee, the faculty, and the executive committee in their handling of the recent athletic situation; that the whole matter be regarded as a closed incident; and that in the future, steps be taken to comply with the rules of the Southwest Conference. The resolution added that athletics were believed to be on an honorable plane and that any irregularities that did occur were due to the rapid growth of the university.[88] It is interesting to note that this was the first admission by the board that any "irregularities" ever had existed. Despite the tone of this resolution a gulf had been created between the board and the faculty, and the tensions left a residue of bitter feelings.

Fundamentalism and Liberalism

During the early part of the twentieth century when the controversy between fundamentalism and liberalism raged through the southern part of the United States, its influence was felt at Southern Methodist on three different occasions. The first, a relatively minor affair in 1917, involved a young English teacher who inadvertently mentioned higher criticism in her class. The other two incidents concerned two professors who were actively and avowedly advocates of liberalism and higher criticism in their classes. The first teacher was retained at the university (until she left of her own accord), but the other two members of the faculty were forced to resign. Southern Methodist University was not able to withstand the pressures of the more conservative religious elements despite the support given by some of the more prominent bishops.

The main issue at SMU was higher criticism, which the fundamentalists feared and attacked whenever it appeared. Higher criticism applies to the Bible those methods which have proved successful in dealing with other ancient writings. This method presupposes that the Bible is like other ancient books and does not require a special method to be understood.

Many southern Protestants clung to an unchanging, infallible Bible as the bedrock of their faith, despite the accumulation of evidence discrediting a full literal acceptance of the scriptures. This desire to cling to the older ways was caused by fear of the rapidly changing events of the postwar years. Militant factions in all churches were shocked by the stirrings in national life. The war itself vastly accelerated change, as did the automobile, the tractor, the radio, movies, mass education, and a host of other factors. The transition to a predominantly urban-industrial society was not accomplished without anguish and contention. Spokesmen for the old order tried to hold onto the older ways of thought and put their faith and belief in a literal interpretation of the scriptures. The critical nature of the decade was reflected in the continuing struggle between the old and the new, between orthodoxy and innovation. By the end of the decade many traditionalists sensed that time was working against them.[89]

Southern Methodist saw its first tensions over the rising influence of liberal theology in the academic year of 1917-1918. Katherine Balderston, who was teaching a sophomore English class, asked the students to read *The Inside of the Cup* by Winston Churchill. This novel deals with two problems: should the church take a stand in politics, and what is a clergyman to do when his belief in the literal inspiration of the Bible has been shaken by higher criticism. The young teacher, who was from the East, was fully aware that this second problem "was loaded with dynamite for the students brought up in the orthodox theological milieu of Southern Methodism," and so she decided, "rather cravenly," as she put it in a letter, "to stick to a discussion of the less controversial question."[90] This approach did not work, and the students insisted upon being told what higher criticism was. This left Miss Balderston without any alternative. She wrote:

I was on the spot and explained it in the least traumatic fashion that my own limited knowledge allowed. Even this watered-down explanation shocked and offended the theological students in the back row, and the upshot was that I reported to the Bishop, and was summoned to a hearing before Bishop Mouzon and the assembled members of the Theological faculty. What an awful Saturday afternoon that was! They decided, when the inquisition was over, that I was not so black as I had been painted, and did not fire me— somewhat to my disappointment.[91]

The news of this encounter leaked out and caused a small furor with a number of faculty and students on Miss Balderston's side (she fails to mention just who). She chose to leave SMU after that academic year to work for the United War Work Campaign. However, after the Armistice in November, she returned to the university for one semester.[92]

The incident indicates the thinking of Methodist leaders in 1918, before the heightened fundamentalist-modernist controversy of the 1920s. They were obviously all opposed to even the mention of such ideas in the classroom by a teacher who had no great inclination to support fundamentalist beliefs. The fact that Bishop Mouzon and the School of Theology could call before them an instructor in the Department of English and subject her to critical questions indicates the climate of opinion. There is no indication what role if any President Hyer played in this affair.

This incident was indeed a tempest in a teapot compared with the Rice affair in 1921. By this time the fundamentalists were defending such an extreme position that they were alienating such moderates as Bishop Mouzon, who now could be classed as a mild modernist. John A. Rice was selected to teach Old Testament in the School of Theology in 1920. He had received the B.A. degree from South Carolina and his theological training from the University of Chicago. He had served at churches in St. Louis and Fort Worth and was widely regarded as a great preacher in the Southwest.[93] Rice had also served on the commission that established the university and had been one of those who, with Bishop Boaz, favored locating the university in Fort Worth.

In December, 1920, Rice's book, *The Old Testament in the Life of Today*, was published. The book had been written before he joined the SMU faculty; in fact, the knowledge that he was to have a book published had enhanced his attractiveness to the university. Rice described the book as "the essence of a life time's thought and study on the vital principles found in the Old Testament, as it applies to the life of this present movement." "It is," he explained, "the gist of lectures that I have given all over the country for twenty years."[94] The book was designed to be used as a textbook in Old Testament courses throughout the country.

In his book Rice puts himself clearly with those who advocate the use of higher criticism. He could be classed as a modernist, but only a mild one. In the introduction to the book, Rice states four things he is trying to accomplish:

First, to trace in broad outline the growth of the Old Testament. . . . It came gradually out of the unfolding life of the Hebrews. . . .

Another end in view is the shifting of attention from texts and verses to men and books. We miss the power of this literature by minute dissection . . . . They [the Old Testament writers and prophets] are dealing with questions we ourselves are now grappling with. . . .

. . . Finally, it is hoped that this interpretation may bring relief to some who are still distressed about the results of scientific biblical criticism. . . . The new knowledge only makes faith easier.[95]

This book did not make life any easier for fundamentalists either inside or outside of Methodism. By the spring of 1921 Rice's book had been read and word had gotten around about what he said in the classroom. Starting in April letters began appearing in the *Texas Christian Advocate* denouncing Rice, his book, and his teaching. Rice himself summed up the charges well. He was accused of being

"a German rationalist," with being "worse than Nietzsche," a "destructive Higher Critic," a "Darwinian evolutionist," with holding the Old Testament to be but a conglomeration of myths, legends, and fairy tales; with making Moses only a great magician and the prophets roving dervishes; with denying that the Bible is a sufficient guide and standard in matters of faith and practice; with denying the supernatural and classing the Bible as mere literature, on a parity with all other literature; with undermining the faith of our fathers. . . .[96]

The author of a weekly column in the *Advocate* also joined in the chorus of criticism of Rice's book:

It is a warp of gold and a woof of cotton. . . . It will cause many a believer to mourn. According to Dr. Rice, the Old Testament is a sort of compilation of mythology, tales of ancient firesides about on a par with the rhymes of Mother Goose, with here and there a bit of authentic history.[97]

Another writer said, "I am glad he has dug to the bottom, but he has no right to put the slush into the young preachers of our land. Let the shavings remain with him, but for God's sake don't ruin the finished product."[98]

Not all of the voices that were raised were critical ones. Some of the most powerful men in the church, such as Bishop Moore and Bishop Mouzon, rose to Rice's defense. Mouzon wrote a long letter to the *Advocate* in which he explained that he had been instrumental in bringing Rice to the School of Theology:

The Committee knew that Dr. Rice's view of the Old Testament was the view of all Old Testament scholars at the present time. The Committee also knew that Dr. Rice was . . . brought up in the lap of Methodism, and that he was true to the great doctrines of Christian experience which are the essential doctrines of Methodism. For these reasons Dr. Rice was chosen.[99]

The bishop went on to support Rice's contention that some parts of the Old Testament are of more value than other parts and that the Old Testament is not the supreme and final book of Christianity, since it was followed by the New Testament. He added that it should not be overlooked that the attack on SMU and Rice began with

certain well known Baptists whose chief interest just now is looking after other people's business. We should let them know that we are able to attend to our own affairs. We Methodists are not in the habit of trying to manage the affairs of the Baptist Church.[100]

The Baptist who was in the center of the agitation was J. Frank Norris, a minister in Fort Worth. Norris early became the belligerent champion of a movement to expose what he considered unsound instruction in the colleges and universities throughout the state. His views won many, not only in his large congregation in Fort Worth but also throughout the state.[101] He soon discovered that a sensational use of conservative themes resulted in numbers in his church and subscribers for his magazine. His tactics in the pulpit and his continuous crusades made his church by 1925 the largest Baptist church in the world with a congregation of some eight thousand, a Sunday school of seventy-five hundred, a nonprofessional choir of six hundred, and an orchestra of forty instruments.[102] He published a magazine, *Searchlight*, which he mailed all over the South. Norris did not restrict his fire to the Baptists. He also pointed to the liberalism of John Rice for all to see. He was shortly joined by Methodists in Texas who were fundamentalists of various shades and who demanded the resignation of Rice from the faculty of the School of Theology. The whole issue was brought up at the fall meeting of the annual conferences in 1921.[103]

The pressure became strong enough that Rice felt in the best interest of the institution he should resign. He was a gentle soul, not by nature a fighter or crusader for causes. He was a devout minister, most beloved by his students and respected by the faculty; but his book was simply too close in spirit to the higher criticism of modern scholarship to be acceptable to average Methodists in Texas. Rice became convinced that the institution would suffer if he remained on the faculty.[104] It was in this spirit that Rice offered his resignation to the board on October 3, 1921.

However, Rice was in a strong position and was sufficiently well respected to be able to attach certain conditions to his resignation that the board felt obligated to accept. Indeed, the price set by Rice was high. He attached four conditions to his resignation. First, he wanted a full statement covering his work in the university as a teacher and member of the faculty. Secondly, he desired an appointment equal to those he had held for twenty years. In the third place, he asked the university to assume any financial loss he might incur, and lastly he wanted the board to repudiate the charges in the *Advocate* and to make a satisfactory statement of the reasons for accepting his resignation.[105]

These stringent conditions were not those of a man who was down and out but those of a man who was helping the university ease itself out of a difficult situation. SMU met all of Rice's conditions. The chairman of the board, Judge J. E. Cockrell, issued a statement covering the first and last points of Rice's conditions. The statement contained nothing but praise for Rice and his teaching. Cockrell said that Rice had come to the university without any solicitation on his part:

The brightest young men in the Church, who have sat at his feet, testify with unanimity to his loyalty and to his religious enthusiasm and convictions. No one has had his religious faith impaired, much less destroyed. . . . So far as Dr. Rice's work in the University as a teacher and member of the faculty is concerned, it has been of the most satisfactory character. . . . The University cannot consent that any unjust imputation shall be permitted to rest on the good name of Dr. Rice because of conditions arising which have led to his presenting his resignation. . . . He was at all times in favor with many leaders of the Church and with the great masses of our people. . . . Yet it is considered expedient that the resignation be accepted to take effect as soon as proper adjustment for his work can be made.[106]

Clearly Rice retained the respect and admiration of the faculty and the board, who found him to be an excellent teacher and an acknowledged scholar. Why, then, would the board accept his resignation? Both the board and Rice agreed on what was expedient. Rice said in his official letter of resignation:

Concisely put, it seems that the doctrine of expediency, which is so often far from right, but which is also often close to the right, must be adopted in this emergency, and that for the greater immediate good I must sever my connections with the University and continue my labors elsewhere.[107]

This surrender to expediency would appear to be a surrender to the vocal, fundamentalist element in Texas Methodism; the fundamentalists were able for the time being to dominate the situation. The faculty members of the university were displeased with the actions of President Boaz and the board, who had bowed to the forces of conservatism and reaction very quickly. Indeed, it never seems to have occurred to them that any other course of action was possible. Neither the president nor the board felt Rice guilty of heresy or false doctrine. According to Boaz's own statement, he had never heard Rice say anything with which he disagreed;[108] but neither the president nor the board defended Rice before his resignation or considered retaining him. It also seems not to have occurred to Boaz that other able scholars would leave, or would hesitate to come to a university so vulnerable to criticism. This was manifest during the next decade.

Not only did the executive committee issue a statement praising Rice, but it also awarded him a substantial financial settlement. He was paid the remainder due him on his two-year contract with the university, which amounted to $1,013.34. He also received an adjustment on the financial loss he had suffered by moving to Dallas. Rice submitted an itemized claim which was extremely detailed (even to the point of including $150.00 for a chicken and cow house) and totaled $8,005.27. He had been charged rent for a furnished house at the rate of $100 a month for the fifteen months he served the university. This $1,500 was deducted from the $8,005.27, which left Rice with a cash settlement of some $6,500 plus his salary through the following June.[109]

This was an expensive settlement for an institution that was beset with severe financial difficulties. The board evidently felt so strongly that Rice must leave that they were willing to pay the price he asked despite the shortage of funds. It is possible to assume, then, that Rice was in a sufficiently strong position that the board feared if his terms were not met, he would not have resigned. This was a situation the board was not willing to confront. The university, then, obligated itself to pay Rice over $7,500 at a time when it was running an annual deficit of $35,000 and when an intensive campaign was being waged to raise money in order to qualify for the grant from the General Education Board. The fear of condemnation by the fundamentalists was extremely strong.

Bishop Mouzon assigned Rice to a pastorate in Okmulgee, Oklahoma, and later moved him to Tulsa, where Rice became pastor of the Boston Avenue Church. Rice led the congregation there in building an unusual, modern sanctuary which is still an architectural landmark[110] and created

for himself the reputation of a prominent and respected Methodist
leader. Rice wrote to Bishop Mouzon in 1922: "You can never know
what your courage has meant to me. I shall walk in the afterglow of it
all to the end of the journey." The bishop answered:

> I was, to a large degree, responsible for your coming to Southern Metho-
> dist University and I was unwilling to have you leave the University and
> suffer inconvenience because of your connection with the School of Theology.
> I have never thought that it required any courage to do right. Doing my duty
> has become the habit of a life time, so that when I am sure a thing is right,
> I never think of the consequences.[111]

Rice's reputation did not suffer because of this episode. Macmillan
Company published an enlarged second edition of Rice's book in November, 1921.[112] The publisher regarded the book as a distinct addition to
Macmillan's list of books and informed Rice that if he had any more
manuscripts the firm would be interested in seeing them.[113] The incident
also attracted nationwide publicity because it coincided with two other
situations involving the same issues, one concerning a professor of law at
Montana University and the other a professor of sociology at Baylor
University.[114] These cases were given national publicity by Upton Sinclair
in 1922 with his satire on American higher education, *The Goose-Step*:

> These reactionaries are busy in all the Southern colleges, plying their
> brooms against the tide of modern thought. They succeeded in driving . . .
> Professor Rice from the Southern Methodist University at Dallas, Texas. . . .
> In Fort Worth is a Baptist preacher, who publishes a paper called the
> "Searchlight," and has grown rich out of waging war upon modern thought;
> in what delicate language his controversies are carried on you may judge
> from one sentence, referring to the expulsion of Professor Rice: "While the
> Methodists have put their orang-outang out, we [the Baptists] are keeping
> ours in!"[115]

Sinclair turned his biggest guns upon the Baptists in the South, who more
warmly embraced fundamentalism than did the Methodists.

The third professor who was involved in the fundamentalist-modernist controversy was Mims Thornburg Workman. He taught religion in
the College of Arts and Sciences and also espoused liberal ideas. Unfortunately, he did not have the prestige or position of John A. Rice
and was fired rather summarily and given no financial settlement. Workman had done his undergraduate work at Henderson Brown College in
Arkadelphia, Arkansas, where his father was president, and had received
a master's degree from Emory University. He came to SMU to work

on a divinity degree in 1920, at which time he also began teaching.[116] Later he became a full-time faculty member. He taught the commonly accepted beliefs of liberal scholars of that day, which proved to be sufficiently modern to disturb the fundamentalists.

Workman's ideas were brought under fire in May, 1923, at a meeting held in Fort Worth of the World's Christian Fundamental Association, a layman's movement to oppose modernists. In the beginning the association had consisted largely of Baptists, but by 1923 it included other major protestant denominations; this reflected the growing nationwide importance of the fundamentalist movement. J. Frank Norris played host to the association. The high point of the meeting was a

full-scale trial of Texas colleges charged with teaching rationalism, evolution, and higher criticism, three labels the Fundamentalists used interchangeably to designate beliefs unacceptable to them. Six students, appearing as witnesses against Southern Methodist, Southwestern, Georgetown, and Texas Women's College, testified that evolutionary instruction was so rife in their institutions that safe teaching was no longer possible.[117]

One of Workman's students testified that she could not believe Workman "when he said that the first eleven chapters of the Bible were myths, or when he said that it was questionable as to whether Christ had risen bodily from the dead." She continued:

At Christmas I realized that my faith would be shaken if I remained in the course. I dropped it and wrote a letter to my father and mother in China, telling them of the teachings contradictory to the Bible and warning them not to send my brothers to SMU.[118]

These accusations did not go unanswered. A group of SMU students and faculty had gone over to see the show. These included Forest E. Dudley, Harvie Branscomb, R. J. LaPrade, and Sherwood Gates. After the testimony of this young lady, Norris remarked that he would like to play fair and, if anyone wished to speak a word of defense for the university, he would be welcome to do so. Dudley later wrote:

To our utter amazement, and I am sure to Mr. Norris's utter chagrin, a small man, about forty, stood up from way up in the central part of the balcony. In a loud and clear voice, he said: "I am an attorney; I do not know the accused, or the young lady who sat in two of the accused's classes. But if I were to attempt to convict a man for heresy, I would get testimony from his finished product, and not from a little foreign born freshman who had sat in only two classes." He sat down, and to our supreme delight and surprise, that throng of people burst into ear-splitting applause. The whole attack of Mr. Norris went down the drain.[119]

Others on the campus raised their voices to defend SMU. Charles W. Ferguson, student editor of the *Campus*, pointed out in the newspaper that evolution had been offered as a theory and not as a proven fact. He also added that the courses in Bible had taught him to exalt God and Jesus Christ as never before.[120]

When these charges were made against Workman, the board appointed Bishop Moore and the newly elected President Selecman to confer with Workman and advise him in this matter.[121] Evidently his answers were satisfactory, because no action was taken against Workman until two years later. Perhaps at this time Selecman was deterred from acting too decisively because he did not feel he was in a strong enough position to do so. However, by May, 1925, Selecman was convinced by the "numerous complaints and criticisms of the teachings of Professor Workman" that he was expressing "unsound" doctrine and doubting "some of the cardinal tenents of the Christian faith."[122]

The reasons for firing Workman were never formally presented. But all the evidence points in the direction of Workman's being too liberal in his teaching of the Bible. Workman issued a statement in his defense:

If I did not believe in the immortality of the soul and the Divinity of Jesus Christ, I should never have entered the Christian ministry of teaching and preaching. They are the very foundations of my faith.[123]

Despite this protestation, Selecman felt that the criticism leveled against Workman was strong enough to interfere with his future usefulness to the university. Selecman therefore requested Dean Jennings of the arts and science college to encourage Workman either to take a leave of absence or to resign. Selecman claimed that he did this "for the purpose of befriending and shielding" Workman.[124]

The students rallied to Workman's defense. He was an extremely popular teacher who had great concern for his students and could communicate with them easily. Students with inquiring minds idolized him, even if they were not primarily concerned with religion.[125] He was selected by the seniors as their favorite teacher for 1925. The dedication to him in *The Rotunda* described his idealism and enthusiasm as the "expression of the true fire and zeal for service." The senior class believed that he had opened their eyes to things that really mattered.[126] Workman was also chosen to be the speaker for Senior Vespers, an honor the graduating class bestowed upon an admired faculty member.[127]

In an effort to retain Workman, a petition was signed by six hundred students and a mass meeting held.[128] When the board met on June 1, 1925, a committee of ten seniors attended and presented each board member with testimonies of students who appreciated Workman.[129] All of this proved to be of no avail. The board supported the recommendations of the president, and Workman was asked to resign:

> It is reprehensible on the part of any teacher to speak to classes of students in criticism of the administration of the University. . . .
> . . . A situation has been created at Southern Methodist University which makes it unwise for [Workman] to remain here . . . .[130]

Selecman wished to get rid of Workman probably because he appeared to be a nuisance and embarrassment to the administration. Wealthy Methodists and others who might aid the university would have little sympathy or patience with a man they might consider an irresponsible intellectual who unsettled the minds of the students. The overwhelming support of Workman by the students and most of the faculty doubtless seemed divisive to Selecman, who was always interested in internal harmony.[131]

Workman appeared to his friends as a bright young man, warm hearted, gregarious, who genuinely loved people. He was transparently honest, constitutionally unable to avoid telling students what his own study and reflection made him believe to be true. To many he appeared to be a destructive critic, and he failed entirely to see this. He was, in short, an impractical idealist who was unaware that others lacked his qualities of mind and spirit. He did not realize that he could or should fight for his academic life.[132]

Workman's career never quite recovered from these events. Bishop Mouzon secured for him a teaching position at an interdenominational school of religion at the University of North Carolina. He remained here only two years before it was learned why he left SMU.[133] He then taught three years at Vanderbilt before he decided to return to the ministry. He served a series of churches in the Little Rock and, later, Missouri conferences, moving almost every year.[134]

The firing of Workman was not supported by the faculty. In fact, there was much criticism of Selecman's position. The younger faculty applauded Workman, and the older members were at least tolerant of a bright young man with new ideas.[135] Not many thought he should lose his position because of a few critical voices raised outside SMU. In order to quiet the dissent, John Beaty, of the English department, introduced a resolution at a faculty meeting on May 29, 1925, which stated: "We as a faculty express our confidence in the administration this year."[136] The Workman case was not mentioned, but the resolution was widely interpreted as a statement supporting the president. The motion passed unanimously, but there were several faculty members who did not vote at all.[137] When the account appeared in the newspapers, however, the impression was given that the faculty voted full confidence in Selecman's administration and all its policies.[138]

Harvie Branscomb of the theological faculty took exception to this interpretation of the faculty vote. He claimed that it did not mean an endorsement of policy in regard to Workman. Branscomb made it clear that he was opposed to any effort to dismiss Workman. No charges of heresy had been brought against him. The criticism came almost entirely from outside the university. Branscomb further stated:

> If the faculty members of good training, acknowledged orthodoxy and wholesome influence are to be discharged because of the no doubt sincere objections of those outside the University who misunderstand them, I see little hope of building here in SMU the spirit necessary to a great university.[139]

When Selecman read this statement in the morning paper, he called Branscomb very early on the phone and informed him that he should sever his connections with SMU. Branscomb considered himself "fired before breakfast in his pajamas," a story which he told widely.[140] Branscomb appeared before the board on June 2, 1925, and presented his resignation with a statement of the circumstances that had made this necessary.[141] He then accepted a position as a professor in the Divinity School at Duke University, and SMU lost an excellent faculty member.[142]

The fundamentalists remained a force until the end of the decade. By then the peak of their power had been reached. They failed to capture any major denominational body. Their agitations had led to schism in several churches. New leadership was, for the most part, no longer affiliated with the larger denominations but with some independent body or with none at all. Thus the center of gravity in fundamentalism shifted to its own institutions and into isolation from the affairs of the church at large. The fundamentalist-modernist issue came to be regarded as a regrettable past chapter for most denominational bodies.[143]

As far as Methodists in Texas were concerned, fundamentalism was dealt a blow when Texas failed to pass an antievolution law in 1929. Bishop John M. Moore took a strong stand against this bill, which was in keeping with the mild modernism he had espoused in the Texas conferences.[144] The bishop also wrote a scholarly article opposing the law in which he made the point that the "real question is not the road by which man came, but the power by which he came."[145] This article evoked a sheaf of letters from the faculty members of SMU supporting the bishop's stand against antievolution laws.[146]

Bishop Edwin D. Mouzon had taken a stand against the fundamentalists even earlier. In 1923 he wrote a small book, *So-Called Fundamentalism*, in which he attributed the interest of Methodists in fundamentalism to ignorance of their own theological basis. The bishop maintained that fundamentalism is a religion of the letter while Methodism is a religion of the spirit.[147] With these two strong bishops opposed to fundamentalism, by the late 1920s it ceased to be a threat to the faculty, and the board and the administration ceased to be influenced by charges of modernism or liberalism. Unfortunately, this more secure posture came too late for the three faculty members who earlier had suffered for expressing religious opinions hardly more liberal than those of the two bishops.

CHAPTER VI

Years of Growth, 1925-1940

BY 1925 Southern Methodist University had reached a turning point in its career. The financial problems which had plagued the university from the beginning were at least partly solved. As a result of the contract made with the General Education Board in 1920 the university had been forced to put its financial house in order, since it had to do so before it could qualify for the board's grant. This meant instituting a businesslike system of accounting which kept the endowment funds and School of Theology monies separate from the general funds and preparing a yearly budget. For the first time the university was free from debt. SMU had collected two-thirds of a million dollars, which qualified it for the grant of one-third of a million from the General Education Board. As a result, the endowment of the university increased from $709,346 in 1921 to $1,734,-072 in 1925.[1] Southern Methodist University had weathered its first decade and now, instead of leading a hand-to-mouth existence, had sufficient strength to make plans for the future.

Building Program

Until 1924 all the classrooms and offices of the university were centered in Dallas Hall. This building had been adequate for 706 students in 1915, but the facilities were severely strained for 2,500 students in 1924. During this period the number of students had increased more than 300 percent, while the rooms available for instruction had increased 44 percent from twenty-five to thirty-six rooms.[2] Until 1924 Dallas Hall housed the College of Arts and Sciences, the School of Theology, and School of Music (including the piano practice rooms), the library, the administrative offices, the chapel, the post office, the bookstore, and the barber shop. Virtually every department was appealing for more space.

104

Since the endowment was increased and the university free of debt, it embarked upon a building program which added nine new buildings to the campus by 1939. The new group of buildings represented the first expansion of the university and provided much-needed instructional facilities. This newly expanded campus was to constitute the physical plant of the university until the 1950s, when a second building program was launched.

The first of the additions was an administration and classroom building for the School of Theology made possible through the gift of $100,-000 from Harper and Annie Kirby of Austin, who were devoted Methodists. The Kirbys presented their gift through W. D. Bradfield, their former pastor and by 1924 a professor in the School of Theology and a member of the Board of Trustees. The Kirbys were greatly pleased with the choice of Charles C. Selecman as president of the university and chose to make the announcement shortly after his election to illustrate their faith in SMU's future.[3] The new building released the theological school from its cramped quarters in Dallas Hall and also, according to Dean Paul B. Kern, "set forth before the public and particularly our own large student body a material evidence of the dignity and importance of ministerial education."[4]

Kirby Hall, completed for use in September, 1924, contained a library and a chapel in addition to classrooms and offices. The chapel, a replica of a New England colonial church, was a model of beauty and simplicity. President Selecman remarked that to "enter it is to feel the subtle spirit of worship and reverence."[5] The exodus of the theology faculty from Dallas Hall made available much-needed space for other purposes. The total cost of the building was $142,000. Since the Kirby's gift was only $100,000, the balance was paid by the university.[6]

The next building constructed was also a gift, an auditorium given by R. M. McFarlin, a wealthy oil producer and dedicated Methodist layman of San Antonio. Bishop John M. Moore approached McFarlin in December, 1923, concerning the possibility of his giving such a building, and this request was strongly supported by Bishop Edwin D. Mouzon, a long-time friend. The desire of the two bishops was to have an auditorium large enough to accommodate all the student body at one time for chapel and assemblies,[7] a wish President Selecman shared. Such an auditorium, said Selecman, would help increase school spirit:

This auditorium will meet one of the greatest needs of Southern Methodist University student body, and will make it possible for us to get our entire group together and develop a college spirit of loyalty, reverence and enthusiasm without which our work is rendered complex and difficult in the extreme.[8]

The McFarlins intended the building to cost $300,000, including the price of a $25,000 pipe organ. However, the final figure was nearer to $500,000, all of which was paid by the McFarlins. This building was the only one SMU received during this period which was completely paid for by the donor. Usually a fixed sum was given, and the university was expected to provide any additional money that was needed.

The auditorium, opened in March, 1926, had a seating capacity of thirty-five hundred in addition to a stage which would seat two hundred. Besides its campus uses this building was made available to various groups from Dallas and thus helped weld the university to the city. Eventually the School of Music moved into the smaller rooms surrounding the auditorium, which aided in relieving noise and congestion in Dallas Hall.

Despite the advantages gained from McFarlin Auditorium, the university would have been better served if the half-million dollars could have been used to build a science building and a library. These would have been much more useful to the crowded university. But both Bishop Moore and Bishop Mouzon encouraged McFarlin to donate his money for a meeting place for all the students, revealing a greater concern for the moral and spiritual unity of the student body than for the academic and intellectual aspects of university life. The result was that SMU had an excellent place for holding chapel (which by now was held only once a week) while lacking adequate classroom and library space.

At the same time that McFarlin Auditorium was being constructed, two other buildings were also being erected. But the money for these buildings was much harder to come by, and the work progressed more slowly. One building was designed to provide classroom and office space for physical sciences and was to be financed by the students and friends of Robert Stewart Hyer. President Selecman said in 1923:

For a long time the friends of Dr. Robert Stewart Hyer have desired to see him and his department properly housed in a great science building. His popularity with his former students and with Methodist people generally throughout Texas would indicate that if the movement were properly launched in the near future this building might be secured.[10]

The sciences were severely handicapped by a lack of laboratory space. In 1924 Ellis W. Shuler, professor of geology, noted that fewer courses were then being offered in the sciences than had been offered in 1918. He felt that this "condition reflect[ed] the lack of facilities for science work, and the lack of attractiveness of science courses to students under such conditions."[11] A campaign to collect funds was carried on for a couple of years before enough money was collected to begin construction of a new building. The actual building got underway in early 1925, with Hyer himself breaking the ground. But the construction went slowly because of insufficient funds, with the result that it was not until the fall of 1926 that the building was ready for use. Hyer was able to teach in this new building three years before his death in 1929.

The total cost of the building was $140,469, of which the friends and students of Hyer collected only $58,856. The balance of $82,774 was taken from the general funds[12] and was carried as a debt by the university through the depression to the Second World War. Hyer Hall contained lecture rooms and laboratories for the departments of physics, biology, and geology, with each department having a floor. Again the moving of these departments from Dallas Hall greatly aided the crowded conditions in that building.

The chemistry department was not allotted space in Hyer Hall, probably because that department was the smallest and, as we have seen, the chairman, E. H. Heuse, was not aggressive in expressing the needs of his department. All during the late 1920s President Selecman spoke of the urgent need for a chemistry building. What the department finally got, in 1928, was a "shack" which cost $7,517.[13] After these temporary quarters burned in 1930, the chemistry department was located in the basement of Atkins Hall, the men's dormitory,[14] where it remained until after World War II.

The other building under construction in 1925 was the first story of what eventually became the administration building. At this time it did not house the administrative offices but instead provided space for a cooperative bookstore, three classrooms, three offices, and the post office. The initial money for this building came from P. L. Turner, who provided $27,500 in cash as an advance payment on a fifteen-year lease for a part of the building in which to operate a bookstore and a "co-op."[15] The total cost of the one-story structure was $51,100, and the difference between this figure and the advance lease payment was to be met by the sale of real estate. Evidently the real estate sale did not bring in the amount desired, because the university carried as a debt $24,679 on the administration building in 1928.[16]

The Co-op was the nearest thing the university had to a student union until after World War II. It sold "everything collegiate" including all prescribed textbooks, school supplies, athletic goods, college jewelry, fountain drinks, and light lunches.[17] It was, naturally enough, the favorite meeting place on the campus.

The administration building remained a one-story building until 1938, when J. J. Perkins of Wichita Falls, a member of the board, announced his gift of $75,000 to complete the building. When the second and third stories were added, office space was provided for the president, the vice-president, the dean of the arts and science College, the registrar, and the business department.[18] These offices had occupied a whole wing of Dallas Hall which was now available for classrooms and offices. Perkins Administration Building balanced Hyer Hall, both of which flanked Dallas Hall and enclosed part of the quadrangle.

J. J. Perkins became one of the more generous benefactors of Southern Methodist University, especially later in the 1950s. He made a fortune from the Ranger oil fields and was founder and manager of the Perkins-Timberlake Oil Company and the Perkins Oil Company. During the 1920s Perkins was a leading oil producer in Wichita Falls.[19]

In 1926 SMU built two new dormitories for women, not entirely out of choice, however. In February of that year the three smaller dormitories for men burned to the ground. These had been hastily and inexpensively constructed in 1915 just before the university opened and were never intended to be permanent. One of them had partly burned in 1918 but was rebuilt. These buildings were housing 140 men in 1926 when, in not much more than an hour, the buildings and personal belongings of the occupants were destroyed. No one was injured because the fire occurred in the middle of the afternoon when few students were in the dormitories. But the city of University Park even lost a new $10,000 fire truck.[20]

This situation obviously presented the university, as well as the men, with an acute problem. For the remainder of that semester the men lived in private rooms around the campus, but a better solution had to be found before fall. C. W. Snider of Wichita Falls made a business proposition. He offered to build a reinforced concrete, fireproof, fifty-room dormitory for women, all equipped and furnished, for $150,000. This dormitory would be arranged in suites of two bedrooms plus a study room and private bath.[21] However, Snider was not making a gift but was looking for a way to invest his money. In return for this dormitory, the university made two annuity contracts. One was for $100,000 at 6 percent payable to Snider during his lifetime and then willed to his wife. The other was for $50,000, also at 6 percent, payable to Snider and then to his daughter after the death of both parents.[22] This proved to be a profitable arrangement for Snider because every year until his death in 1955 he received $9,000 from the university. His wife now receives $6,000 annually and after her death, her daughter will receive $3,000 annually until her death.[23] For the university, though, the arrangement was unwise. By the time of Snider's death in 1955, the university had paid him approximately $261,000. Since then his widow has received $96,000, making a total of $357,000 paid to the Snider family on a building that cost $150,000. Under the pressure of building a dormitory quickly, the university entered into an arrangement that cost it in the long run far more than it gained. SMU would have been better off borrowing the money at 6 percent interest and paying off the principal rather than paying indefinitely on an annuity contract. But, doubtless, in 1926, the advantages seemed to outweigh the disadvantages.

At the same time that Snider Hall was built, the university also constructed a companion building to house another hundred women. This building was financed largely by money from the fire insurance on the three men's dormitories, which totaled $80,949. A special campaign was organized and some $74,000 pledged for the construction of this building. To these two sums was added $7,000 that had been raised earlier by Virginia K. Johnson for a woman's dormitory, and in honor of her the dormitory was named Virginia Hall.[24] However, not enough money was collected for the building since the total cost ran to $181,959, so that in 1931 the university still owed $83,025 on Virginia Hall.[25] Both of these buildings were ready for use by the fall of 1926, and the university was able to accommodate all the women who applied. The men were then housed in what had previously been the Woman's Building. This building, which had been originally planned for men in 1915, was renamed Atkins Hall after Bishop James Atkins, who was instrumental in founding SMU.[26]

The last major construction during the 1920s was characteristically enough a football stadium. Nationwide this was an era of stadium and field house building. In this golden age of football, every university was expected to have a team. Dallas expected it of SMU and both President Boaz and President Selecman felt obligated to fulfill this desire. Football was first justified on the basis that it was good public relations in that it advertised the university and brought additional funds to it. It was only a short step from football as public relations to football as business. It became a game not for the players but for the spectators. This development had already taken place at SMU when President Boaz made it a deliberate policy to build up a football team. SMU built well enough to win the championship of the Southwest Conference in 1923.[27]

The first playing field SMU had was sodded and graded by the coach, Ray Morrison. There were no seats at all for the spectators, who simply ran up and down the sidelines with the team. In 1923 Jordan C. Ownby of Dallas, an alumnus and a strong supporter of athletics, gave to the university two steel stands which would seat about five thousand spectators.[28] But by 1926 football at SMU demanded something more pretentious. Occasional games were played at Fair Park Stadium in east Dallas, but the administration and board preferred that the games be played on the campus. The business manager of athletics, R. N. Blackwell, was especially prominent in the drive for a stadium.[29]

The result was that by 1926 the executive committee of the board set up the Stadium Corporation, which entered into an agreement with the Bennett Mortgage Company of St. Louis for a loan of $175,000 to erect the first unit of permanent, concrete stands faced with brick to blend with the other buildings. The total cost of the project including the new stands, the moving of the old steel stands to the opposite side of the field, the grading and sodding, and the erection of fences was not to exceed $190,000. Of this amount Jordan Ownby subscribed $10,000 and the stadium was named for him.[30] The executive committee felt that the whole project would be self-liquidating from the gate receipts of the football games. With this in mind the university obligated itself for a fixed payment of $10,000 annually and promised to pay off the entire debt in ten years.[31]

The stadium was opened for the first game in the fall of 1926. The new concrete stands seated twelve thousand people, while the older steel ones across the field still provided seating for five thousand, making it possible for a total of seventeen thousand people to see a game. The ground floor of the new stands was used for workouts in unfavorable weather. An adequate number of showers and lockers was available for the varsity, freshmen, and visiting teams. A modern press box that would accommodate twenty-five correspondents was included. All the athletic offices were situated in these new quarters.[32]

The expectations of the president and the executive committee that athletics would pay for itself and make a profit proved to be unfounded.

Even after the successful 1926 football season, President Selecman stated at the annual board meeting that the athletic funds would have to be carefully supervised if the annual payments for the stadium were to be provided for. The total income from athletics for that year had been $118,758, while the expenses were $100,918, which left a balance of only $17,840.[33] By 1931 the situation had not improved and Selecman stated at the board meeting:

> The general impression that college athletics are quite profitable financially has not been substantiated by our experience at Southern Methodist University. Since 1923, our athletics have produced a debit balance every year with the exception of 1925, the total indebtedness over this period being $52,547.[34]

The result of this situation was that during the depression the university had a fixed payment of at least $10,000 a year and an obligation to liquidate the entire debt in 1935. This obligation aggravated the near-desperate financial condition of the university during the 1930s. SMU clearly overextended itself regarding the stadium. Like other institutions, it found itself trapped in a vicious circle. It had encouraged football and built an expensive stadium as a promotional technique for publicizing the university in hopes of attracting endowment money, only to find that it had to place increasing emphasis upon the recruitment of a winning, professionally coached football team in order to attract gate receipts that were needed to pay off the debt.

The last of the major buildings to be constructed in the years prior to World War II was the library in 1939. The need for a library was apparent all during the late 1920s. It was discussed at nearly every board meeting after Selecman became president.[35] Indeed, Selecman even erected a sign on the campus which read, "Site of Future Library." The library had been housed in the east wing of Dallas Hall ever since the university opened in 1915. The money available for books had always been meager. The poverty of the library was made clear in a report by the librarian, Dorothy Amann, to the board in 1928. The library was especially lacking in books for advanced and graduate courses. Amann pointed out that in 1927 the University of Texas had spent $14.39 per student on books, Tulane had spent $5.92, the University of Georgia spent $3.91, while SMU spent $1.42. In the number of books per student SMU again ranked very low. Southwestern had seventy-four books per student, Duke fifty-eight, Emory twenty-nine, Texas Christian twenty-seven, but SMU had only fourteen.[36] Since these were the institutions with which SMU was trying to compete, clearly it was being outclassed and needed to increase its library resources.

However, this goal was not accomplished. In the building spree of the mid-twenties funds for a new library and new books were always near the bottom of the list. The order in which the buildings were constructed indicates something about priorities at SMU. Money was found to construct a football stadium because a winning football team was considered important for the public relations of the university. But the library building that would have increased the university's academic standing was forced to wait. Clearly the board and administration felt athletics to be more significant than an adequate library. The board did intend to build a library earlier than it actually did; but the depression interfered, and the university had all it could do to remain solvent.

At long last, in 1938, W. W. Fondren of Houston gave the university 6,600 shares of Humble Oil stock, which had an estimated value of $400,000.[37] Fondren, who was one of the founders of the Humble Oil Company, had been on the board since 1919 and was well aware of the needs of the university. After one of the board meetings, Fondren asked Selecman to show him the plans for a library and to tell him the cost. Selecman evidently was taken by surprise, because it took him a little while to locate the plans. When asked to name a figure, Selecman hesitated a moment, desiring to name a figure that was reasonable and yet would cover the cost. He finally suggested $400,000. To this Fondren agreed.[38]

Construction was delayed because the bids exceeded the amount available. The board wanted to wait until the "return of normal business conditions" before beginning the project. Finally in 1939 the contract was let, and the building was ready for use in the fall of 1940.[39]

For its time the library was an impressive building. The final cost was $458,000, essentially all of which was given by Fondren. The building had three stories and a basement, with eight levels of stacks. These stacks had a capacity of three hundred thousand books, but at the time the library opened it contained only about eighty thousand books plus assorted pamphlets.[40] For the convenience of the library workers there was an elevator in the stacks and also an electric book conveyor. The main reading room could seat five hundred, and the third story contained nine seminar rooms and ten faculty research rooms. The entire building was air conditioned, the first such structure on the campus and one of the first in the area.[41]

With the construction of the library, the central group of buildings on the campus was completed. Dallas Hall stood in the center facing the open end of the quadrangle toward Bishop Boulevard.[42] Hyer Science Hall and Fondren Library were located on one side of the quadrangle, with Perkins Administration Building and McFarlin Auditorium opposite. These five buildings formed and still form the heart of the campus, and all face inward to the fountain in the center of the quadrangle.[43] All the buildings are similar in architecture and follow the pattern set by the first president, Robert Stewart Hyer. They are built of red brick in Georgian style and are trimmed with white stone.[44]

During the administration of President Selecman every effort was made to beautify the campus with trees, shrubs, and plants, not an easy task in the dry Texas climate. By 1940, instead of the original acres of Johnson grass, there was a landscaped campus with carefully laid out sidewalks, shade trees, and shrubs. A. D. Schuessler of the German department supervised this effort and even maintained a nursery on the campus to keep an ever ready supply of stock. In 1928 alone over six hundred trees were planted, some thirteen hundred shrubs, thirteen hundred hedge plants, and many flowers and bulbs.[45] After a quarter of a century the campus was beginning to resemble the one visualized by President Hyer in 1911.

By 1940 virtually all the departments were reasonably well housed and even provided with a little growing space. The classes of the arts and science college were held in Dallas Hall and Hyer Hall. The School of Theology had its own building, Kirby Hall. The School of Engineering was located in an inexpensive structure which appeared to be adequate for its limited enrollment.[46] The law school still met in the basement of Dallas Hall, but its enrollment was also small. The School of Music used classrooms in McFarlin Auditorium. All the administrative offices were in Perkins Administration Building. The men students were living in Atkins Hall and several fraternity houses that had been built. The women were comfortably housed in Snider and Virginia halls. Sororities were not allowed to have houses until the dormitories had been filled to capacity. For athletics there was the gymnasium built in 1919 and the newer stadium. The physical plant was adequate for a student body of approximately three thousand, which was considered the maximum enrollment in the prewar years.

Expanded Academic Program

In addition to the physical growth of the campus in the period 1925 to 1940, Southern Methodist University also expanded the scope of its curriculum and increased its course offerings. In 1925 both the School of Engineering and the School of Law were established, adding two professional schools to the original ones of theology and music. The following year the graduate department was elevated to a school with its own dean. The departments of education and commerce experienced the greatest growth, reflecting nationwide interest in these expanding fields of study. The department of education increased its course offerings as well as its faculty members at a phenomenal rate, until a School of Education was established within the College of Arts and Sciences. The commerce department grew, thanks to the demands of mercantile and industrial interests in Dallas, until in 1941 a separate School of Business Administration was established. By the time of World War II, SMU still had at its center the College of Arts and Sciences, but grouped around it were the six professional schools: theology, music, graduate studies, law, engineering, and business.[47]

The School of Engineering was organized as a result of the cooperative efforts of the university, the Technical Club of Dallas, and the North Texas Chapter of the American Institute of Architects. The original impetus came from the Technical Club, a group of two hundred men from the various branches of engineering in the Southwest. These men, who were graduates of four-year engineering schools, desired to see similar training offered at SMU.[48] The board consented to this request and in February, 1925, authorized the establishment of a cooperative School of Engineering.[49]

Under the cooperative plan, students were to alternate between theory in the classroom and practice in the industries. Students would then be able to apply their theoretical knowledge to actual industrial conditions. Under this plan the student body was divided into two groups. While the students of one section were in the classroom, members of the other section were at work in industries. At the end of four weeks the students exchanged places. This alternation between work and school continued throughout the year and after a period of five years led to a bachelor of science degree in engineering.[50]

The cooperative plan had been used with success at the University of Cincinnati and the Georgia Institute of Technology. C. A. Nichols, head of the department of education, visited the University of Cincinnati School of Engineering, which then served as a model for Southern Methodist. The cooperative plan offered two distinct advantages to students; first it provided them with practical experience in industries under actual working conditions; second, the wages the students received for this work paid a large part of their expenses.[51] Doubtless without this financial assistance there would not have been enough students for an engineering school.

The Technical Club was highly instrumental in the development of this school. The university planned to pay the teachers' salaries from the students' tuition, but it had no money for laboratory equipment. Indeed, the board probably would not have agreed to the establishment of the school if it had meant any outlay of cash. But the Technical Club agreed to provide $10,000 for laboratory equipment,[52] which was the only cash the school had. The club also aided in the recruitment of students and in locating the jobs which provided half of the students' training.[53] Until the depression thirty to forty Texas industrial firms cooperated with the university, including railroads, public utilities, municipalities, and a diversity of private engineering and manufacturing companies. These firms were located in Dallas, Fort Worth, Waco, San Antonio, Houston, Tyler, Marshall, Denison, and Beaumont.[54] However, after the depression hit, it became increasingly difficult to find businesses that were willing and able to employ students.

The engineering school began its first year with only a freshman class; each year an additional class was added until in five years all the levels of instruction were offered. Each freshman class was limited to 120 students. During the first two years the school was self-supporting, but at the beginning of the third year, the students divided into three groups for specialization in civil, electrical, and mechanical engineering.[55] At this time (1927-28) the university was forced to provide its first funds for the school, which further strained resources. There is every indication that the board lacked a realistic understanding of what this kind of instruction would cost. The board members seemed to believe that the school would always be self-supporting and were not prepared for the outlay of cash that third and fourth year work would cost in terms of faculty salaries and laboratory equipment.[56]

The man chosen to head this new engineering school was E. H. Flath, a native of Ohio. Flath was only thirty years old when he became dean, but he brought to the position an understanding and knowledge of how a cooperative engineering school worked. He had received his engineering degree at the University of Cincinnati under the cooperative plan in 1919 and for two years had directed the co-op courses at Georgia Tech. His industrial experience was with National Cash Register Company and Bell Telephone Laboratories. He was thoroughly convinced that a cooperative plan was an effective way to learn engineering, and he understood how to make one operate. He was also capable of working well with the business community, which was essential to the successful operation of the program.[57] Dean Flath remained with the university until his retirement in 1960.

The engineering school had a substantial enrollment from the beginning compared with other professional schools, which indicates that the creation of the school fulfilled a need of the business community. The initial enrollment in 1925 was 126, at which time the graduate school had 145, theology 252, and music 141. The peak enrollment was reached with 312 in 1930, when engineering was larger than any of the other professional schools. The year 1930 also saw the first graduating class of seventeen students. However, the engineering school was badly hit during the depression, when its registration dropped to 126. By 1940, though, the enrollment had climbed to 174.[58]

The School of Engineering provided all of the instruction for its students in all fields. It had its own departments of chemistry, physics, mathematics, economics, geology, English, and commerce. Since these subjects were already taught in the arts and science college, the university was supplying duplicate service. This arrangement was regarded as necessary, though, in order to maintain the cooperative nature of the engineering program with the students working half-time. In order to teach this wide range of courses, the engineering faculty grew from four in 1925 to twenty-three in 1930.[59] However, when the depression caused a drop in enrollment, this duplication of services was abolished and the engineering school was reorganized. The cooperative program was dropped at the freshman and sophomore level, and all engineering students took their first two years of work in the College of Arts and Sciences.[60] This was disastrous for some of the engineering faculty, who suddenly found themselves without a job in the middle of the depression. The arrangement, though, lasted only two years; in 1935 the engineering school was again responsible for the sophomore class. However, the freshmen engineering students still continued to take their work in the arts and science college.[61]

In 1937 the engineering school hoped to meet the minimum re-

Edwin D. Mouzon, Jr., Professor of Mathematics.

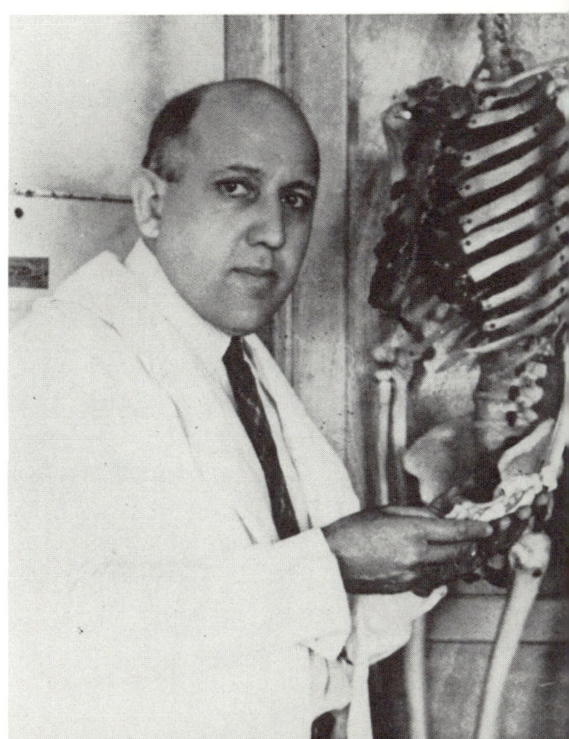

Samuel Wood Geiser, Professor of Biology; editor of *Field & Laboratory* from 1943 to 1959 and of its successor, the *Journal of the Graduate Research Center* in 1960 and 1961.

Herbert Gambrell, Professor of History.

Cornerstone laying, Kirby Hall (now Florence Hall), 1924

Faculty of the School of Theology, 1940. Back row, from left to right: John Hicks, Paul A. Root, Robert Goodloe, Wesley C. Davis. Front row: J. T. Carlyon, Eugene B. Hawk, James Seehorn Seneker.

Paul Van Katwijk, Professor of Piano; Dean of the School of Music from 1918 to 1949.

Charles S. Potts, Professor of Law
and Dean of the School of Law
from 1926 to 1949.

Eugene B. Hawk, Professor of Homiletics and Dean of Perkins School
of Theology, 1934-52; Acting President from September 1, 1938, to
March 1, 1939.

Earl H. Flath, Professor of Electrical
Engineering and Dean of the School
of Engineering from 1925 to 1960.

Elzy Dee Jennings, Professor of Education; Dean of the College of Arts and Sciences, 1922-38; Vice-President, 1933-38.

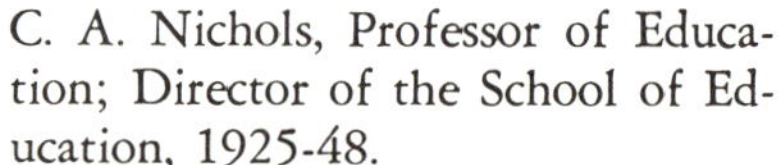

C. A. Nichols, Professor of Education; Director of the School of Education, 1925-48.

G. O. Clough, Professor of Education; Director of Dallas College, 1934-48.

A. W. Foscue (left), Professor of Accounting and Statistics, and Laurence H. Fleck, Professor of Accounting, Dean of the School of Business Administration from 1946 to 1963.

Albert C. Zumbrunnen, Professor of Religion; Dean of Students, 1926-48.

William F. Hauhart, Professor of Finance; Director of the School of Commerce, 1921-40; Dean of the School of Business Administration, 1940-46.

J. D. Boon (right), Professor of Physics, and J. W. Blanton, in the Blanton
Student Observatory, erected in 1934, of which Mr. Blanton was the donor.

Mayne Longnecker, Professor of Biology; Dean of Students, 1954-64.

Edwin Jay Foscue, Professor of Geography; editor, together with Stuart McGregor, of the *Texas Geographic*, 1937-49.

Walter T. Watson, Professor of Sociology from 1929 to 1960.

Comparative Literature faculty members: from left to right, F. D. Smith, Gusta Barfield Nance, Lon Tinkle.

Members of the English faculty: from left to right, John Bowyer, Ima Honaker Herron, George Bond, John Lee Brooks.

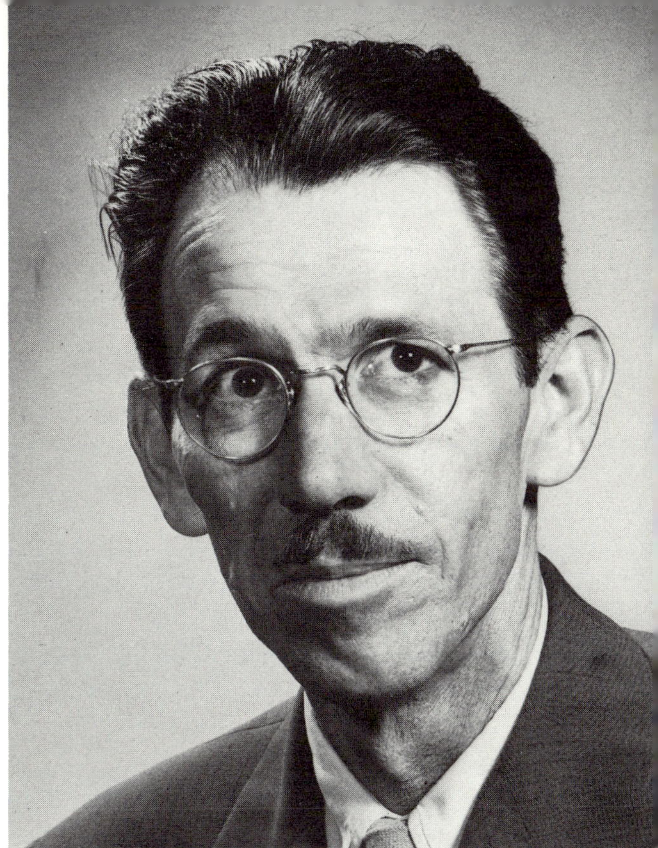

Jerry Bywaters, Professor of
Art.

Frank Rader, Professor of Finance.

Group of early faculty members. Back row: John O. Beaty, Elise Hay Golden, Stanley Patterson. Front row: Itasca Perkinson, S. W. Martin, Evelyn Sellers, Ernest E. Leisy, J. U. Yarborough.

Business Office administrators: from left to right, Layton W. Bailey, Business Manager–Treasurer; Ella Conley, Cashier; Wiggs N. Babb, Auditor; Bill Wright, Assistant Auditor.

The campus as it appeared about 1940.

quirements for accreditation by the Engineer's Council for Professional Development, the highest accrediting agency for engineering schools, but failed to do so. The university then put forth every effort to meet these standards. Again the Technical Club came to the rescue, this time with $25,000 for new laboratory equipment. The major improvements included

entirely new laboratory equipment for soil mechanics and foundations; installation of machine tools for a course in shop practice; addition of steam turbine generator and dynamometer for engine testing . . . ; and additions to electronics and communications equipment.[62]

The value of the equipment was $77,866 in 1939, an increase of $32,180 over the previous year. With these improvements the School of Engineering was accredited in July, 1939, which put the school in a position where it could go forward.[63]

The School of Law was established by the board at the same time as the engineering school, but it did not grow as rapidly. Judge Joseph E. Cockrell, who was chairman of the board and a lawyer, was especially interested in the establishment of this school. He believed that Dallas was the ideal location and that SMU should provide this educational service "provided money could be raised outside of the regular budget."[64] Again the board seemed to believe that additional colleges could be made to pay for themselves. Establishing a law school would doubtless be less expensive than establishing an engineering school had been, but even a law school would need some additional funds for a library. The Dallas Bar Association gave its support and approval to the new law school,[65] but there is no record that it aided the school with money in the manner that the Technical Club had helped finance the engineering school.

The law school got off to a shaky start in the fall of 1925 with a faculty of two and a student body of twenty-four. Only first year courses were offered in 1925-26. An additional year's work was added during each of the next two years until the three-year course was completed. Students were admitted to the law school after two years of college and, after the completion of the three-year law course, received the LL.B. degree. Students could receive a B.A. degree as well as the LL.B. degree after the completion of a six-year course.[66] The enrollment remained small all during this period; the peak number was reached in 1934 with ninety-seven students, after which it fell, as did the number of students throughout the university. Even by 1940 there were only eighty-six law students.[67]

The faculty increased slowly also. During the 1930s there were four full-time members plus a few part-time teachers.

Despite the lack in quantity of law enrollments the quality of the work of the law school was recognized earlier by accrediting agencies than was that of the engineering school. As early as 1927 the School of Law was placed on the list of law schools approved by the American Bar Association. Also at this time it was recognized by the Texas Supreme Court and the State Board of Legal Examiners as a school whose graduates were licensed to practice law in Texas without examination. In 1929 it was admitted to membership in the Association of American Law Schools.[68]

The man who guided the new school for twenty years was Charles Shirley Potts, who served as dean from 1927 to 1947.[69] Potts, a native Texan, received the LL.B. degree from the University of Texas in 1909 and the S.J.D. degree from Harvard in 1926. He taught at Texas A&M, at the University of Texas, and just prior to coming to Dallas at Washington University. He was author of several books and was chairman of the editorial board of the *Texas Law Review*. Potts was a quiet, gentle man, not a promoter but a scholar who was well respected by his colleagues and other lawyers and who offered this infant law school wise leadership.[70]

In 1938 the Dallas School of Law, which had been established in 1925 by the Young Men's Christian Association of Dallas, was merged with SMU's School of Law. The merger was intended to be mutually beneficial. The SMU School of Law had declined in enrollment to sixty-nine students, which was making it difficult to operate. The Dallas School of Law was having trouble in meeting the new higher standards set by the American Bar Association and the Dallas Bar Association. It was felt that if the two law schools combined, they would be of mutual assistance to each other. SMU's School of Law had the standards, while the Dallas School of Law had the students.[71] An elaborate agreement was entered into whereby SMU would operate a day division on the university campus and an evening division in the YMCA building in downtown Dallas. The terms of this merger were prepared by the Council on Legal Education of the American Bar Association and the Association of American Law Schools as an experiment in upgrading substandard schools. The evening division classes were taught by the faculty members of SMU and classrooms were provided by the YMCA. Full credit was received by the evening students, and full tuition was paid.[72]

This merger proved to be completely satisfactory. The idea of evening downtown classes had been proposed by both Judge Cockrell and President Selecman when the school was first organized, but it had been abandoned. Now the evening classes were far more popular than the day classes and enrolled twice the number of students.[73] However, this arrangement of holding the classes in two locations was designed to be a temporary one. Under the terms of the merger, classes could be conducted at two separate places for two years; then the law school had to choose one or the other place for a permanent location. In 1940 the decision was made to hold all classes on the campus, retaining, however, the day and evening sessions.[74] This did cause a slight drop in the evening enrollment, but it was not until the end of World War II that the number of day students exceeded the number of night students.[75]

The two older schools of music and theology saw some changes also in this period. The School of Music remained under the leadership of Dean Paul van Katwijk and experienced an impressive growth from 141 students in 1925 to 287 in 1940.[76] The School of Theology underwent several changes of deans but actually lost students. The total enrollment in 1925 was 252; this fell to a low of 125 in 1936 and rose to 222 by 1940.[77] These changes, though, reflect the decline of overall enrollment during the depression. Paul B. Kern, who was on the original faculty, was made dean in 1920 and served until 1926,[78] when he became minister of the Travis Street Methodist Church in San Antonio. In 1930 he was elected bishop.

James Kilgore, who also had been on the original faculty and had served as acting president in 1922, was chosen by Selecman to be acting dean. He retained this post until 1933 when a permanent dean was selected, Eugene B. Hawk. Hawk had received the B.A. degree from Emory and Henry College (1903) and the B.D. degree from Vanderbilt (1909). He had served various churches in Texas, including First Church in Fort Worth. Immediately prior to his coming to SMU, he was a minister in Louisville, Kentucky. Besides serving as dean, he was also professor of homiletics and pastoral theology. In 1939 he became vice-president of the university, a position he held until his retirement in 1951.

In the College of Arts and Sciences the major developments during this period were the growth in the departments of education and commerce. As these two fields began to attract a larger and larger number of students, the course offerings and faculty members increased proportionally. Eventually both departments achieved independent status within the arts college, as the School of Education and the Dallas School of Commerce.

The education department began its growth in the early 1920s. At the beginning of this decade, there were only two teachers in this field, but by 1926 there were five full-time teachers and eleven part-time.[79] This number remained fairly constant until 1940. The course offerings increased even more dramatically. In 1920 there were only fourteen courses listed, but by 1925 there were more than three times as many courses, forty-six. The number increased by twelve during the following ten-year period and remained constant until 1940.[80]

With this tremendous increase in faculty and course offerings, it would be logical to expect a corresponding growth in the number of graduates with a B.S. degree in education, but such was not the case. The graduates increased, but not in proportion to the growth of courses in the department. As can be seen from Table I, in the five years between 1922 and 1926 there were only ten degrees granted in the field of education. In the next five-year period this number increased four and one-half times, to forty-five, where it remained until 1937. During the last period, 1937-40, the number rose to seventy-four. Most of the students taking education courses were doing so not to earn a B.S. degree in the field but simply to certify themselves to teach while taking a B.A. or B.S. in an academic subject. In 1922 only 17 percent of the graduating class held teaching certificates; but by 1926, 39 percent received certification.[81] The Department of Education also produced the largest number of master's degrees. Between 1921 and 1938, 38 percent of these degrees were in education. The nearest competition was the English department, which had over 18 percent.[82]

The man who guided the education department through this period of growth and who had the insight and imagination to see what possibilities existed was C. A. Nichols. Nichols was a native Texan who had a doctor's degree from the University of Havana (1906). He taught at a number of colleges in Texas, including Southwestern, before he came to SMU in 1919. After teaching several years at SMU, he took a leave of absence and earned another Ph.D. from Columbia University in 1930.

Nichols, who was a strong promoter of teacher training, saw unlimited possibilities for the influence of SMU in this field. He presented his ideas to the board in 1925 and 1926 in two lengthy reports which illustrate his vision. He arranged to have SMU students do their practice teaching in the Dallas public schools, since the university had no labora-

TABLE 1

NUMBER OF GRADUATES IN COLLEGE OF ARTS AND SCIENCES 1922-40*

Year	B.A.	B.S.	B.S. Commerce	B.S. Education	B.S. Physical Education	B.S. Journalism	B.S. Home Economics
1922-26	475	12	65	10	1	0	17
1927-31	650	32	160	45	14	21	32
1932-36	616	58	232	45	27	44	10
1937-40	424	64	261	74	20	32	13

TABLE 2

NUMBER OF M.A. DEGREES AWARDED IN VARIOUS FIELDS 1921-38*

English	123	Government	27	Biology	11	History	48
French	12	Philosophy	9	Chemistry	1	Geology	0
Latin	22	Psychology	12	Mathematics	37	German	0
Spanish	27	Sociology	25	Education	257		

* These figures were compiled from the annual *Bulletins of Southern Methodist University.*

tory school. He was aided by the fact that the city schools had discontinued a teacher-training program, leaving this field open to SMU. He also advocated that courses of study could be organized in a wide variety of fields: home economics, commercial subjects, public school music, physical education, rural education, religious education, and school administration.[83] Nichols evidently convinced the board of his ideas, because in 1926 his department was elevated to a School of Education within the arts college. For several years he gave reports to the board along with the deans of the various colleges.

The other department which saw tremendous growth in this period was commerce, also a utilitarian, technical subject. Collegiate training for business had been introduced into the colleges and universities during the first two decades of the twentieth century. Business education had, of course, begun at SMU in 1919 at the urging of the Dallas Chamber of Commerce. After a short-lived experiment in a separate college, the department of commerce became part of the College of Arts and Sciences in 1922. At this time the department was organized as the Dallas School of Commerce and was a two-year upper level program with a preliminary requirement of two years of college work. The degree of bachelor of science in commerce was conferred after the successful completion of these four years. The first graduating class in 1922 was composed of two students.[84]

In 1925 the department consisted of six faculty members and offered work in accounting, finance, commerce, marketing and secretarial training. By 1930 the curriculum had been broadened to include statistics, but the secretarial work had been dropped. In 1935 several courses in public administration were added. The faculty remained approximately the same size during this period, but the number of course offerings increased from twenty-four in 1925 to a high of thirty-eight ten years later. By 1940 they had dropped slightly to thirty-four. The department early (1925) became a member of the American Association of Collegiate Schools of Business.[85]

Unlike the education department, the department of commerce produced a sufficient number of graduates to justify creating a separate school within the arts college. Between 1922 and 1926 there were 65 bachelor's degrees in commerce awarded. In the following five-year period the number rose to 160, more than twice as many. Despite the depression, from 1932 to 1936 there were 232 degrees awarded, and the number even increased between 1937 and 1940 to 261.[86] At this point the B.S.

degrees in commerce equaled half of the B.A. degrees, which had always been by far the largest number. By 1940 the academic courses of the arts college were in danger of being overshadowed by the courses of the commerce department. With the substantial number of graduates, the establishment of an independent School of Business Administration in 1941 was a logical step. This new school was still an upper level school (the first two years being taken in the arts college) and it awarded a degree of bachelor of business administration.[87]

William Frederic Hauhart guided the development of business education at SMU, first as chairman and later as dean. Hauhart, a native of Missouri, had a Ph.D. in German from Columbia University (1909) and taught German at the University of Michigan until World War I. When the demand for German dropped off during this period, Hauhart was given a job teaching economics, which he found to his liking. He continued in this field, coming to SMU as chairman of the department of commerce in 1921, and remained on the faculty until 1945.

When Hauhart came to SMU, he brought with him a young colleague also from the University of Michigan, L. H. Fleck, who joined the accounting department and in 1946 succeeded Hauhart as dean of what by that time was called the School of Business Administration. Fleck held a master's degree (1919) from the University of Michigan and had become a certified public accountant in Texas in 1926.

With the stress that was placed upon technical and vocational courses during this period, the concept of a liberal arts college, upon which Southern Methodist University was founded, was in danger of being diluted. By the late 1930s the number of graduates who majored in business, education, physical education, journalism, and home economics nearly equaled those who majored in traditional liberal arts subjects. During the period 1922-26, 84 percent of the graduates received degrees in liberal arts subjects, while only 16 percent of the degrees were in vocational fields. By the period 1927-31 the vocational degrees had risen to 28 percent, and for the next five-year period the number was 35 percent. By the end of the decade nearly half, or 45 percent, of the graduates were receiving degrees in vocational fields.[88] These figures indicate the major problems of the liberal arts college during the 1930s. The pressure of an industrial and commercial society put a premium upon specialized skills and vocational subjects and threatened to overwhelm the tradition of a liberal education that had been the central concept in the educational philosophy of Southern Methodist University and similar institutions.

The problems of education were complex and confusing during this period. How were colleges and universities to reconcile the professional and vocational with the liberal? How to adjust to the competing claims of quantity and quality in an age of mass education? How many subjects could be effectively taught in an age of specialized knowledge? Was there any longer a common body of knowledge to which all college students should be exposed? What kind of liberal education was meaningful in an age of specialization?[89]

Educators with widely differing opinions were to be found. Abraham Flexner saw in the American university a beehive of triviality and vocationalism and drew up a major indictment. He criticized universities for being "service stations" for the general public.[90] A similar verdict was rendered by Robert M. Hutchins in *The Higher Learning in America.* He felt the colleges did too many things besides teach and there was too much emphasis upon athletics and social life. He particularly attacked the idea that education should be immediately useful. He advocated a forthright return to the old scholastic curriculum, to a general education in the classics.[91]

Defenders of the newer university were not lacking. Harry D. Gideonse answered Hutchins by writing *The Higher Learning in a Democracy.* Gideonse claimed that Hutchins failed to recognize the forces that had created the American university. It would be impossible for colleges to be more consistent than the society in which they exist. How could education be unified? Truth is not a single, complete, and static entity. Boundaries of knowledge have expanded, and hence the content of education must be diversified.[92] John Dewey found Hutchins's ideal of philosophical unity and authority something "akin to the distrust of freedom and the constant appeal to *some* fixed authority that [was] overrunning the world." Dewey felt that higher education, instead of escaping from present evil social tendencies, should study social needs and potential.[93]

Basic to the ideal of a liberal education was the idea that all men should have the same kind of education. They should at least read in common a body of classical literature that would help them to make a community of the educated. But with the advent of the elective system and the need for mass education, this unity was difficult to achieve. How could a liberal education be made into a general education? The pioneering attempt to answer this question was begun by Columbia University in 1919 with its course in Western Civilization. By the 1930s solutions were sought to this problem of how to transform a liberal education into a general education.

SMU first attempted to attack these problems in 1934. A college curriculum committee was organized by the College Council[94] to study the "changing conceptions, aims, and trends of education," to study the revised programs of other colleges and universities, and to make recommendations for revising the curriculum of the College of Arts and Sciences.[95] Fully a third of this report was devoted to the concepts of education espoused by Hutchins, Gideonse, Flexner, and Dewey.

The most meaningful conclusion that the committee reached was that with the type of students who attended SMU, it would not be possible to inaugurate experimental programs incorporating some of the more radical educational ideas of the day. The university could not, for example, devote itself exclusively to a classical liberal arts program such as Robert M. Hutchins was suggesting. On the other hand, the university desired to avoid placing too much emphasis upon vocational and professional training. The committee reached the conclusion that the aim of Southern Methodist University should be

a conservative middle ground between emphasis upon cultural, humanistic principles and the practical preparation of young men and women to adjust themselves to modern society and making a living in it.[96]

With this in mind, two interdepartmental majors were established, one in the social sciences and the other in American civilization. The social science major was inaugurated in 1935 under the direction of Herbert Gambrell of the history department. Included in this division were the fields of economics, government, history, philosophy, psychology, religion, and sociology. An elementary course, Introduction to Social Sciences, was set up as a prerequisite to any other course in the division. This course was originally taught by Linus Glanville of the history department and I.K. Stephens of philosophy.[97] These two gave weekly lectures with discussion sections led by various teachers from the other fields. These discussion sections were supposed to "integrate" the course and expose the students to the various fields.[98]

A student could major in social science or he could major in any one of the seven departments. Twelve semester hours of elementary and intermediate work were required for a major plus twenty-four semester hours of advanced work, distributed among at least three departments. A major examination was required of all majors.[99]

The primary motivation behind this social science major was a desire to imitate the integrated courses offered at Chicago and Columbia which attempted to generalize liberal education. A secondary motivation was to allow students to be exposed to other fields of study, since history was the only discipline offering a freshman level course. Few students who had taken the required course in Western Civilization at Columbia turned to the other fields as a major. In short, creating the social science major was an attempt to strengthen the other departments in the social science division which were weak.[100]

This course did not live up to expectations. The discussion leaders were not masters of all the fields involved nor were they even interested in mastering these fields. Despite the heroic efforts of Glanville and Stephens, good students complained that the superficial touching on the whole field of social science was of small value and the poor students were bewildered and apathetic. A new approach was attempted in 1940, but this was no more successful than the first. By 1950 the whole idea was abandoned, and the experiment ended about where it started. Freshmen took the required history, and the other disciplines did not enroll the students until after the first year.[101]

The other interdepartmental major was the History of American Civilization, which was introduced in 1940. This course allowed students to center their attention upon the civilization of the United States without regard for departmental categories. Requirements for a major were Introduction to the Social Sciences, History of the United States, and History of Ideas in America. An additional eighteen semester hours were to be selected from courses in the Geography of North America, Economic Development of the United States of America, Political Theory, American Philosophy, History of Churches of America, and American Literature.[102] Without a doubt this program was the brain child of Henry Nash Smith, who directed it. Smith, who had been teaching at SMU since 1925, had just returned from Harvard, where he had received in 1940 a doctor's degree in American Civilization. He taught the crucial courses for only one year, though before he left SMU for the University of Texas, after which the program was shortly dropped from the curriculum. This program was far more successful than the social science program had been, because Smith had actually been trained in the field. Later in the 1950s the History of American Civilization major was revived under new leadership.

One of Umphrey Lee's first acts, after he assumed the presidency in

March, 1939, was to ask the College Council to appoint a committee to make a self-study of the College of Arts and Sciences.[103] President Lee desired this study partly because, as a new president, he needed to know more about the university and also because the college needed to know more about itself. This survey was conducted by the faculty members, who simply added this extra chore to their already full schedule.

The report, which was presented in April, 1940, contained much material which had been collected by the 1934 curriculum committee. But the specific recommendations were new.[104]

These recommendations embraced many of the concepts of general education and indicated the desire of the faculty to raise the academic standards of the university. The first step suggested was a plan of selective admission which would raise the academic ability of the students and make possible such innovations as honors courses, tutorials, and comprehensive examinations. The desire was expressed to integrate the departments to a greater degree, to develop further interdepartmental courses of study like the one in social science. It was recommended that introductory courses be established for those who planned to major in the field which were separate from courses for those who did not. Emphasis on breadth in early work and specialization later could be achieved by dividing the arts and science college into a junior and senior division. The liberal arts work of the college could be greatly enhanced by removing from it the vocational courses. This was largely accomplished with the establishment of the business school in 1941. A need was also felt to provide some guidance and advisory services for the students.[105]

However thoughtful this report was, it evidently suffered the fate of many such documents. It served as an exercise for the faculty, aided them in evaluating themselves, and then it was filed. None of the recommendations was enacted (except the establishment of the business school, which was on its way regardless). The failure to put into practice any of the recommendations did not reflect on the quality of those suggestions but was due more to the lack of funds and the depressed state of affairs at the beginning of the Second World War.[106] As an indication of the soundness of the ideas, virtually all of the recommendations became a reality in the 1950s.[107]

CHAPTER VII

Faculty and Intellectual Life, 1925-1940

THE INTELLECTUAL ATMOSPHERE at Southern Methodist University during the years 1925 to 1940 was not highly conducive to research, writing, or publishing. The university was still young, and its main efforts were directed toward teaching. The teaching loads were heavy, usually fifteen hours a week. Not many faculty members had the time or the inclination to attempt any scholarly research on top of such a load. There is no indication that encouragement was given to the faculty by President Selecman or Dean Jennings. Indeed, Selecman was known to discourage faculty members from using their offices at night because they used extra electricity.[1] Without a doubt, it was an all-consuming task to create a university out of a Johnson grass pasture, and the conditions under which the early faculty worked simply did not stimulate research.[2]

Despite these handicaps, however, some writing and some publishing were done. The university acquired the *Southwest Review*, a literary magazine, in 1924 and published it continuously even through the slim days of the depression. In 1932 the science departments began publication of *Field & Laboratory*, the Arnold Foundation issued its Studies in Public Affairs (quarterly, 1932-43) and the Proceedings of its Institute of Public Affairs (annually, 1934-39), the sociology department issued Studies in Sociology (1936-40), and in 1937 the university established its own press. The faculty members who gave of their time and efforts to these publications deserve to be commended.

The publication of the *Southwest Review* was the most ambitious project undertaken by the relatively small number of dedicated faculty members. This magazine was acquired from the University of Texas by SMU in 1924 through the efforts and persistence of Jay B. Hubbell, chairman of the English department. The *Review* had been established in 1915 as the *Texas Review*, with Stark Young, professor of general literature, as editor. Young shortly left for Amherst College, however, and the policies and pattern for the magazine were established by the next editor, Robert Adger Law, a Shakespearean scholar. The *Review* did not flourish and Texas intended to discontinue it, when Hubbell requested that it be transferred to SMU. This act consisted simply of turning over to Hubbell the list of subscribers, of which there were only sixteen.[3]

Hubbell was editor of the *Southwest Review* from 1924 to 1927, when he left for Duke University. During this period he was teaching full time and serving as chairman of the English department, in addition to his duties as editor. He was ably assisted by George Bond of the English department and Herbert Gambrell of the history department, both of whom were young instructors. The members of the advisory board were chosen from every state in the Southwest in the hope of having regional backing. Hubbell aspired to achieve a balance between articles written by southwesterners or about the Southwest and articles from writers in other areas, including some who had a national reputation.[4]

Hubbell and Bond marked out the main lines of a coherent editorial policy and discovered a number of writers capable of carrying it out. When both of these men departed in 1927, a crisis in the affairs of the magazine developed. The *Review* obviously belonged to the English department, and the most logical successor was John McGinnis. A serious difficulty lay in the fact that *Review* work was not recognized by the university as a legitimate part of the teachers' duties. It had to be carried on in spare time. McGinnis taught full time and also edited a weekly book page for the *Dallas Morning News*. Nevertheless, he "reluctantly accepted custody of the orphan."[5]

McGinnis's plan for meeting this crisis was to use the assistance of his more capable advanced students in performing a major portion of the editing job. Thanks to the presence of highly capable students and the excellent leadership that McGinnis provided, the system worked. Henry Nash Smith, then a young English instructor, evaluated the experience later:

> . . . it may well turn out that the *Review's* greatest importance during McGinnis' editorship lay in the fact that it was a sort of super-graduate seminar, an Institute of Higher Studies, in which were enrolled his older students, younger colleagues, and even contemporaries, on the faculty or not, who were writing or reading proof or merely running errands for the *South-*

west Review. Certainly the University has received its money's worth from the project in this fashion alone. At least three members of its faculty came up through this curriculum, besides others who later went into journalism, publishing, teaching elsewhere, or writing.[6]

The McGinnis method succeeded because it was exciting, authentically Socratic. McGinnis detested formalism and made an art of conversation. He would usually begin his work late at night.

A manuscript would be brought out and read aloud, sentence by sentence, and subjected to a scrutiny of almost unimaginable rigor. The etymology, the semantic history, the denotation, the connotations of a word; the rhythm of a sentence; the progression of thought in a paragraph; transitions; even punctuation and spelling—all these were debated, altered, restored, marked for future discussion.[7]

This method was highly instructive, but also extremely time-consuming. Charles W. Ferguson, one of McGinnis's students, wrote that those who assumed they were trying to get out a magazine were often surprised to learn that McGinnis assumed they "were engaged in the only enterprise worthy of rational beings, the pursuit of clarity and elegance in thought and phrase."[8] With this time-consuming process, the issues of the *Review* were nearly always late by several months. But McGinnis was not editing for a deadline; he considered it vulgar to sacrifice excellence for mere routine.

The magazine was in chronic financial trouble. During the late 1920s the university granted the *Review* an annual subsidy of $1,000.[9] With this sum plus the subscription fee of two dollars and occasional donations from Dallas citizens, the magazine managed to operate. During the first year the subscriptions increased from 16 to 750. By 1932 the *Review* had 937 paid subscriptions.[10] Despite this substantial subscription list, the magazine nearly folded during the depression until a plan was devised to save it.

From the Autumn 1932 issue through that of Summer 1935 SMU collaborated with Louisiana State University in publishing the magazine jointly. McGinnis feared the magazine might be made into an organ for the propagation of agrarianism, since Robert Penn Warren was on the board of editors and the agrarian manifesto, *I'll Take My Stand*, to which Warren was a contributor, had just been published. And indeed, controversy did arise between the Dallas and Baton Rouge editors over a review by Albert Russel Erskine, Jr., of LSU, of Stark Young's novel, *So Red the Rose*. The disagreement was settled amicably, however, and the collaboration ended amid expressions of mutual esteem when the Baton Rouge people secured a subsidy from LSU to publish their own magazine. At this point SMU doubled its former appropriation, and the *Review* continued.[11] McGinnis served as editor until 1943.

Without the devotion of a passionate few the *Southwest Review* would never have been kept alive. The major responsibility was assumed by McGinnis, but much of the drudgery and hard work fell on younger men, such as Henry Nash Smith, Lon Tinkle, and John Chapman. Smith's substantial contribution to the *Review* occurred during the depression, when the magazine certainly would have died had Smith not given up everything else but his teaching to keep it going.[12]

Both Tinkle and Chapman were McGinnis's "boys" as students and continued their association with him after graduation. Chapman was the first student McGinnis selected to help him when he took the magazine over in 1927.[13] He learned much about writing and editing before he received the B.A. degree (1927) and the M.A. degree (1928). Most of his later career has been spent on the faculty of Southwestern Medical School in Dallas, and over the years he has continued to contribute articles to the *Review*. Tinkle remained more closely associated with the *Review* because, after his graduation in 1927, he returned to SMU in 1932 to earn the M.A. degree and to teach French and comparative literature. He followed McGinnis as literary editor of the *Dallas Morning News* and is the author of some eight books on a wide variety of subjects. With his wit and charm, Tinkle has stimulated countless students to appreciate good writing, good literature, and good taste.

McGinnis had the ability to perceive what was vital in the life of a region and to find the right people to describe it. This talent is represented by a series, "Naturalists of the Frontier," by Samuel Wood Geiser, the first of which appeared in the *Review* in October, 1929. Geiser was a professor of biology, having come to SMU in 1924 with a doctor's degree from Johns Hopkins (1922). Almost by accident, he became interested in a man named Jacob Boll, of whom little was known except that he had collected snakes and butterflies and had lived in Dallas for some years before his death in 1880. Geiser found himself drawn into an almost unknown chapter of Texas history—scientific exploration during the frontier period.[14] A series on naturalists like Boll was printed first in the *Review* between 1929 and 1937. The collected articles were then published in 1937 as *Naturalists of the Frontier*, the first book by the newly organized SMU Press, called in the early years University Press in Dallas. Geiser was doubtless encouraged by McGinnis and Smith to develop his studies into a series of articles because there was at hand the means of publishing them.

Closely associated with the *Review* was the establishment of the SMU Press. McGinnis was a prime mover in this enterprise. The Press was begun with the approval of the Board of Trustees, the encouragement of the faculty committee on publications, and $1,000 from the Schoellkopf family.[15] The original working staff on the SMU Press consisted of Henry Nash Smith, George Bond (who had returned from New York and was teaching English), Jerry Bywaters of the art department, and Herbert Gambrell of the history department.[16]

Establishment of a press at SMU in 1937 was a rather audacious move. There was no money in sight to pay even for secretarial services, let alone to employ a full-time staff. The thousand dollars in hand was enough to pay only for publication of one book. After Geiser's volume was published, no further activity could be contemplated until the Schoellkopf Fund could be replenished by sales. John McGinnis did find a way to keep things going by using some of the regular funds of the *Review*. In 1939 the press's second book appeared, J. Frank Dobie's *John C. Duval: First Texas Man of Letters*, essentially a bound reprint of pages that had earlier appeared in the *Review*. In its earlier years the press had only one paid employee, Allen Maxwell, who began work part time in 1939. Maxwell was also concerned with the *Review,* of which he became managing editor in 1941. When he was called into war service in 1942 Donald Day became the first full-time director of the press. He held that post until 1945 and served as *Southwest Review* editor from 1943 to 1945. When Allen Maxwell returned after the war, in 1946, he became the full-time director of the press and editor of the *Southwest Review*.[17]

The pages of the *Southwest Review* provided an outlet for those faculty members who had any desire to do research or writing. McGinnis and Smith were constantly searching for articles, encouraging, cajoling faculty and others to write for the magazine. The *Review* was not dominated by the faculty (McGinnis did not want to turn it into an academic organ), but the faculty quite naturally was well represented.

A frequent contributor as well as active worker with both the *Review* and the SMU Press was Herbert Gambrell of the history department. He served as managing editor of the *Review* from 1924 to 1927 and as chairman of the Board of Publications, governing body of the press, from 1939 to 1964. His reputation as an authority on Texas history was early established with "James Stephen Hogg: Statesman or Demagogue?" and "Anson Jones,"[18] which appeared in the *Southwest Review*. He also published articles in the *Journal of Modern History* and the *Dictionary of American Biography*.

The chairman of the history department, H. A. Trexler, whose fields of interest were southern history, the Confederate Navy, and western travels, contributed a series of articles to the *Review* during the early 1930s.[19] Trexler came to SMU as chairman in 1929 from Birmingham-Southern College following the death of R. A. Hearon and remained until his retirement in 1954. He did his undergraduate work at Hastings College, Nebraska (1906) and received the Ph.D. degree (1914) from Johns Hopkins University. In 1938 his studies on the Confederate Navy culminated in a book, *The Confederate Ironclad "Virginia."* He also had articles in the *Mississippi Valley Historical Review*, the *South Atlantic Quarterly*, and the *Missouri Historical Review*. Trexler was not a strong chairman; he disliked administrative duties and gave them to the other department members, Herbert Gambrell and Linus Glanville. The history faculty remained completely stable; no one resigned and no new members were added.[20]

A young member of the art department, Jerry Bywaters, published a series of articles during the 1930s on art in Dallas and the Southwest which added up to a serious analysis of the meaning of regional art. He reviewed virtually every art show in the pages of the *Review* as well as writing substantial articles on southwestern architecture and new Texas painters.[21] Bywaters had graduated from SMU in 1927 and continued his art studies at the Art Students League, New York, as well as in Europe and Mexico. He was a practicing artist and art critic for the *Dallas News* (1933-39) and returned to SMU in 1936 to teach art. He later (1943) became director of the Dallas Museum of Fine Arts. Bywaters was mainly responsible for the interest shown in art and architecture at the university and in Dallas.

The interest that Ernest E. Leisy had in research and writing was partly directed toward the *Review*. Leisy, who taught American Literature, joined the SMU faculty in 1927 and remained until his retirement in 1952. A native of Kansas, he had received his master's degree from Harvard (1914) and his doctor's degree from the University of Illinois (1923). He was a contributing editor of the *Review*, writing numerous book reviews as well as articles in his field.[22] He wrote a number of textbooks, edited new editions of American novels, and in his later life became an authority on Mark Twain. He published *Mark Twain: The Letters of Quintus Curtius Snodgrass* (1946) and *The American Historical Novel* (1950). He was also a frequent contributor to *American Literature*, the magazine established by Hubbell at Duke, *Modern Language Notes*, and the *New England Quarterly*.

The sole member of the philosophy department, I. K. Stephens, wrote an article for the *Review* on Edmund Montgomery, who was a hermit philosopher of a small Texas town.[23] Stephens discovered this little-known but substantial scholar and brought him to the attention of the public. Stephens had joined the SMU faculty in 1921 after receiving the M.A. from the university. He received the Ph.D. degree in 1927 from Harvard. Stephens remained on the faculty until his death in 1956, teaching philosophy and writing philosophical criticism. Even though he published little, he was regarded highly by his colleagues because he understood the meaning and purpose of a liberal arts college in a small but growing university.[24]

The efforts of the *Review* and its numerous writers all add up to a rediscovery of the Southwest as a region, a recognition that it had made a contribution to the fields of literature, history, art, philosophy, and science. With its emphasis upon regionalism (hopefully balanced by national interest), the magazine as well as the university played a role in developing knowledge of and pride in a region that had a substantial history.

Another magazine published on the campus during this period was *Field & Laboratory*, a small journal sponsored by the science division: the departments of geology, geography, physics, biology, and chemistry. The idea for this journal, which was to include articles by both faculty and students, originated with Samuel Wood Geiser and John Daniel Boon, chairmen of the biology and physics departments respectively. These two men presented their plans to the science division, which agreed to publish the journal semiannually. Again there was no money. But the plan was devised for each department to contribute one hundred dollars a year from its laboratory fees toward this publication, and with the sum of four hundred dollars[25] the project was launched. It was soon discovered that this sum was not adequate, and the magazine acquired a patron, Jack Frost, an alumnus of SMU who was successful in the oil business.[26]

The first issue of *Field & Laboratory* appeared in November, 1932, with the statement that the magazine would be devoted to the publication of the results of work done by students and teachers of science "with the belief that the discipline of writing and the possibility for publication will promote a spirit of research."[27] Since the magazine was being sponsored by the entire science group, it was intended that there should be at least one article from each field in each issue. In addition to promoting research, it was hoped that establishment of the magazine would give wider publicity to scientific study of the Southwest, since few scientific journals had articles dealing with general scientific topics related to this area.

The first editor was a young geographer, Edwin J. Foscue, who had graduated from SMU in 1922 and earned his doctor's degree at Clark University (1927). He began teaching at his alma mater in 1923 and remained until he retired in 1965. Foscue continued to edit the magazine until 1943, when he went to Washington for war work, at which time Geiser became editor. Foscue was editor with Stuart McGregor from 1937 to 1949 of the *Texas Geographic Magazine* and was a frequent contributor to the *Journal of Geography, Economic Geography*, and *Geographical Review*. He was also the author of *Gatlinburg: Gateway to the Great Smokies* (1946) and *Taxco: Mexico's Silver City* (1947), and coauthor with Louis O. Quam of *Estes Park: Resort in the Rockies* (1949). The assistant editor was Mayne Longnecker, a young biology teacher from Iowa who later (1937) earned his doctorate at the University of Chicago. Frank C. McDonald of the physics department was circulation manager. McDonald had come to SMU in 1929 with a Ph.D. degree (1926) from the University of Chicago. These men were primarily responsible for the publication of *Field & Laboratory* for the first ten years.

Student participation was high in this publishing venture. The first five volumes of the magazine, 1932-37, contain a total of sixty-nine papers, eighteen of which involved student participation, a total of 26 percent. During the next five volumes, students wrote or aided with an even greater number of papers. Of a total of forty-six, twenty-seven involved students, or 59 percent.[28] This high percentage did not continue, but nevertheless these figures indicate that students were active participants. Most of the student articles were associated with master's theses.

The bulk of the articles were, of course, written by the faculty members. Geiser and Boon contributed the largest number of papers. Geiser, with his ever-inquiring mind, found time to write for *Field & Laboratory* as well as for the *Southwest Review*. Boon offered the scientific journal as much support as Geiser did. He continued to support it at a period when it seemed as though it would not succeed. Boon had only a B.S. degree from Granbury College (he did graduate work at Chicago and Wisconsin but never received an advanced degree). He had come to SMU in 1919 from Polytechnic College and had been made chairman of the physics department in 1929 at the death of Robert Hyer. Boon collaborated with Claude C. Albritton, Jr., a younger member of the geology department, in formulating "the 'Boon-Albritton theory' in explanation of the formation of lunar craters, and the terrestrial formation of so-called 'crypto-volcanic structures' by meteoritic impacts."[29]

Albritton, a major contributor to the journal, was a 1933 graduate of SMU who had received the Ph.D. degree in geology from Harvard in 1936, at which time he returned to SMU to teach. During his first year as a teacher, he published three articles in the *Journal of Paleontology*. Later in his career he became dean of the faculty of the College of Arts and Sciences (1952) and dean of the Graduate School (1957).

Two other faculty members who wrote numerous articles for *Field & Laboratory* were Ellis W. Shuler and Elmer P. Cheatum. Shuler, a member of the original faculty, was chairman of the geology department and also dean of the Graduate School. Throughout his long career he encouraged research, writing, and publishing. In 1945 he published *Rocks and Rivers of America*, and he also contributed articles to *American Journal of Science* and *Scientific American*.[30] Elmer Cheatum came to SMU in 1925 to teach biology just after he received his master's degree from Kansas State College. He earned the Ph.D. from the University of Michigan in 1932 and remained with SMU during his entire academic career.

Among the activities which the university sponsored during the 1930s were the Institutes of Public Affairs. These were begun in 1934 with the support of the Arnold Foundation. The Arnold Foundation had been established in 1924 by Ora Nixon Arnold of Houston as a memorial to her husband, George F. Arnold. Mrs. Arnold gave $120,000 to SMU endowment funds with the stipulation that the interest be used "to further the training of young men as civic leaders and to promote a better realization of the problems and responsibilities of citizenship."[31]

With this money the political science department became the department of government, and by 1929 it was called the Arnold School of Government, with Harvey Guice as director. It offered courses in U.S. government, international government, politics, citizenship, administration, legislation, and diplomacy.[32] By 1934 this department had a separate status within the arts college, like the School of Education and the School of Commerce. At this time S. D. Myres, Jr., emerged as the director, and under his leadership the Institutes of Public Affairs were inaugurated.[33] Myres was a native Texan who had received the B.A. (1920) and M.A. (1925) degrees from SMU, and the doctorate (1929) from the University of Texas. He joined the faculty of SMU in 1925 and remained until 1954.

The Institutes of Public Affairs, held annually between 1934 and 1939, were a series of conferences on various topics of current interest. The subject in 1934 was "The Government of Texas"; in 1935, "The Cotton Crisis"; in 1936, "The Southwest in International Affairs"; in 1937, "International Institutions and World Peace"; in 1938, "Mexico and the United States"; and in 1939, "America and the World Crisis." At each of these conferences Myres arranged for a series of papers to be given by experts in various fields. These were then collected and edited by Myres and published by the Arnold Foundation.[34]

The great majority of these papers were written by experts from throughout the state. Only a small minority were written by faculty members at SMU. Myres himself wrote only two of them for the conferences, but he wrote some eight other monographs on various phases of government which were published by the Arnold Foundation.[35]

A more frequent contributor to the Institutes was J. Linus Glanville of the history department.[36] Glanville joined the faculty in 1925 after receiving the B.A. (1917) and M.A. degrees (1918) from SMU. Later he obtained the Ph.D. degree from Johns Hopkins (1931). His other writings include *Italy's Relations with England, 1896-1905* (1924); *Colonialism in the New Italy* (1934); and *The Struggle for Security in Europe* (1936). He also contributed articles to the *Southwestern Social Science Quarterly* and the *Historian*.

Another publication effort carried on at Southern Methodist University in these years was a series entitled Studies in Sociology, sponsored by the sociology department between 1936 and 1940. This series was the brainchild of Walter T. Watson, who came to SMU in 1929. The next year he received the Ph.D. from the University of Chicago. Watson exemplified and perpetuated the Chicago approach at its best, and he worked for the development of sociology as a science in the whole Southwest.[37]

Studies in Sociology represented almost completely the work of the sociology students, whom Watson challenged and inspired. Two of the more revealing studies were done by Elbert L. Hooker, one on the urban tourist camps and the other on the fraternity system at SMU.[38] These articles illustrate the effect Watson had in stimulating students to go out observing into the community.

The research, writing, and publishing done during the twenties and thirties were carried on by a minority of the faculty. Only a handful of dedicated souls was able to surmount the obstacles and produce an article or two, a book review, or sometimes a book. The great majority of the faculty were solely engaged in teaching and gave little thought to scholarship. This is a characteristic of a new university; a university needs some maturity before it can engage in research. A large part of the writing that was done appeared in local or regional publications. However, occasionally an article or a book review appeared in a widely circulated, scholarly magazine. In the early twenties almost nothing was published, but by 1939 Umphrey Lee could list thirty-nine separate articles or books which had been published by faculty members in the past year.[39] Clearly, the faculty was beginning to realize the value and need of such activities.

During the 1930s the arts faculty was small, between sixty and seventy members.[40] Everyone knew everyone else, and what affected one department affected the whole campus. The entire university was thrown into an uproar when in 1932 the chairman of the English department, John O. Beaty, tried to fire Henry Nash Smith. Beaty, who had joined the faculty in 1919, became chairman in 1927 when Hubbell left for Duke University. Beaty's undergraduate work was from the University of Virginia, and his doctor's degree from Columbia (1921). He was an active, ambitious faculty member who published several textbooks in collaboration with colleagues as well as other works: *John Esten Cook, Virginian* (1922); *Race and Population* (1928); and a novel, *Swords in the Dawn* (1937). He also contributed articles to the *Dallas Morning News*, the *Publications of the Modern Language Association*, and the *Southwest Review*. He was awarded the Kahn Fellowship for foreign travel in 1926, at which time he made a trip around the world. Beaty had a first-class mind, was an inquiring scholar, and knew his field; but he possessed a streak of Puritan self-righteousness and moralist determination which made him difficult to work with and decreased his effectiveness. He saw himself as a self-appointed guardian of the moral standards of the university and in this capacity attacked Smith.[41]

Smith's offense in the eyes of Beaty was that he had written the preface to a short story, *Miss Zilphia Gant*, by a then relatively unknown and obscure author named William Faulkner. Smith had secured this story from Faulkner with the idea of publishing it in the *Southwest Review*, but McGinnis felt it would not be wise to do so. As a result, the story and Smith's preface were published by the Texas Book Club, which was sponsored by a patron of the *Review*, Stanley Marcus.[42]

Beaty described the short story as "the foulest book I have ever read—a book which parades sex abnormalities in a hideous way and also contains a particularly scurrilous attack on Jesus Christ."[43] Beaty convinced President Selecman that Smith's writing the introduction was behavior entirely unfit for a professor at SMU; and Selecman wrote Smith, who was in London teaching extension courses for Oxford University, that he should resign. Selecman characterized the book as "salacious and immoral in tone." He continued:

. . . We consider the situation as very serious and entirely out of keeping with the standards of an institution such as Southern Methodist University.

In view of this, I am suggesting your resignation to take effect August 31. . . . This course, I think, will be less detrimental to you and the University than any procedure that would involve wider discussion of the problem and probable publicity.[44]

This attack seemed ludicrous to those who were acquainted with the "cherubic nature of Henry's truthfulness."[45] Smith refused to resign and instead took the next boat home to fight for his job. His friends gathered around and one of them, Edwin D. Mouzon, Jr., suggested that the best course of action was to get Bishop John Moore, chairman of the board, on his side. Mouzon talked with the bishop, who was a long-time friend of his family, and convinced him that Smith should be retained and the matter smoothed over. By this time President Selecman had come to the conclusion that the offense was not so great and agreed with Moore.[46]

Beaty, however, had not changed his mind and refused to accept Smith back into the English department. Selecman evidently did not feel that he could force Smith on Beaty. As a result, on September 21, Selecman and Dean Jennings made another attempt to encourage Smith to resign. They offered him a year's leave of absence with full pay provided he would leave town and never return again and never discuss the matter.[47] Smith again refused, making it clear that he could not accept the financial settlement. He argued:

The controversy involved not a breach of departmental discipline or any incompatibility between myself and the members of the department, but did involve an assertion that a particular act of mine had proved me not a fit person to teach at SMU.

. . . Inasmuch as I am a member of the faculty, the performance of whose duties has been suspended, I feel that my departure without explanation would be with damage to my reputation and to my self respect.[48]

Selecman was caught between Beaty, who refused to tolerate Smith, and Smith, who refused to resign. The president evidently felt he had to acquiesce in Beaty's desires, and yet he was afraid to fire Smith. Eventually a compromise was reached whereby Smith was retained on the faculty and given a position in the comparative literature department. This small department was headed by F. D. Smith, a short, mild-mannered man who had been brought to SMU by President Hyer in 1920.[49] F. D. Smith was not offended by the actions of Henry Smith and was willing to make a place for the younger man in his department. Lon Tinkle, a close friend of Henry Smith, gave up his part-time teaching in comparative literature and returned to teaching French full time. I. K. Stephens also gave Henry Smith a course in philosophy.[50] With this arrangement then, Henry Smith resumed his classes in the spring semester of 1933.[51]

This compromise satisfied everyone except John Beaty, who was incensed that Smith was retained on the faculty in any department. On November 28, 1932, he wrote a letter to all board members expressing regret that the administration had been forced to accept a compromise, "which really represent[ed] a surrender to the subversive elements," and maintaining that the university should take a positive stand.[52] As though this were not enough, on December 1, 1932, Beaty wrote a letter to all the Methodist ministers in Oklahoma and Texas enlightening them about the situation and encouraging them to write to the trustees and demand a full investigation. His letter was full of innuendoes, never mentioning Henry Smith by name nor stating what he had actually done:

A situation has arisen which threatens to destroy all the Christian usefulness of Southern Methodist University: to make it a center for the propaganda of obscenity and degeneracy and to make it the sponsor of a dastardly attack on Jesus Christ.

Is this the goal for which consecrated people have given their money to Southern Methodist University? . . . If you fail to act now, Southern Methodist University will be lost to the Church under far worse conditions than those under which Vanderbilt was lost. Ought this to happen? When Methodism understands the issue there can be but one answer—"With the help of God, No."[53]

By this action Beaty made manifest the intolerance, the hypocritical prudery, and the antiintellectualism that were to characterize his later career even further.[54]

As soon as Beaty's letters went out, the board and the administration were flooded with inquiries about what was going on. The faculty rushed to Smith's defense. A letter signed by virtually every member of the faculty was sent to President Selecman protesting Beaty's letter and repudiating the charges and innuendoes as false and unjustified.[55] Several board members, notably Ivan Lee Holt, protested Beaty's actions in going over the heads of President Selecman and the board members by writing letters to the Methodist ministers.[56] At the board meeting in January, 1933, Beaty appeared and apologized for committing "a breach of etiquette" in writing letters to people outside the university without consulting the administration. He maintained that he had felt compelled to do so because the matter was of such grave importance.[57]

The board regarded Beaty's action as more than a breach of etiquette. They evidently must have discussed discharging him, because they amended the bylaws with a provision for dismissing anyone from the faculty who presented grievances about the university to anyone other than the president,[58] but they did not make it retroactive. J. J. Perkins favored at least suspending Beaty for a time as punishment for his unwarranted actions,[59] but not even this was done. A later generation of SMU administration may well have wished that the board had seen fit to discharge Beaty in 1933. Beaty continued his role as watchdog for the university's well-being. During the McCarthy era of the 1950s, he was busy hunting out all the communists and subversives on the campus. He wrote *The Iron Curtain over America* (1951), which indicted the Jews as the leaders of a giant communist conspiracy. After he mailed three thousand copies of "How to Capture a University" to parents of SMU students describing "communist infiltration of the university," Beaty was censured by both the board and the faculty; but he remained in his position until his retirement in 1957.[60]

It is, indeed, a little surprising that some action was not taken against Beaty, not because he attacked Henry Nash Smith (most Methodists in the early 1930s would have been shocked by Faulkner's books), but because he defied administration officials and went over their heads. This kind of insubordination was not easily accepted by Selecman, as will be seen in the following chapter. But Selecman had a high regard for Beaty. He believed Beaty stood for high ideals in teaching and personal life and felt at least considerable sympathy with him in his attack on Smith.[61]

Both Selecman and Beaty tended to be stern moralists who wished to root out anything that was alien. Probably because of this similarity of viewpoint, Selecman was willing to overlook the insubordination on Beaty's part.

During the twenty-five years between 1915 and 1940, the faculty of the arts college underwent considerable change. It had grown from fifteen members in 1915 to sixty-six in 1940. At this latter date there were five (one-third) of the original faculty still teaching. These were John McGinnis, John McIntosh, A. D. Schuessler, Ellis W. Shuler, and Samuel A. Myatt. In 1940 these men were all granted a year's leave of absence with pay[62] as a reward for their twenty-five years of service.

The faculty in 1940 was better trained, at least in terms of advanced degrees, than the earlier faculty. As pointed out in an earlier chapter, President Hyer had managed to put together the initial faculty with a relatively high percentage of Ph.D. degrees. In 1915, 40 percent held a terminal degree. However, this high percentage could not be maintained, and it quickly dropped to 25 percent. During the depression the figure rose to 48 percent in 1935, while the number of faculty dropped. These figures would indicate that those faculty members who had Ph.D. degrees were retained over those who did not. By 1940 over half of the faculty (55 percent) held a doctor's degree.[63]

One of the obvious characteristics of the SMU faculty was the amount of inbreeding, the marked tendency of the university to hire its own graduates. During the twenties most of these graduates held only B.A. or M.A. degrees and made up the bulk of the lower ranks of the faculty. By the thirties, however, many had gone away to secure doctor's degrees from the strongest universities in the country and had then come back to teach at SMU, so that by 1940, 35 percent of the faculty with the rank of assistant professor or above held a degree from SMU. The practice of hiring SMU graduates was sharply curtailed after World War II.[64]

This policy is a common one among new universities, and SMU simply followed it. Whether or not this was a wise course or whether there was an alternative, SMU was well served by the loyalty and quality of its own graduates who rose to key positions on the faculty. These people were the backbone of the faculty during the thirties and even longer. Such members as Gambrell and Glanville in history; Bond, Herron, Brooks, and Smith in English; Mouzon in mathematics; Foscue and Albritton in geography and geology; Tinkle in French; Stephens in philosophy were the substantial, contributing members who made the

TABLE 3

SMU FACULTY 1915-1970*

Year	Total Arts & Sciences Faculty	Percent of Ph.D. Degrees	Percent Having M.A. Degree as Highest Degree	Percent Having B.A. Degree as Highest Degree	Percent of Asst. Prof. or Above with SMU Degree	Percent of Instructors with SMU Degree
1915	15	40%	60%	0	0	0
1920	28	25%	57%	18%	0	88%
1925	59	25%	49%	24%	20%	83%
1930	71	35%	48%	16%	28%	62%
1935	63	48%	43%	8%	30%	40%
1940	66	55%	41%	4%	35%	47%
1950	128	56%	38%	6%	19%	45%
1960	124	82%	10%	8%	23%	36%
1970	208	87%	10%	3%	13%	32%

* Information compiled from the annual *Bulletins of SMU*. These figures include only those with rank of assistant professor or above, except for the final column.

growth of the institution their life work.[65] During the depression years the faculty remained almost static. Virtually no vacancies were created, and everyone held onto the position he had. But as soon as World War II was over, there appeared on the faculty men and women from different universities and different sections of the country.

CHAPTER VIII

The Depression Years, 1930-1940

DURING THE DEPRESSION years of the 1930s Southern Methodist University suffered the same financial difficulties as the rest of the United States. The SMU faculty was reduced in number, salaries were cut, and the university faced a mounting debt. Money-raising campaigns were canceled, and building programs came to a halt. In the early years of this period Southern Methodist University was strained even further by tensions between President Selecman and the executive committee of the board on the one hand and the faculty on the other. These two sets of controversies coalesced in 1931 and even spilled over into two meetings of the North Texas Annual Conference. Selecman found himself fighting to save his presidential career and, in a larger sense, his career as a minister in the Methodist church. From Selecman's viewpoint, he won the battle against the executive committee when the chairman, R. H. Shuttles, resigned and Selecman retained the presidency. But he was forced to give some ground in his contest with the faculty, and a reorganization of that group was the result.

Turmoil of the Selecman Years

Selecman had always been a controversial figure in the university and the church. He possessed a strong will and a determination to carry through his own program. He was an intelligent, capable man who had a powerful and impressive voice and an imposing bearing. He had been the pastor of several large churches in St. Louis, Los Angeles, and New Orleans before coming to Dallas. As a minister his strong will and determination were assets, since a ministry is more or less a one-man show. But when he attempted to deal with a group of individualistic faculty members, he ran into difficulty.

145

Selecman's election to the presidency came only after the list of candidates had been exhausted and the university had been drifting leaderless for nearly a year.[1] Even then his selection was not unanimous. The chief drawback to Selecman's appointment was that he did not have even a B.A. degree, much less any advanced work, and he lacked any experience in academic administration. However, as minister of the First Methodist Church in Dallas, he had enough influential Methodists backing him to secure the position.

In his novel *Pigskin*, Charles Ferguson satirized Selecman's administration and described Selecman as "a cross between the Apostle Paul and Benito Mussolini."[2] This is an apt description. As a minister Selecman always emphasized the Christian aspect of education and was anxious to make it felt at SMU. He desired a completely Christian faculty, who would present a Christian view of the world in every class. He felt that moral standards and a sense of right and wrong were nearly lost to his generation. In the teaching of mathematics or physics or literature, the Christian teacher, he held, should try to turn the thoughts of the students to "deity, duty, and destiny." He further felt that the university should try to

combat the influences on the campus that destroy character, such as filthy literature, false doctrines of sex, social follies and shallowness, cheating and laziness, booze and bootleggers, dishonesty and every petty crime, meantime holding aloft a standard of uncompromising manhood and high principle that will be the very atmosphere of college and university life.[3]

In dealing with the faculty Selecman used high-handed and dictatorial methods, not unlike those of Mussolini. He was never hesitant to assert his authority and put faculty members in their places, whether they were deans or lowly instructors. He always let the faculty know where the power lay.[4] It might be suggested that perhaps Selecman used his authority as he did to compensate for his feelings of inferiority, since he lacked the proper academic degrees. What better way to show the faculty, who held Ph.D. degrees, that he was as good as they were? His summary manner caused much bitterness and hostility to develop among the faculty toward him. Several faculty left during the late twenties with feelings of animosity toward the university.[5]

Selecman could not tolerate criticism and tended to discharge faculty members for relatively minor and insignificant reasons. One incident related to an adviser to the annual. In the 1927 yearbook, the *Rotunda*, there appeared a dedication to Selecman which was intended as a joke but which hit a little too near the truth. It read:

> We are familiar with the high-handed methods of Prexy in running the school and all its occupants by his big stick policy. We have all heard and seen him enter Chapel (ha! ha! ha! etc.) and in that MODEST and SELF-RETIRING way, tell how good he is and that he is still in charge of the University.[6]

Selecman was deeply offended by this spoof, demanded an apology, and further demanded that the offending page be removed from the yearbook. The two students involved sent a letter of apology[7] and spent several weeks searching down the yearbooks, which had been distributed, and tearing out the offending page. Selecman tried to prevent one student from returning to SMU and tried to withhold the diploma of the other, but was persuaded to relent.[8]

The faculty adviser, Joseph D. Doty, was not as fortunate as the students. Doty was a 1916 graduate of SMU who had been awarded a Rhodes Scholarship in 1920. He was a brilliant teacher, but Selecman did not forgive him for allowing the offensive statement to be published in the *Rotunda*. Before the incident Doty had been granted a leave of absence to study for his doctorate with the understanding that he could return to SMU. After the episode, Selecman decided he did not want Doty back. The president did not inform Doty until his graduate work was completed. Doty was then forced to find a professorship elsewhere, and SMU lost an excellent history teacher.[9]

Selecman's concept of what a university should be was often at variance with that of faculty members who were educated in the liberal arts tradition. He encouraged and developed the practical and vocational courses, such as business, education, and engineering, and these fields grew at a rapid rate.[10] Selecman also sought and received the support of Dallas business interests, partly with this utilitarian curriculum, but largely by supporting the development of a winning football team. The emphasis upon athletics and the preferential treatment given athletes was one of the major characteristics of the Selecman administration.[11] SMU built a football stadium before it had adequate classroom space and long before it had a library.[12]

As far as many of the faculty were concerned, the emphasis was simply put in the wrong place. They viewed a university primarily in terms of the liberal arts tradition and felt that money and effort should be put into teachers' salaries and the library. Furthermore, they resented the influence that Dallas businessmen had in the university. The character who was the arch proponent for this view in Ferguson's book states the case well. He says to the president:

I stand . . . for a college which shall not be forever playing to a stupid constituency with devices and courses calculated to arouse the interest of a populace drunk on practicality. I stand for a college in which the faculty shall not be forced to bow to an absentee board of business men who operate through a hireling to control the college as though it were an industrial plant for the manufacture of widgets and gadgets.

. . . I stand also for an intelligent ethics in the conduct of college affairs, an ethics which shall recognize the pursuit of truth as a legitimate undertaking and the cultivation of learning as a worthy pastime. I fear I stand for a college which to you and your Board of Regents would be a shocking failure, but which none the less turns out happy men and women who could read books and talk of something besides real estate.[13]

Another obvious aspect of President Selecman's character was his overwhelming desire to be elected a bishop in the Methodist church. Few men openly express a desire for the episcopacy, since in theory a bishop is called by God. But Selecman's actions and appointments appeared to be dictated more by the politics of the General Conference than by the needs of the university.[14] Some of the faculty thought that he viewed the presidency as a stepping stone to the episcopacy. There is no doubt that the man in the position of president or that of dean of the School of Theology would be a logical choice for bishop.

When the General Conference met in 1930, it was widely known that Selecman was a candidate, along with several others.[15] At this time Selecman was fifty-six years old and had been president for seven years. In the election he placed fourth on the first ballot but dropped thereafter,[16] while men who were younger than he were elected.

His defeat was a great disappointment to Selecman. When he returned from the conference, his friends organized a dinner for him, as a sort of consolation prize, at which his administration was praised.[17] At the meeting the following day, the board recommended a salary increase and expressed to the president its "very highest esteem and hope that he [would] make the Presidency of the University his life work."[18] Selecman's desire to be bishop continued, but it was not until 1938 when he was sixty-four years old that this honor was bestowed upon him.[19]

Shortly after his great disappointment at not being elected bishop in

1930, Selecman found himself attacked outside the university by the supporters of the football team and attacked inside the university by dissatisfied faculty members. The attack from the Dallas citizens concerned the firing of R. N. Blackwell, the business manager of athletics. Blackwell had been accused of drinking on several occasions, and in February, 1931, Selecman decided that Blackwell was doing the university more harm than good and his connections with the university should be severed. Selecman was aware that the case must be handled with care, because Blackwell was liked by the Dallas backers of the football team as well as by several members of the executive board. With this in mind Selecman wrote a letter to the executive committee on February 5, 1931, explaining the situation and showing that he had the backing of the correlation committee, which was composed of the deans, as well as the faculty athletic committee.[20]

The indications are that the charges against Blackwell were more extensive than the amount of liquor consumed. Blackwell himself indicated that the case against him was expanded at a meeting February 11, 1931, but failed to mention what the other charges were.[21] It may have been that the university feared to bring stronger charges against Blackwell because they would reflect upon the university or it may have been that they were unable to prove stronger charges. Whatever the reason, Selecman chose to rest his case against Blackwell on the drinking issue, one on which all Methodists could unite, especially during the days of Prohibition.

As Selecman expected, he immediately ran into opposition from the executive committee and from the Dallasites who backed the football team. A majority of the committee was opposed to firing Blackwell and the chairman of the board, R. H. Shuttles, was reported to have said that if Blackwell were fired it "would 'wipe Dallas off the map,' in so far as further support of the University was concerned."[22] W. D. Bradfield, who was a member of the board and also on the theological faculty, replied that he favored high ideals and if Blackwell were not fired, the Methodist church would be wiped off the map. Bradfield made it clear that he understood the dilemma, since Dallas had always been more than generous with its support. Indeed, during the early days, its help kept the doors of the university open. But he made it clear that the university should not emphasize the material over the ideal.[23]

In a private meeting between Selecman, Shuttles, and Blackwell, a compromise was reached which provided that Blackwell would voluntarily resign but not until January 1, 1932—in other words, after the next football season. It was hoped that delaying the matter would give Blackwell an opportunity to find another job (a difficult task during the depression), would save the university from criticism, and would pacify the citizens of Dallas.[24] Just exactly the opposite occurred.

A veritable storm broke out when it became known at the June board meeting that Blackwell would resign. Letters were written, articles appeared in the newspapers, and a petition was circulated. An article in the *Dallas Morning News* stated:

> A strong counter movement to have him retained was launched by his friends, many of whom are citizens in Dallas and elsewhere, who felt that his record in the management of the athletic affairs during the last few years has been such as to warrant keeping him in the service during slack times.[25]

The supporters of Blackwell hoped that enough pressure could be brought to retain him and force Selecman to resign. There was much speculation that arrangements would be made for Selecman to be called as minister to one of the larger Methodist churches.[26] To many the firing of Blackwell represented another example of Selecman's high-handed tactics. However, in this case Selecman probably should have taken action sooner.[27]

The support for Blackwell was most clearly stated in a petition which was circulated in January, 1932, after his resignation became effective:

> We are the loyal supporters of Southern Methodist University and appreciate its remarkable growth and wide recognition. . . . Aside from its great benefit to the Church and its influence on Christian education, its record in athletics has brought great advertisement to and been worth much in a business way to Texas and especially the city of Dallas.
>
> We would regret to see a final separation of Dr. Blackwell from the institution at a time when we look upon what seems to us success. . . . We feel the organization that exists would be handicapped by Dr. Blackwell's separation. . . .[28]

The board took no action on this petition.

This controversy began as a fairly simple one of the firing of a business manager and developed into a larger one over whether it was the Board of Trustees or the citizens of Dallas[29] who controlled the university. Once the answer to this question became clear, the majority of the board supported Selecman's policies and refused to be controlled by the business interests of Dallas. The university found itself in this awkward situation because it had leaned heavily upon Dallas for financial support and was not interested in offending those who had aided it. And yet the university needed to be in control of its own affairs. The middle ground was difficult to define. The decision of the board to accept Blackwell's resignation indicated that the majority of the board desired to make clear that they were running the university.[30]

At the same time that Selecman was subjected to these pressures from outside the university, the pressures within the university, which had been under cover for some time, surfaced and developed into another movement to remove Selecman from the presidency. As early as 1930 a group of faculty members went to Shuttles, as chairman of the board, with the request that Selecman be replaced as president. Shuttles listened with sympathy and gave the faculty members to understand that he would consider their request carefully.[31] In general the faculty objected to Selecman's high-handed methods of running the university, but they also had some specific complaints.

In June, 1930, the Board had raised Selecman's salary from $8,000 a year to $10,000. At the same time the salary of the football coach, Ray Morrison, was raised to $12,000, and he was given a five-year contract.[32] During the same period a full professor received approximately $3,500, and an instructor $1,800.[33] These actions were taken at a time when the debt of the university had been increasing. In 1927 the debt was $410,000; in 1928 it was $436,948; in 1929 it had risen to $442,-335; and in 1930 it reached $520,283.[34]

By November, 1930, the economic situation appeared more grave. Selecman sent a letter to all the faculty and staff pointing out that the receipts were $15,000 short of what they had been the year before. He asked each member to join with him in making a "voluntary contribution" to aid the university, adding that if this plea failed a "greater misfortune may befall us . . . all next year in the nature of policy retrenchment by the Board of Trustees."[35] Hence, five months after his own salary was raised 25 percent, Selecman asked faculty members whose average salary was barely more than a quarter of his to contribute a portion of their salaries to the university to pay its debts. Eighty members responded by giving approximately 2 percent, fifty-five gave 1 percent, and twenty-five made no contribution at all.[36]

This request of Selecman's caused widespread discontent among the faculty and increased the bitter feelings between the administration and the faculty.[37] Obviously, faculty members feared for their jobs if they did not contribute, and yet none of them had extra money.

Shuttles, the chairman of the board, became determined to force Selecman's resignation. He may or may not have believed that the faculty had some legitimate complaints against Selecman, but he doubtless saw the advantage of attacking Selecman on two issues at the same time. Shuttles asked the aid of Bradfield, making it clear that with Bradfield's assistance Selecman could be forced out. However, Bradfield refused to go along with Shuttles, because he felt Selecman needed support in the Blackwell case.[38]

At this point in the maneuverings Horace M. Whaling, Jr., emerged as a possible successor to Selecman. Whaling, who had a B.D. degree (1907) from Vanderbilt, had joined the faculty in 1916. He was made vice-president in 1920 and become an active spokesman for the administration during the athletic troubles of 1922-23.[39] Bradfield, who also was in the School of Theology, realized that Whaling was becoming critical of President Selecman's administration and suspected he was trying to undermine the president.[40] Selecman himself soon became aware of the situation and informed the board that he could no longer work with Whaling.[41] Within a few months Whaling left the vice-presidency and became the minister of the Oak Lawn Methodist Church in Dallas. With this move Selecman helped to secure his own position.

During the month of May, 1931, the campus was in a turmoil. The pressures against Selecman from Blackwell backers and from the faculty were heading for a climax at the June board meeting. The faculty circulated a petition with forty-one signatures requesting the right to appear at the meeting:

Realizing that the genuine cooperation and mutual confidence between administration and faculty which is essential to the sound development of any university does not and cannot exist at Southern Methodist University under the present President, we, the undersigned members of the faculty, agree that, if the Board of Trustees cares to consider our opinion, we stand ready to confer with the said Board at its annual meeting in June 1931.[42]

This petition was signed by three deans: Potts of law, Flath of engineering, and Van Katwijk of music; and eight department heads: Stephens of philosophy, McIntosh of classical languages, Hauhart of commerce, Zeek of French, F. D. Smith of comparative literature, Geiser of biology, Jones of mathematics, and Guice of government. The other thirty signers included McGinnis, Fleck, Longnecker, Gambrell, Henry Smith, Mouzon, Watson, and Leisy.[43] Conspicuous by their absence were the supporters of President Selecman: Vice-President Whaling, Dean

Jennings of arts and science, Acting Dean Kilgore of theology, Nichols of education, Chairman Beaty of English, and virtually all of the theological faculty. Out of a total faculty of ninety-five members of assistant professor rank or above,[44] forty-one, or almost half the faculty, expressed various forms of dissatisfaction with the Selecman administration and were willing to sign a petition to that effect.

On the fateful day of the board meeting, the president's secretary told as many of the signers as could be located on short notice to await a call. Gambrell and Stephens waited on the front portico of Dallas Hall for a call that never came.[45] The board took no action against either Selecman or Shuttles but ended by expressing a voice of confidence in both the president and executive committee, in spite of their obvious differences.[46] The issues were thoroughly discussed and this compromise reached, probably because of the moderating influence of Bishop John M. Moore.

Even Chairman Shuttles supported by almost half of the faculty was unable to persuade a majority of the board, which was largely composed of Methodist ministers, that Selecman should be fired. Indeed, the whole movement really had little chance of success, because such a board would always stand behind a fellow preacher under fire, except perhaps in matters of major crimes.[47] Also, by this time Shuttles appeared to be in the position of turning the faculty against Selecman, of trying to keep a drunkard on the staff, and, perhaps worst of all, of trying to secure lay control of the university.[48] On all these issues the ministers on the board were sure to flock to Selecman's defense.

As a result of the board meeting, Selecman had won at least a partial victory, for he was still president. But Shuttles was still chairman of the board. The dispute between these two men was carried over to the fall meeting of the North Texas Annual Conference. The conference elected two members to Southern Methodist University's Board of Trustees, one lay and one clerical. At this time Shuttles was the lay representative, and Selecman the clerical representative.[49] Opponents of Selecman introduced a ruling prohibiting members of the faculty from serving on the board. This was an obvious slap at Selecman and prevented him from being re-elected when his term expired.[50]

During the debate on this issue Shuttles was attacked so violently that he asked that his record as chairman be investigated. This was done, and the investigation was conducted on six counts. In addition to the charges of desiring to keep a drunkard on the staff, of trying to secure lay control of the University, and of turning the faculty against Selecman, Shuttles was also accused of "allowing conditions to exist which if known would ruin the University," of failing to "cooperate with the president," and of failing to handle financial affairs well.[51] The investigating committee reported that these charges were completely false. The committee praised Shuttles highly and attributed the dispute between the two men to an honest difference of opinion. Despite such vindication, Shuttles's resignation, which had been presented to the board in June, 1932, was now accepted by the Annual Conference, but not until after a further exchange of angry words between Shuttles and Selecman.[52] Shuttles was no longer on the board, but he received the support of the conference for his position. Selecman retained the presidency, but with a slightly tarnished reputation.

As a result of these pressures on Selecman, the faculty was able to secure a measure of control over its own affairs. The almost complete power of the president was slightly modified by his having to listen to the faculty with their different viewpoints. In February, 1933, Selecman appointed, with the approval of the board, a committee on faculty reorganization headed by J. D. Boon, chairman of the physics department.[53] This committee found that a majority of the faculty were "eager to attain a more satisfactory sense of partnership, opportunity and security in their relations to the University." Since there was no "suitable group which could study larger educational problems and policies and utilize the thinking of the faculty as a whole," the committee recommended the formation of a University Council and the reorganization of the College Council.[54]

The University Council, created as a result of this recommendation, was composed of the deans of all the schools, the dean of students, the registrar, and ten elected members, one from each of the six groups in the arts colleges[55] and one from each of the other four schools, law, engineering, theology, and music. This meant that each school had two representatives, one being the dean, while arts and sciences had seven representatives. No departmental chairman was allowed to serve unless he first resigned as chairman. The duties of this council were carefully written out, but they were largely advisory. Originally the Boon committee hoped to have a committee on tenure which would have the power to investigate all cases of faculty dismissal,[56] but in this they were not successful.

The committee on faculty reorganization also changed the organization of the College Council. This council, organized in 1919 when Hyer was president, consisted of representatives from each of the divisions of instruction within the college of arts and sciences.[57] Until 1922 these representatives were elected by the faculty;[58] but beginning in 1922, for reasons not stated those representatives were appointed by the president. The 1933 faculty reorganization committee desired a return to the former method of electing the representatives. The duties of the College Council were actually written down for the first time, but they tended to be advisory. The committee recommended that the council should have the power to make standard salary scales, to consult with the dean concerning the budget, and to investigate the inequalities in rank and salary. But none of these duties was granted to the College Council.[59]

The net gain of the reorganization for faculty members was a lift of their morale, a chance to have a voice in the university, and the power to have a measure of control over policies and practices. The University Council, as a new organization, provided a forum in which elected representatives of the faculty could speak. However, this group was large and unwieldy, and very probably the deans tended to dominate it. The old College Council achieved a new sense of independence, in fact became a different organization, after its members were elected. Prior to the reorganization, when the president had appointed the representatives, they tended to remain in office year after year. Beginning in 1933 a whole new set of names turned up on the College Council, men and women who had never been appointed by the president.[60] The terms of office were limited, with the result that there was a turnover in the representatives. By increasing the number of faculty members who served on the council, the work of the council was not necessarily better, but at least more faculty members had a knowledge of university problems and a voice in trying to find answers. After this period Selecman tended to be more restrained in his actions and ceased to make as many unilateral decisions as he had earlier. He may have mellowed slightly, or he may have simply worn a velvet glove on his iron hand more often than before;[61] but in any case, the last five years of his administration were his best.

One action of the University Council which could be used to illustrate the council's usefulness and Selecman's willingness to listen was the appointment in January, 1935, of a Committee on Better Teaching. The chairman of this committee was John Bowyer of the English department, who was a caustic critic of the administration. Bowyer had become a member of the SMU faculty in 1928, after doing his undergraduate work at Washington and Lee and his doctoral work at Harvard. His was perhaps the clearest and most forceful voice on the faculty in defining and implementing a liberal arts education.[62]

The report which Bowyer wrote and presented to the University Council in November, 1935, was highly critical of the current administration:

The Committee feels itself obligated to mention the fact that many members of the faculty regard the conduct of academic policies and other academic matters at S. M. U. as haphazard. They commented . . . on the lack of regularity in making nominations for the addition of new members to the faculty, in examining instructional policies in faculty meetings, in recognizing increased ability to serve the University. . . .[63]

Bowyer indicated that his report was not aimed at specific techniques of teaching but stressed the formulation of teaching objectives and analysis of the factors that condition good learning. His goal was to improve the whole foundation of intellectual life on the SMU campus.

One of Bowyer's main recommendations was to upgrade the quality of the faculty by requiring adequate advanced training (Ph.D. degree for all professional ranks), discouraging inbreeding, refraining from giving faculty members teaching assignments outside their special fields of study, and eliminating part-time teachers. Bowyer also suggested that research and further study be encouraged by rewarding these with rank and salary increases, by encouraging attendance at national conventions of scholarly societies, and by establishing a system of sabbatical leaves. In order to make these changes possible financially, he suggested a smaller faculty of better-trained scholars, fewer course offerings, and fewer departments. Bowyer saw the primary duty of the university as teaching and suggested that better teaching be rewarded, not with administrative posts, but with higher salaries.[64]

Bowyer's report is interesting partly because it indicates that he had sound ideas about the way a university should operate, but largely because it is an indication that these policies were absent from SMU academic practices. The lack of such policies could be somewhat excused in the past when SMU was young; but as the university approached its twenty-fifth year, such changes became imperative. It is to the credit of the University Council members that they were able to think in terms of broad academic policy. However, these newly recommended policies and practices to raise academic standards were forced to wait until after World War II.

SMU and the Depression

Another factor that was highly important in these controversies of Selecman's with both the executive committee and the faculty was the deepening economic crisis of the university. Shuttles and the executive committee were highly concerned about the rising debt and falling income. To the businessmen in these pre-New Deal days, it was absolutely unthinkable that the university should continually show a deficit. They tended to hold Selecman solely responsible for the situation,[65] which was hardly justified. The indebtedness of the university had been initially incurred by the extensive building program and increased instructional program of the late 1920s, which the executive committee had approved. It was not the result of poor management on the part of the administration.

In 1931 at the high point of its indebtedness the university showed a debt of $643,505. Of this figure $439,753 represented the balance due on five buildings and the stadium. The difference between these two figures was the operating deficit, $203,752, about half of which went to pay the interest on the money borrowed for the building program.[66] In other words, the executive committee was unrealistic if they expected that the university could have built five new buildings and established an engineering school and a law school without increasing its expenses. Of course, what they did not anticipate was the depression of the 1930s.

During the period that the debt was increasing, the income was also going up, but not as fast. In 1924 the total income of the university was $573,769, but in 1930 it had risen to $833,954. The endowment saw a notable increase from $519,692 in 1922 to $1,793,100 in 1930. Plant assets rose even more, from $1,372,099 in 1922 to $3,251,560 in 1930.[67] These figures were all used by President Selecman in 1931 to defend his administration against attack. He also pointed out that the university had sufficient resources in secured notes and lands, outside endowment and plant assets to cover the indebtedness, with the exception of its stadium bonds. No mortgage existed against any of the university property. This line of argument was unconvincing to the executive committee, who saw only that the university was not living within its income and had a large interest payment to make every year.

An allied cause for dismay was the constant deficit of the athletic department, which was supposed to make money to pay off the stadium bonds. President Selecman admitted in 1931 that the general impression that college athletics were financially profitable was not substantiated by SMU's experience. From 1923 to 1931 athletics had produced a debit balance every year with the exception of 1925. The total indebtedness of the period from 1925 to 1931 amounted to $60,909.[68]

In June, 1932, the board took the drastic step of reducing all salaries and wages for the next academic year by 20 percent. The faculty had been warned that such a cut might be forthcoming, but it doubtless worked hardships on all involved. By the following year the situation had further deteriorated. The School of Engineering expected a deficit of $20,000, and the athletic department one of $23,000. The board had agreed that the debt must not be increased and had prohibited the administration from borrowing any further funds. This decision meant another salary cut, 50 percent for the months of April, May, and June, 1933. It was at this point that the engineering school was reorganized and combined with the College of Arts and Sciences.[69] The engineering faculty members who were teaching subjects that were duplicated in the arts college were simply out of a job. Minimum salaries were set for all faculty and administration members. The president's salary was reduced from $10,000 to $7,500, but the salary of the football coach, which had been set by a five-year contract in 1930 at $12,000, remained intact.[70]

As it might be expected, the faculty was extremely bitter about a salary cut that went to pay for athletics, particularly since many of them were not in sympathy with the athletic program anyway. The football coach received a salary more than four times as great as most faculty members. This was without a doubt the low point in morale during the depression.[71] However, when the financial situation improved at the end of 1936, the university repaid 42 percent of these latest deductions, with the understanding that it was repaying the athletic debt.[72] It was assumed that the faculty would simply have to bear the debt of the engineering school. In fact, what actually happened all during the depression was that the faculty and staff were asked to bear the deficit of the university in the form of salary deductions.

A crisis arose in 1935 that even salary cuts could not aid. In December of that year the final payment of $85,000 was due on the football stadium. When the stadium was built in 1926, the University had agreed to pay $10,000 annually in interest and principal and in 1935 to pay off the entire sum.[73] This $10,000 a year payment accounted in part for the yearly athletic deficit. The board was in the process of arranging to postpone this final payment on the stadium when the football team came to the rescue. Bishop Moore in his autobiography describes the events:

> The stadium gave me some anxiety. It cost $225,000. Friends in sums of $10,000 and less gave $50,000; the athletic surplus receipts paid about $90,000. The debt left was $85,000; no money; creditors were pressing for payment. In St. Louis I persuaded the Bonding Company to hold until January. I was hoping for a "windfall." The Conference football game in Ft. Worth between S.M.U. and T.C.U. would decide who would go to the Rose Bowl. Physical indisposition kept me at home alone, but the radio was open. I never had two such nervous hours. I will not say that I prayed for victory, but I cannot say that I did not. We won! We went to the Rose Bowl. By feasting and folly we lost that game; but our receipts were $90,000! The stadium was cleared by the "windfall" and our credit was preserved.[74]

SMU actually cleared only $78,183, but this substantially paid off the bonds.[75]

Another source of revenue that the university found was the sale of lands it owned north of the campus. The land had been given to the university in 1911 by W. W. Caruth as an inducement for the university to locate in Dallas. This land, 273 acres of it, was put upon the market in 1934.[76] At first buyers were hard to find, but by 1936 several acres had been sold. In that year Texas celebrated the centennial anniversary of its independence from Mexico, which brought an upturn in the economy of Dallas, where the main exposition was held. All of this aided the university to realize $83,221 from the sale of land by 1938.[77] Unfortunately, this amount of money was only a small fraction of what the land would have brought if it could have been held until after World War II.

A third source of income was a financial campaign waged in 1936 to raise a million dollars. The campaign was conducted in a well-organized manner with salaried leadership, but it fell miserably short of its goal. The total collections amounted to $127,289, of which $25,637 went for expenses, and $9,349 toward sidewalks and a tunnel; only $92,305 was applied to the debt.[78]

With these combined sources the debt was reduced from a high in 1931 of $643,505 to $330,594 in 1938 when Selecman left the presidency. Salaries began to edge back up in January, 1937, with a 4 percent increase, bringing them to 84 percent of their level before the cuts had begun. By the fall of that year, they were up to 90 percent of the base salary, but they did not reach 100 percent level until 1943.[79]

Students at SMU

Despite the financial difficulties and tensions within the university during the 1930s, students continued to enroll in Southern Methodist University, attend their classes, participate in organizations, and eventually graduate without even knowing that such problems existed. By 1940 Southern Methodist University had a total enrollment of just under four thousand students, but not all these students were on the campus at one time because this figure included the summer school enrollment and those taking extension work. Excluding these latter figures the total number of students "on the hill" during the two regular semesters in 1939-40 was around two thousand.[80]

The overall enrollment increased throughout the first twenty-five years from 706 in 1915 until the depression, when the numbers fell. The high point prior to the depression was reached in 1930-31 with 3,218 students. Beginning the following year the enrollment fell, hitting a low of 2,445 in 1933-34, at which point it began to rise slowly until by 1939-40 there were 3,921 students enrolled.[81]

The decline in the number of students so alarmed the administration that President Selecman recommended to the board in January, 1934, that two field workers be employed to recruit students.[82] Employing two new people was a drastic step for an institution that had already cut the salaries of the faculty 20 percent. Those two recruitment officers must have produced some results, though, because they were retained by the university for two years. In a further effort to raise enrollment Dean Jennings was appointed head of a committee to conduct a campaign for students among the churches and alumni of Dallas.[83] These efforts evidently were at least partly successful, because the number of students rose from 2,445 in 1934 to 3,112 the following year and then to 3,264 in 1936.[84]

The overwhelming majority of the students during the thirties came from Dallas and the surrounding area. Between 50 and 65 percent came from Dallas,[85] and between 70 and 75 percent came from within a hundred-mile radius of Dallas.[86] These figures would indicate that Southern Methodist University was largely a local institution supported by the local area. The registrar and the president often quoted figures to show that the students came from a wide geographical area by enumerating the students from foreign countries, from different states, and from different counties in Texas.[87] Yet these figures remained low, and the average Southern Methodist University student was not more than one hundred miles from home. This remained a characteristic of the university until after World War II, when the population of the United States became much more mobile.

Not only were the students from one geographical area, but they were largely from one economic class, the middle class and upper middle class. Between 50 and 60 percent of the parents or guardians of Southern Methodist University students were engaged in business. The professions of law, ministry, medicine, and teaching comprised 15 percent. Of the students from Dallas in 1935-36, 77 percent came from sections of Dallas where middle class and upper middle class families lived. The other 20 percent came from neighborhoods lower in the economic scale.[88]

The religious backgrounds of the students also were similar. Between 40 and 50 percent of the students were Methodist, which might be expected. The Baptists comprised around 12 to 14 percent, and the Presbyterians 9 percent. The remainder was divided among the smaller Protestant sects with the Catholics and Jews in a decided minority, 4 percent Catholic and 3 percent Jewish.[89] The total impression of all these figures indicates that the student body of Southern Methodist University was a fairly homogeneous group drawn largely from an area surrounding Dallas with a middle class to upper class background and with similar Protestant heritage.

Fraternities and sororities played a large role in the life of the students during the 1930s. Given the time, the place, and the type of student who attended Southern Methodist University, this is not surprising. There were eleven fraternities and fourteen sororities on campus. Most of these were established the first year the school opened, but they did not acquire their dominant position until the years of the depression. When the university opened in 1915, only 28 percent of the students were Greek. The number continued to rise until by 1933 over half the students, 52 percent, belonged to fraternities. For the remainder of the decade the number fluctuated between 45 and 50 percent.[90]

The rise in fraternity membership during the depression is surprising. One would anticipate that as finances became strained, a large proportion of students would be unable to afford the cost of fraternity membership and the additional expense of fraternity life. But such was not the case at Southern Methodist University. As the economic conditions became worse, the proportion of fraternity students became greater. As the depression lifted in some degree, the number of nonfraternity students increased. These figures substantiate the conclusion that fraternity men and women were of higher economic status and hence were able to remain in school while others were obliged to leave.[91]

The major social division that existed at Southern Methodist University was between the fraternity and nonfraternity students. The only social life at Southern Methodist University revolved around the fraternities and sororities. As a result, the independents were virtually excluded from campus social life, but this exclusion was only occasionally perceived by the Greeks. There existed at SMU two separate worlds, and only seldom did they meet. "The independents reacted to the situation with feelings of antagonism and resentment toward the fraternity system. They definitely felt excluded from the campus social life and were looked down upon as being inferior by the fraternity students."[92] The independents came from varying backgrounds, but they had two things in common on the Southern Methodist University campus. They were not members of a fraternity, and they were members of a lower economic class. The independents made slightly better grades than the fraternity students, despite the latter's superior cultural and economic background.[93]

This social division between the fraternity members and independents was accentuated by the refusal of the university to hold dances on the campus. The discipline of the Methodist church did not allow dancing, and, even though dancing was widely accepted and no longer regarded as a sin, a Board of Trustees composed largely of Methodist ministers simply could not bring itself to go on record as approving social dancing. The fraternities, however, organized "teas" and "receptions" nearly every weekend at a country club or a downtown hotel.[94] These affairs were, of course, dances, and everyone including the administration knew they were; but nothing was done to prevent them.

Since the fraternities and sororities were the only organizations which had any social activities, the nonfraternity student was excluded from the major portion of the campus social life. It was not considered proper for a fraternity man or woman to attend a dance with a nonfraternity date.[95] As a result of the university's ban on dancing, any hope of unifying the students or even modifying the cleavage between the two groups was virtually nonexistent. What the campus needed was a school dance to which all students could come, or class dances which members of the various classes could attend without regard to fraternity membership.

In 1935 the pressure on the administration and board became intense, and it appeared as though the dancing ban might be lifted. In late 1934 a committee was appointed by the University Council to study the social life of the university. This committee recommended that the students should be allowed to dance, pointing out that campus dances would aid the unity of the campus and would allow the university to have some control over the students' social life.[96] This recommendation was supported by virtually every student organization as well as by the dean of students and the dean of women.[97]

Despite the wide support for this proposal, the board refused to approve the recommendation at its January meeting.[98] The issue did not die but continued to be brought up at virtually every board meeting, where it was either rejected outright or else tabled. In February, 1936, the board used as a basis for its stand article 805 of the Methodist Discipline, which forbade dancing. Since the article had been adopted in 1858, the editor of the *Campus* poked fun at the absurdity of being bound by such a ruling. He pointed out that just a few things had been changed since 1858—including the abolition of slavery.[99] The decision of the board sufficiently provoked the students that on March 3 they held a "folk dance" in the gymnasium. It was an unscheduled, spontaneous affair that moved President Selecman to speak disapprovingly at the board meeting of the "spirit of continental youth, the Revolt of Youth movement on the campus."[100]

Here the situation remained until the first board meeting of the newly elected president, Umphrey Lee, in June, 1939. The time was propitious for resolving a vexing issue. The new president, who was widely supported, had more freedom of action than the former one. In addition, just a few months earlier the much delayed union of the northern and southern Methodist churches had occurred.[101] At this time the discipline was sufficiently modified to allow dancing. President Lee presented the matter in such a way that it was easy even for a conservative clergyman to agree with him. He simply asked the board to allow administrative officials to work out the matter "with such diligence and good sense as they possess." He added that he felt the board could trust the administration to handle such matters as might arise without embarrassment to the church or the board. To this proposal the board consented,[102] and thereafter dances were held on the campus without fuss or fanfare.

Earlier during the 1930s, though, the dean of students reported on several occasions that the social life of the campus was overemphasized and that the number of scheduled events was far too numerous.[103] A glance at the social page of the *Campus* supports these contentions. The newspaper was issued twice a week, and it listed from ten to twenty social activities per issue. These activities were carried on almost exclusively by the fraternities and sororities and included two major dances per fraternity per school year in addition to numerous smaller affairs, such as dinners, luncheons, teas, and smokers.[104] From reading the *Campus,* one would never suspect that the United States was then in the throes of a major depression. Considering the number of social events and the number of sororities and fraternities, each group must have had an average of from four to five functions a month.[105] All this activity was confined to about half of the student body, or less than a thousand students. Small wonder that the Greek students failed to have as high a grade point average as the non-Greek students. Southern Methodist University acquired the reputation of being a "country club," or "play boy," school, during the 1930s,[106] an image which persisted well past the Second World War.

Like all general images and reputations, this picture does not present the whole story. There were in effect two Southern Methodist Universities existing side by side, one dominated by the fraternities, sororities, and their parties, and the other composed largely of independents, many of whom were interested in the intellectual activities of the campus.[107] These students wrote for John McGinnis, worked on the *Southwest Review,* acted in the Arden Club plays, wrote and presented the yearly Pigskin Review, conducted investigations for *Field & Laboratory* and *Studies in Sociology,* and generally took part in the intellectual life of the campus.

Many of these students tended to be more serious because they had to earn money to put themselves through Southern Methodist University. During the depression, students were employed by the National Youth Administration, a division of the Works Progress Administration. In 1935, for example, five hundred students applied for 167 jobs.[108] Two years later there were 250 NYA jobs. These jobs paid undergraduates thirty-five cents an hour and graduate students fifty cents an hour for working in the library and as teachers' assistants.[109] The university also provided from sixty to seventy-five emergency scholarships for students who could not otherwise attend college.[110] These students were not financially able to join fraternities and doubtless had a more serious attitude toward education.

As further evidence that Southern Methodist University did possess some serious students, the university had produced, by 1940, a number of distinguished graduates. In 1948 the Committee on Qualifications for Phi Beta Kappa asked the university to prepare a list of these graduates as part of Southern Methodist University's application for a charter of Phi Beta Kappa. This report listed 126 distinguished graduates during the first twenty-five years. It would not be difficult to enlarge this list, because it contained only those who had received a B.A. or a B.S. degree. It did not include those who had received professional or graduate degrees, or those who attended but did not graduate.

Of those 126 notable graduates, seventeen were listed in *Who's Who in America*, twenty-five in *American Men of Science*, and five in *Leaders of Education*. There were three Rhodes Scholars, eight college presidents, and two bishops of the Methodist church. Exactly half of the 126 had attained the rank of associate professor or above at a reputable institution, and fifty-six had received the Ph.D. degree. Some of these degrees were earned at the most respected institutions in the United States, ten from Harvard, seven from Illinois, nine from Chicago, and four from Michigan. This group of graduates had also done writing and publishing. Twenty-one of them had published one or more books exclusive of textbooks.[111] This list of graduates indicates that during the first twenty-five years, some capable men and women chose to attend Southern Methodist University and received a valuable education, despite the struggle of a new university to survive, despite the turmoil of the Selecman years, and despite the overwhelming interest of large numbers of students in fraternities, football, and an active social life.

Election of Umphrey Lee as President

At the meeting of the General Conference of the Methodist Episcopal church, South, in May, 1938, Charles C. Selecman was elected bishop. At the June board meeting in the same year a committee was appointed to nominate a new president of Southern Methodist University. Bishop Ivan Lee Holt, member of the board who had served as the first chaplain of the university, was chairman of the committee.[112]

The man most often mentioned as successor to President Selecman was Umphrey Lee, who was currently dean of the School of Religion at Vanderbilt University. All during the 1930s the talk among the faculty expressed the hope and desire that Lee might be made president.[113] Lee was a native Texan who had done his undergraduate work at Trinity University and had received the M.A. degree from Southern Methodist University in 1916. Indeed, he had even been the first president of the student body. Later he received the Ph.D. degree in history from Columbia University (1931). As a Methodist minister he had served a couple of small churches in Texas before becoming pastor in 1922 of the Highland Park Methodist Church, which is located on the campus of Southern Methodist University and serves the surrounding area. While at this church he taught occasionally in the School of Theology. He was minister of the church until 1936, when he went to Vanderbilt University.

In spite of faculty support, Lee's election to the presidency does not appear to have been a foregone conclusion. The nominating committee considered many names and talked to faculty and alumni before narrowing the choice down to six laymen and two clergymen. These men were all well qualified for the position; a majority of them held doctorates and had academic experience. All of these men had interviews with the board except Umphrey Lee, who felt that board members knew him well enough that such an interview was unnecessary. It is difficult to determine which candidate afforded Lee the most competition, because reports differ.[114] The competition must not have been great by the time the board met, since Umphrey Lee was unanimously elected on the first ballot.

Lee's election was greeted with enthusiasm by the faculty, the alumni, the student body, and the citizens of Dallas. It would have been impossible to imagine a more widely accepted and acclaimed choice. Umphrey Lee was a scholar who had a broad and liberal mind and was completely respected by the faculty. He had an earned doctor's degree, the only Southern Methodist University president to possess one, and he was the author of several books: *The Lord's Horseman: John Wesley the Man* (1928), *Historical Backgrounds of Early Methodist Enthusiasm* (1931), and *John Wesley and Modern Religion* (1936).[115] John Bowyer of the English department expressed the tremendous lift in faculty morale that the election of such a man brought to a dispirited, depressed faculty. Suddenly there was new hope for the future, for interest in liberal studies, and for higher academic standards.[116] Lee's biographers, Weiss and Proctor, described him as

a versatile, complicated man who exuded an aura of simplicity and unassailable dignity, [and who] captivated those he met informally. . . . [He] also possessed a genius for making you feel better, bigger, and more intelligent than you really were.[117]

President Lee made it clear at the beginning of his administration that he desired to stress the liberal arts college concept and hoped that

Southern Methodist University could hold that place of leadership in the Southwest that Vanderbilt and Duke held in the Southeast and Oberlin held in the Middle West:

In view of the territory to be served, Southern Methodist University should emphasize its college of liberal arts. There is a place in the Southwest for a school which will attempt to be in this region what some of the older and better institutions are for the Eastern and Middle Western sections of the country. Unless the emphasis is upon sound scholarship and upon intellect and sympathetic guidance of the individual student, there is little excuse for the existence of the university. But an institution which is abreast of the best that is being thought and done in the educational world and at the same time is committed to a unified philosophy of the nature of the world and of man may well have a significant place in a disturbed generation.[118]

At his first board meeting President Lee called attention to the publications of the faculty during the last year, indicating that he was aware of the value of such activities. He listed twenty-six faculty members who had published one or more books or articles and gave praise to the *Southwest Review, Field & Laboratory,* and the SMU Press. He particularly stressed the importance of the library and the science departments. Lee, always a gracious individual, was careful to give credit to others. After he had stressed the needs of the university, he said he did so "not in order to suggest . . . or to hint that Southern Methodist University is in a dire condition." "On the contrary," said Lee,

the stability and future of this institution have been assured by the sacrificial work of the people associated with the University and by its benefactors through the past quarter century. But I mention these things in order that you may see what is necessary if Southern Methodist University is to carry out the desires of its founders and the dreams of those who have given largely in order that the University of the Church might have a dominant position in a great region.[119]

Here was a president who understood the purpose of a university, who was interested in promoting scholarship and high academic standards, and who would support faculty members who had similar views. Since Umphrey Lee had a vision of what Southern Methodist University might become, the second twenty-five years could begin with confidence.

By 1940 the early awkward years of youth and adolescence were over and Southern Methodist University had the opportunity to mature into a real university or remain a local college mirroring rather than leading the community.[120] Under the leadership of President Lee, and later

President Willis Tate, the university followed the former path. But these two presidents built upon the work of the first twenty-five years.

Conclusion

When Southern Methodist University was founded, it was called a "university"; but no one, least of all President Robert S. Hyer, thought Southern Methodist University could live up to its name. The title was more a promise for the future than a statement of fact for the present. In 1915 Southern Methodist University was a small liberal arts college with even smaller theological and music schools attached to it, all of which were inadequately financed. President Hyer gave years of service to Southern Methodist University before the doors opened. He was largely responsible for the original planning and eventual establishment of a university in Dallas, and he served as its president for nine years, including four years before any students were admitted. Hyer had more understanding of what a university should be than any other Methodist in Texas. He was a scholar who set high standards for this infant institution in a field of Johnson grass, but he lacked financial skill. During an economic crisis in 1920, Hyer was forced to resign.

At this point there was speculation that Southern Methodist University might be forced to close its doors. It almost looked as though the Methodists had undertaken a bigger task than they could adequately finance. But the second president, Hiram Abiff Boaz, had the confidence of the board and the Methodists and set about to raise more money. President Boaz, too, had been associated with the university at its founding; but his tenure as president was short because two years later he was elected bishop. During this time, however, he made an excellent start on putting the financial house in order. He received a second grant from the General Education Board, this time for a third of a million dollars, providing the university would raise two-thirds of a million. President Boaz also had to deal with such diverse matters as football and heresy, but neither one of these issues was completely resolved before his election to the episcopacy.

As a result, when Charles C. Selecman became the third president of Southern Methodist University in 1923, he had his hands full of unfinished business. The first and most pressing task was to complete the collection of funds to qualify for the grant from the General Education Board. Despite additional obstacles that appeared, this task was accomplished by 1924. At this point the university had increased its endowment by a million dollars, was free of debt, and was no longer forced to lead a hand-to-mouth existence. For this accomplishment President Selecman deserves most of the credit. As a strong administrator, he introduced some order and system into the operation of the university, and the institution was run for the first time with businesslike efficiency.

By the mid-twenties Southern Methodist University had survived the difficult early years and had reached a new stage in its development with its financial house in order, a growing body of students and alumni, and a nucleus of capable faculty. At this point the university embarked upon a program of expansion. Within a relatively few years the campus had grown from two buildings to ten, and the instructional program had increased to include the law and engineering schools. This period saw increased emphasis upon practical and utilitarian courses and upon the football team as a method of increasing support for the university.

As a result of this expansion, when the depression hit in the 1930s, the university found itself burdened with a large debt and interest payments at a time of decreasing income. The thirties, then, were lean years with salary cuts and faculty dismissals. The problems absorbed the energies and time of President Selecman. Little attention was paid to larger academic goals or to evaluation of the direction in which the university was moving. When Umphrey Lee became president in 1939, with his scholarly background and desire to emphasize the liberal arts college concept, it was clear that Southern Methodist University would receive more positive academic guidance.

The faculty of Southern Methodist University tended to be dominated by its own graduates during the twenties and thirties. Many of these men and women earned doctorates at the older universities of the North and East and returned to become the backbone of the faculty. Others came from nearby colleges and universities. Only a few came from farther away. The faculty was drawn largely from the local region and during the depression remained almost completely stable.

The students were very largely products of the local area and were a homogeneous group with similar economic, social, and religious backgrounds. Despite the similar backgrounds, the students tended to be divided into those who came to college to enjoy the social life of parties and football games and those who came to get an education. This division could, of course, be found at most institutions. But during the 1930s the party and fun group appeared to be dominant. The serious student, however, could find support and encouragement from the small group of faculty members who wrote and published under adverse circumstances. The result was that there existed side by side two Southern Methodist Universities.

By 1940 the College of Arts and Sciences still stood at the center of the university, although its liberal arts tradition had been diluted by practical and vocational courses. Clustered around it were the professional schools of theology, music, graduate studies, engineering, law, and commerce (retitled business administration in 1940). These schools remained small, but they were the first step toward attaining university status. The next step came in the 1960s when Ph.D. degrees were awarded.

Events proved that Wallace Buttrick, secretary of the General Education Board, had been correct when he said in 1905 that a university would flourish in Dallas. Southern Methodist University and Dallas grew together, each one aiding the other. Dallas supported the university through its formative years with money and with students. Southern Methodist University, in turn, provided the city with services it desired: an evening law school, extension classes downtown, engineering, business and education courses, and a football team. To some extent Southern Methodist University was a "service station" for the community, providing and serving its needs while receiving financial support in return. The two collaborated during the first twenty-five years of Southern Methodist University's existence, and neither appeared in 1940 to regret the collaboration. A broader definition of SMU's purpose and sphere of service were beginning to emerge as the university's second quarter century began.

Southern Methodist University Founders, Trustees, Presidents, General Faculty, 1910-1940

Educational Commission Appointed November 24, 1910

Bishop James Atkins—Chairman of the Commission (North Texas Conference)

North Texas Conference:
    Rev. J. M. Peterson
    Rev. O. S. Thomas
    M. M. Brooks
    J. W. Blanton

West Texas Conference:
    Rev. J. E. Harrison
    Rev. Thomas Gregory
    C. C. Walsh
    J. W. Robbins

Northwest Texas Conference:
    Rev. J. G. Putman
    Rev. G. S. Slover
    L. C. Hawkins
    T. J. Turner

Texas Conference:
    Rev. L. B. Elrod
    Rev. James Kilgore
    J. C. Box
    W. L. Dean

Central Texas Conference:
    Rev. Horace Bishop
    Rev. John A. Rice
    George T. Jester
    J. D. Parr

Chairmen of the Board of Trustees Elected 1913-1940

Rev. Horace Bishop	February 6, 1913–June 8, 1916
Bishop Edwin D. Mouzon	June 8, 1916–June 9, 1919
Joseph E. Cockrell	June 10, 1919–April 7, 1927
Robert Hall Shuttles	June 5, 1927–June 5, 1932
Bishop John M. Moore	June 5, 1932–June 7, 1938
Bishop A. Frank Smith	June 7, 1938–November 4, 1960

Members of the Board of Trustees Elected 1912-1940

Rev. S. E. Allison	1913-26
Rev. S. H. Babcock	1916-22
Frank M. Bailey	1936-58
H. A. Barnard	1930
Rev. Horace Bishop	1912-21
Rev. R. T. Blackburn	1927-43
Clement A. Boaz	1933
Bishop H. A. Boaz	1930-38
J. H. Bohmfolk	1915-16
Rev. C. H. Booth	1922-32
John C. Box	1912-20
Rev. W. D. Bradfield	1916-34
J. S. Bridwell	1939-66
Rev. C. L. Brooks	1923-25
Rev. J. L. Cannon	1916-43
John H. Carlock	1931-35
W. L. Clayton	1921
J. E. Cockrell	1916-26
Harvey C. Couch	1930-41
T. M. Cullum	1930-51
Rev. G. G. Davidson	1920-35
T. S. De Arman	1915-17
Rev. W. W. Drake	1916-33
Rev. R. C. Edwards	1927-30
J. A. Elkins	1922-23
R. W. Fair	1933-64
Rev. J. K. Farris	1916-19
W. W. Fondren	1919-39
Mrs. W. W. Fondren	1939-
M. K. Graham	1930-41
Rev. Thos. Gregory	1912-27
C. C. Grimes	1916-21

Rev. J. T. Griswold	1921-32
R. W. Hall	1915-20
W. B. Hamilton	1933-62
W. H. Hargrove	1923-26
Rev. Gaston Hartsfield	1928-32
Rev. E. B. Hawk	1930-31
Rev. J. O. Haymes	1933-60
W. B. Head	1930-36
J. E. Hickman	1922-62
Rev. C. C. Hightower	1937-39
Bishop Ivan Lee Holt	1918-56
Rev. Forney Hutchinson	1926-30
R. S. Hyer	1912-19
Henry Ernest Jackson	1925-56
George T. Jester	1912-21
Rev. Warren Johnson	1936-40
Rev. James Kilgore	1912-35
Rev. H. D. Knickerbocker	1922-25
Rev. C. A. Lehmberg	1912-21
D. H. Linebaugh	1913-21
Rev. N. L. Linebaugh	1930-35
Eugene McElvaney	1939-71
Frank L. McNeny	1930-49
Bishop Paul E. Martin	1934-68
Bishop W. C. Martin	1934-64
Rev. James W. Mills	1937-49
Bishop John M. Moore	1922-39
Rev. R. E. L. Morgan	1913-25
Bishop Edwin D. Mouzon	1914-21
W. R. Nicholson	1939-59
J. J. Perkins	1927-60
S. B. Perkins	1922-25
E. Gordon Perry	1922-34
Rev. J. M. Peterson	1912-23
George L. Peyton	1934-39
E. H. Pigg	1924-32
Rev. J. T. Pritchett	1916-23
Rev. J. G. Putman	1912-20
Rev. J. D. Randolph	1920-52
Rev. D. B. Raulins	1934-51
Rev. J. A. Rice	1912-15, 1917-18
Bishop Charles C. Selecman	1926-34, 1941-48

E. E. Shipley   1920-21
Rev. J. M. Shockley   1927-57
R. H. Shuttles   1915-32
John B. Slayton   1921-23
Bishop A. Frank Smith   1934-60
Bishop W. A. Smith   1933-34
Ed Stedman   1924-32
Lynn C. Talley   1925-31
Rev. R. A. Taylor   1933-52
Rev. O. S. Thomas   1912-21
Rev. Luther E. Todd   1916-17
Daniel Upthegrove   1939-47
C. C. Walsh   1912-24
Rev. W. W. Ward   1933-59
S. D. Williams   1917-19
J. M. Willson   1933-68
Rev. W. M. Wilson   1916-19
R. L. Young   1915-16

Presidents Elected 1911-1940

Robert Stewart Hyer   April 13, 1911–February 20, 1920
Hiram Abiff Boaz   February 20, 1920–July 7, 1922
James Kilgore (Acting)   October 11, 1922–April 1, 1923
Charles Claude Selecman   April 1, 1923–September 1, 1938
Eugene Blake Hawk (Acting)   September 1, 1938–March 1, 1939
Umphrey Lee   March 1, 1939–May 6, 1954

General Faculty, 1915-1940

NOTE: The information contained in this listing is derived in general from the official annual catalogs of Southern Methodist University. Asterisk indicates that institution and/or date of degree was not listed in the catalog. Rank and degree listed are the highest attained, with additional data where pertinent.

Adams, Francis Marion, 1927-28; Instructor in Biology; B.A. SMU 1926
Adams, Henry Welch, 1921-29; Assistant Professor of English; B.A. SMU 1921
Addis, Elsinore Massey, 1924-26, 1930-34; Instructor in Art; B.S. College of Industrial Arts 1920
Ader, Olin Blair, 1937-39; Instructor in Mathematics; Ph.D. University of Kentucky 1937
Albritton, Claude Carroll, Jr., 1936-   ; Professor of Geology 1936-   ; Dean

of Faculty of College of Arts and Sciences 1952-57; Dean of Graduate
School 1957-71; Vice-Provost for Library Development and Coordination
1971-73; Dean of Libraries 1973-   ; Ph.D. Harvard 1936

Alexander, Gross, 1915-16; Professor of Church History; B.D., S.T.D.*

Amann, Dorothy, 1915-49; Librarian

Anderson, Hans Holst, 1927-30; Assistant Professor of General Literature;
B.A. Iowa State Teachers' College 1923

Anderson, Theodore La Vern, 1935-36; Instructor in Law; J.D. Northwestern
1933

Anglin, Harvey Sherman, 1928-29; Instructor in Religion; B.A. Hendrix 1926

Ashburn, Karl E., 1934-37; Assistant Professor of Commerce; Ph.D. Duke
1934

Atkins, Ernest William, 1925-26; Assistant Professor of Psychology; M.A.
University of North Carolina 1921

Babb, Virginia, 1917-18; Assistant Professor in Home Economics; Diploma
in Domestic Arts, Columbia*

Baker, Harold Dowling, 1930-34; Instructor in Electrical Engineering; M.S.
SMU 1929

Balderston, Katherine, 1916-19; Instructor in English; B.A. Wellesley 1916

Barclay, Dora Poteet, 1925-61; Associate Professor of Organ; B.Mus. SMU
1925; A.A.G.O. 1934

Barnett, Henry Green, 1924-25; Professor of Missions; B.A. Emory 1910

Barnhart, Kenneth Edwin, 1934-35; Instructor in Sociology; Ph.D. Chicago
1924

Barton, John Wynne, 1915-22; Professor of History, Economics, and Business Administration 1915-22; Dean of College of Applied Arts and
Sciences 1920-22; M.A. Columbia 1914

Beaty, John Owen, 1919-57; Professor of English; Ph.D. Columbia 1921

Bell, J. L., 1915-16; Instructor in Church History; B.D.*

Bell, Madison, 1934-64; Instructor of Physical Education; B.A. Center 1920

Bell, W. C., 1916-17; Assistant Professor of Education; M.A.*

Bengert, Edgar Paul, 1925-29; Associate Professor of English; Ed.M. Harvard
1924

Berry, Sellers, 1933-40; Instructor in Flute

Bird, John Macbeth, 1936-38; Instructor in Civil Engineering; B.S. Duke 1934

Bishop, Charles McTyeire, 1925-34; Professor of New Testament; M.A.
Emory and Henry 1886

Bond, George, 1924-27, 1937-69; Professor of English; Ph.D. Michigan 1948

Boon, John Daniel, 1919-45; Professor of Physics; B.S. Granbury 1899

Bowling, Mary Lee, 1927-28; Instructor in Home Economics; B.S. College of
Industrial Arts 1926

Bowyer, John Wilson, 1928-67; Professor of English; Ph.D. Harvard 1928

Bowyer, Lora B. Boarman, 1929-31; Instructor in Speech; B.A. SMU 1929

Bozeman, Virgil, 1938-39; Instructor in Law; LL.B. SMU 1937

Braden, Clarence Camille, 1925-27; Assistant Professor of Mathematics and Drawing; B.S. Texas A&M 1919

Bradfield, William Daniel, 1922-36; Professor of Christian Doctrine; B.D. Vanderbilt 1892, M.A. Chicago 1928

Bradford, Frederick Alden, 1923-27; Assistant Professor of Economics; M.A. Michigan 1922

Branscomb, Bennett Harvie, 1919-25; Professor of New Testament; B.A. (Oxon) 1917; M.A. Birmingham 1920

Brewer, Robert Lee, 1922-49; Registrar; B.A. Southwestern 1911

Brooks, John Lee, 1925-63; Professor of English; Ph.D. Harvard 1933

Brown, William Oscar, 1923-24; Instructor in Sociology; B.A. Texas 1921

Bywaters, Jerry, 1937-   ; Professor of Art; B.A. SMU 1927

Campbell, Robert Douglas, 1927-36; Assistant Professor of Mechanical Engineering; B.S. Texas 1925

Carlyon, James Thomas, 1937-54; Professor of Christian Doctrine; Ph.D. Chicago 1925

Carpenter, John Hall, 1926-27; Instructor in Geology; B.A. SMU 1926

Carrero, Eduardo, 1920-22; Instructor in Spanish

Carson, Hattie Gere, 1921-23; Instructor in Spanish

Cassidy, Mrs. James Harvey, 1915-34; Professor of Pipe Organ; Graduate College of Music, Cincinnati; A.A.G.O. New York 1917

Castetter, Edward Franklin, 1920-21; Assistant Professor of Biology; M.S. Pennsylvania State 1920

Cell, John Wesley, 1930-34; Assistant Professor of Mathematics; M.A. Illinois 1929

Chase, Arthur Sloan, 1930-31; Instructor in Civil Engineering; B.S. North Carolina 1924

Cheatum, Elmer Philip, 1925-65; Professor of Biology; Ph.D. Michigan 1933

Chokla, Sarah, 1931-36; Instructor in English; M.A. SMU 1928

Clark, Edythe, 1927-32; Instructor in Psychology; M.A. SMU 1925

Claunch, John M., 1939-67; Professor of Government 1939-67; Dean of Dallas College 1948-67; Ph.D. Texas 1954

Clough, George Obadiah, 1927-48; Professor of Education 1927-48; Director of Dallas College 1935-48; Ph.D. New York 1931

Cockrell, Joseph Elmore, 1925-27; Acting Dean of the School of Law; LL.B. Washington and Lee 1882

Coe, Aleen, 1918-19; Instructor in English; M.A.*

Comer, John Preston, 1916-23; Professor of Political Science 1916-23; Acting Dean of College of Liberal Arts 1918-19, 1921-22; M.A. Columbia 1915

Conn, Pepway Copeland, 1937-38; Instructor in Brass Instruments; M.S. Oklahoma A&M 1933

Connor, Roma Reagan, 1916-17; Instructor in Art

Cook, John Alfred, 1922-63; Professor of Spanish; Ph.D. Texas 1940

Cooke, Harold G., 1928-31; Professor of City Church; B.D. SMU 1923

Crain, Nuell, 1932-34; Instructor in Religion; B.A. Hendrix 1929

Cuninggim, Jesse Lee, 1917-21; Professor of Religious Pedagogy; B.D. Vanderbilt 1895

Curry, Dudley, 1938-   ; Professor of Accounting; Ph.D. Stanford 1969

Cutler, Ralph Waldo, 1932-36; Instructor in Civil Engineering; M.S. California Institute of Technology 1929

Dalton, Virginia Broadfoot, 1934-48; Associate Professor of Physical Education; M.A. Teachers' College Columbia 1926

Davis, Gaston Joseph, 1938-39; Instructor in Civil Engineering; M.S. Princeton 1937

Davis, Wesley C., 1935-59; Professor of New Testament; Ph.D. Yale 1943

DeBow, Mary Virginia, 1927-48; Assistant Professor of Education; M.A. Columbia 1927

Dennis, Homer Asbury, 1924-32; Instructor in Mathematics; M.A. Illinois 1929

Dewey, Fred A., 1939-45; Assistant Professor of Law; LL.M. Columbia 1934

Dickenson, Robert Edward, 1924-33; Professor of Religion and Chaplain; M.A. Morrisville 1904

Dobbs, Hoyt M., 1916-20; Dean of School of Theology, Professor of Christian Doctrine; B.D. Vanderbilt 1904

Dobie, Mrs. J. Frank, 1918-19; Instructor in English; B.A. Southwestern 1910

Donaldson, Olive, 1915-37; Professor of Art; Ph.B. Chicago 1911

Doty, Joseph D., 1919-28; Associate Professor of History; M.A. SMU 1917; B. Litt. (Oxon) 1923

Dneprov, Ivan, 1932-38; Professor of Voice

Drew, Mary Kay King, 1927-35; Assistant Professor of Education; M.A. Columbia 1929

Dunbar, Ednis, 1924-32; Assistant Professor of Physical Education; Chicago Normal School of Physical Education 1921

Duncan, Catherine Lovell, 1937-45; Instructor in Physical Education; B.S. SMU 1936

Duncan, Frederick N., 1915-26; Professor of Biology; Ph.D. Clark 1906

Dunkle, Herbert Bothwell, 1925-34; Professor of Chemistry; M.A. Yale 1914

Eagleton, Clyde, 1919-23; Associate Professor of History; M.A. Princeton 1914; B.A. (Oxon) 1917

Edmonson, Ruth Whatley, 1924-60; Assistant Professor of Spanish; B.A. Texas 1918

Egger, Roland Andrews, 1927-28; Instructor in Government; M.A. SMU 1927

Emery, Clyde, 1939-64; Professor of Law; LL.B. Harvard 1930

Eubank, Vivian, 1936-37; Instructor in Physical Education; B.S. SMU 1932

Evans, Ethel Rader, 1937-38; Assistant Professor of Voice; Kidd-Key Conservatory 1918

Ewert, Alfred, 1920-21; Assistant Professor of French; M.A. (Oxon) 1920

Faget, Louis, 1934-47; Instructor in Cello

Faulkner, Harry Archer, 1922-27; Instructor in Physical Education

Finean, Isabelle, 1918-19; Instructor in French; B.A. Texas*

Fitzhugh, Nannie, 1939-   ; Instructor in English; M.A. SMU 1934

Flath, Earl Hugo, 1925-60; Professor of Electrical Engineering, Dean of School of Engineering; M.S. Georgia School of Technology 1926

Fleck, Laurence Hobart, 1921-63; Professor of Accounting 1921-63; Dean of School of Business Administration 1946-63; M.A. Michigan 1920

Fleck, Mary Juden, 1925-26; Instructor in French; B.A. SMU 1923

Fleming, Margaret, 1933-37; Instructor in Art; B.A. Oklahoma City 1931

Ford, Gus Lee, 1919-20; Instructor in History; B.A. SMU 1919

Ford, William Roy, 1924-26; Instructor in Spanish; B.A. SMU 1924

Forester, Jesse H., 1922-28; Assistant Professor of French; M.A. SMU 1924

Foscue, Augustus William, 1922-60; Professor of Accounting and Statistics; M.B.A. Stanford 1940

Foscue, Edwin Jay, 1923-65; Professor of Geography; Ph.D. Clark 1931

Foster, Mildred West, 1930-31; Instructor in Physical Education

Foster, William Flenoyd, 1931-62; Associate Professor of Physical Education; M.A. SMU 1929

Fottler, Marion Gertrude, 1924-27; Assistant Professor of Secretarial Training; B.B.A. Boston 1923

Fox, Guy Harold, 1931-32; Instructor in Government; M.A. SMU 1930

Franklin, William Neil, 1928-32; Associate Professor of History; Ph.D. Princeton 1929

Freeland, Ewing Young, 1922-25; Associate Professor of Physical Education; B.A. Vanderbilt 1912

Freeman, Eva Allen, 1922-51; Assistant Professor of Sociology; M.A. Colorado 1916

Freese, Frances, 1927-37; Instructor in Mathematics; M.A. SMU 1926

Fried, Mrs. Walter Julius, 1926-36; Instructor in Violin

Fried, Walter Julius, 1915-26; Professor of Violin

Gallup, Donald Clifford, 1937-40, 1941-42; Instructor in English; Ph.D. Yale 1939

Gambrell, Herbert Pickens, 1924-64; Professor of History; Ph.D. Texas 1946

Garrard, Verna, 1934-64; Professor of Home Economics; Ed.D. North Texas State 1960

Gealy, Fred Daniel, 1939-59; Professor of New Testament, Missions, and Church Music; Ph.D. Boston 1929

Geiser, Samuel Wood, 1924-57; Professor of Biology; Ph.D. Johns Hopkins 1922

George, Paul Charles, 1921-42; Instructor in French; B. es Sc. Brussels 1894

Gibbs, Warren Edgar, 1919-20; Instructor in English; B.A. SMU 1920

Glanville, James Linus, 1925-47; Professor of History; Ph.D. Johns Hopkins 1931

Gohdes, Clarence Louis Frank, 1926-27; Assistant Professor of English; M.A. Ohio State 1922

Golden, Elise Hay, 1919-57; Associate Professor of Voice; Graduate in Music, Arkansas 1912

Golden, Hawkins, 1932-34; Instructor in Law; LL.B. SMU 1930

Goodloe, Robert Wesley, 1920-57; Professor of Church History; Ph.D. Chicago 1929

Grant, C. Boris, 1915-20; Professor of Piano

Gray, Ethel, 1923-24; Assistant Professor of Physical Education; B.A. Texas 1919; B.P.E. American College of Physical Education 1922

Gray, Laurence Roderick, 1924-26; Instructor in Commerce; B.S. SMU 1924

Gray, Mamie Elizabeth, 1924-26; Assistant Professor of Biology; M.A. Texas 1922

Greenburg, Louis, 1923-46; Instructor in Clarinet and Saxophone

Griffith, Frederic Reese, 1916-21; Associate Professor of Biology; M.A. Washington (St. Louis) 1914

Griffith, Margaret Agnes, 1927-28; Instructor in English; M.A. Columbia 1927

Grommet, Clifford, 1939-46; Assistant Professor in Mechanical Engineering; M.S. Georgia School of Technology 1938

Gude, Gerard Egbert, 1919-23; Instructor in Mechanical Drawing and French

Guice, Harvey Hunter, 1922-56; Professor of Government; J.D. Chicago 1918

Guilbeau, Mrs. B. H., 1917-18; Assistant Professor of Education; Dean of Women; M.A.*

Guion, David W., 1920-23; Professor of Piano

Hall, Clabe Washington, 1926-34; Associate Professor of Religion; Ph.D. Yale 1931

Hall, Thomas Ola, 1933-34; Instructor in Mathematics; B.A. SMU 1933

Hamilton, Edna, 1920-21; Instructor in Piano; B.Mus. SMU 1917

Hamilton, Joan, 1915-20; Associate Professor of Home Economics; B.S. Columbia 1916

Hanson, Ruth Ro Jean, 1920-22; Instructor in Public Speaking; B.A. SMU 1919

Harding, Arthur Leon, 1927-34, 1946-72; Professor of Law; S.J.D. Harvard 1932

Hardy, George Chapple, 1930-32; Instructor in Religion; B.A. McMurry 1928

Harrison, Ed McMahan, 1931-53; Associate Professor of Coordination; B.S. Purdue 1910

Harrison, Margaret Irwin, 1926-53; Assistant Professor of History; M.A. Chicago 1922

Harrison, Martin Leigh, 1936-37; Instructor in Law; LL.M. Harvard 1935

Harrison, Roland Wendell, 1921-33; Assistant Professor of Biology; Ph.D. Chicago 1930

Hauhart, William Frederic, 1921-46; Professor of Finance 1921-46; Director of School of Commerce 1921-40; Dean of School of Business Administration 1940-46; Ph.D. Columbia 1909

Hawk, Eugene B., 1934-52; Professor of Homiletics; Dean of the School of Theology 1934-52; Acting President Sept. 1, 1938–March 1, 1939; B.D. Vanderbilt 1909

Hay, Mary Randle, 1925-34; Dean of Women; North Texas Female College 1892

Hearon, Richard Augustus, 1915-28; Professor of History 1915-28; Chairman of Graduate School 1920-23; M.A. Wisconsin 1913

Hemke, Marie Dora, 1920-24; Assistant Professor of English; M.A. Northwestern 1917

Henning, Albert Frederick, 1924-37; Professor of Journalism

Henry, Ruth Doran, 1919-22; Instructor in Biology and French; B.A. SMU 1919

Henson, Richard Carvel, 1926-27; Assistant Professor of Physics; Dr. Eng., Rensselaer Polytechnic Institute 1926

Herron, Ima Honaker, 1927-64; Professor of English; Ph.D. Duke 1935

Heuse, Edward Otto, 1918-50; Professor of Chemistry; Ph.D. Illinois 1914

Hicks, John Harden, 1922-57; Professor of Old Testament; Ph.D. Chicago 1933

Holland, Robert B., 1925-31; Assistant Professor of Law; LL.B. Texas 1925

Holt, Ivan Lee, 1915-18; Professor of Hebrew and Old Testament; Ph.D. Chicago 1909

Holt, Leona Sensabaugh, 1921-41; Professor of Spanish 1921-41; Dean of Women 1934-35; M.A. SMU 1916

Horne, John, 1930-31; Instructor in Mechanical Engineering; B.S. Alabama Polytechnic Institute 1924

Hosford, Hemphill, 1919-29, 1946-62; Professor of Mathematics 1919-29, 1946-62; Dean of the University and Dean of the Faculty of the College of Arts and Sciences, 1946-52; Academic Vice-President 1949-52; Acting

Dean of the Graduate School, 1952-57; Vice-President and Provost, 1952-62; Ph.D. Illinois 1926

Hubbell, Jay Broadus, 1915-27; Professor of English; Ph.D. Columbia 1922

Hubbell, John Wesley, 1920-22; Professor of Voice; Graduate of College of Music, Cincinnati

Huff, Gerald Boone, 1936-46; Assistant Professor of Mathematics; Ph.D. Illinois 1935

Huffman, Harold Funston, 1930-44; Professor of Electrical Engineering; M.S. Illinois 1929

Hunter, Hiram T., 1917-19; Associate Professor of Education; M.A.*

Hyer, Robert Stewart, 1911-29; Professor of Physics 1911-29; President 1911-20; M.A. Emory 1883

Hynes, Mary Adelaide, 1925-26; Instructor in Biology; M.A. Texas 1925

Ingram, Florence, 1916-17; Instructor in Education; B.A.*

Jenness, James Russell, 1928-34; Professor of Physics; Ph.D. Cornell 1928

Jennings, Elzy Dee, 1922-38; Professor of Education, Dean of College of Arts and Sciences 1922-38; Vice-President 1933-38; Ph.D. Texas 1924

Johnson, La Rue, 1932-38; Instructor in Piano; B. Mus. SMU 1931

Jones, Edward Homer, 1915-34; Professor of Mathematics; M.A. Harvard 1910

Jones, Robert Lee, 1923-24; Associate Professor of History; Ph.D. Stanford 1923

Jordan, Gilbert John, 1931-69; Professor of German; Ph.D. Ohio State 1936

Jordan, Lester, 1936-   ; Associate Professor of Journalism 1936-46; Business Manager of Athletics 1945-69, Special Assistant 1969-   ; M.S.J. Northwestern 1927

Keen, John H., 1916-18; Professor of Philosophy; Dean of College of Liberal Arts; M.A.*

Keeton, Morris T., 1938-42; Instructor in Philosophy; Ph.D. Harvard 1937

Keith, Mary Louise, 1927-32; Instructor in English; M.A. SMU 1929

Kern, Paul Bentley, 1915-26; Professor of Homiletics 1915-26; Dean of School of Theology 1922-26; M.A. Vanderbilt 1905, B.D. 1905

Kilgore, James, 1915-34; Professor of Philosophy of Religion 1915-34; Acting President Oct. 11, 1922–Apr. 1, 1923; Acting Dean of School of Theology 1926-34; M.A. Southwestern 1890

Kimball, Justin Ford, 1925-30; Professor of Education; M.A. Baylor 1899

Knickerbocker, Hubert Renfro, 1922-24; Associate Professor of Journalism; B.A. Southwestern 1917

Knight, Fannie, 1923-24; Instructor in Home Economics; B.S. SMU 1923

Knott, Morgan, 1939-47; Instructor in Piano; B.Mus. SMU 1937

Koenig, August George, 1918-20; Associate Professor of Chemistry; B.A. Texas 1909

Kuser, Milton M., 1934-36; Instructor in Mathematics; M.A. SMU 1931

Lamar, Mary, 1931-38; Instructor in English; M.A. SMU 1930

LaMond, Stella Lodge, 1937-59; Professor of Art; M.A. Columbia 1930

Landon, Ransom Durell, 1927-47; Professor of Civil Engineering; M.S. Cincinnati 1927

Langsam, G. Geoffrey, 1938-46; Instructor in English; M.A. Columbia 1937

Law, Henry Marvin, 1926-34; Assistant Professor of Geology; B.S. SMU 1926

Lee, Umphrey, 1927-33, 1939-58; Professor of Homiletics 1927-33; President 1939-54; Chancellor 1954-58; Ph.D. Columbia 1931

Leisy, Ernest Erwin, 1927-57; Professor of English; Ph.D. Illinois 1923

Lewis, Ralph Elton, 1936-38; Assistant Professor of Mechanical Engineering; M.S. Illinois 1931

Lock, Lora May, 1924-34; Associate Professor of Physical Education; B.S. Kansas State Teachers' College 1915

Longnecker, William Mayne, 1927-64; Professor of Biology 1927-64; Dean of Students 1954-64; Ph.D. Chicago 1937

Lowry, Robert Benton, 1939-41; Instructor in Law; LL.B. Northwestern 1937

Lutz, Samuel Gross, 1939-40; Assistant Professor of Electrical Engineering; Ph.D. Purdue 1938

MacCarthy, Thomas George, 1927-34; Professor of Civil Engineering; C.E. Columbia 1917

McCommas, Dorothy Pimm, 1925-31, 1948-54; Instructor in Spanish; B.A. SMU 1923

McCord, Mary, 1915-45; Professor of Speech; M.O. National School of Oratory 1917

McCorkle, Nelle Elizabeth, 1938-48; Associate Professor of Education; M.A. SMU 1932

McCorkle, T. Smith, 1936-41; Associate Professor of Education; M.A. SMU 1936

McCrary, David Switzer, 1936-37; Instructor in Government; M.A. Columbia 1929

McDonald, Frank Cobb, 1929-63; Professor of Physics; Ph.D. Chicago 1926

McDonald, Roy William, 1939-45; Professor of Law; LL.M. Columbia 1941

McElvaney, Lucy-Avis, 1928-32; Instructor in Piano; B.Mus. SMU 1925

McGinnis, John Hathaway, 1915-54; Professor of English; M.A. Columbia 1915

MacGregor, Rob Roy, 1927-28; Instructor in History; M.A. SMU 1926

McIntosh, Helen, 1924-30; Instructor in English; M.A. SMU 1925

McIntosh, John Strayer, 1915-45; Professor of Latin and Greek; Ph.D. Chicago 1909

McIntosh, Russell, 1927-31; Assistant Professor of Physical Education; B.A. SMU 1925

MacLean, Eloise Manthorne, 1939-40; Instructor in Speech; B.A. Manitoba 1924

McPherson, Nenien Cotesworth, Jr., 1935-37; Professor of Philosophy of Religion; Ph.D. Northwestern 1930

McReynolds, John Oliver, 1915-16; Professor of Physiological Optics; M.D. LL.D. F.A.C.S.*

Malone, Frank, 1938-48; Assistant Professor of Brass Instruments; B.P.S.M. SMU 1938

Matchett, Rebecca Pegues, 1921-24; Instructor in Physical Education; B.A. Mississippi State College for Women 1920

Matson, Ray McKinley, 1938-61; Professor of Mechanical Engineering; M.S. Georgia School of Technology 1932

Meents, Richard Ommo, 1931-32; Assistant Professor of Geology; Ph.D. Oklahoma 1930

Metler, Alvin Velbert, 1937-41; Instructor in Chemistry; Ph.D. Duke 1932

Metzenthin, Waldemar Eric, 1920-23; Assistant Professor of German; M.A. Columbia 1904

Miles, Henry James, 1936-37; Instructor in Mechanical Engineering; M.S. Rutgers 1931

Million, Elmer Mayse, 1938-39; Instructor in Law; LL.B. Oklahoma 1935

Mims, Staley Wood, 1928-30; Instructor in Engineering Drawing; B.S. Texas A&M 1925

Minnis, Margaret, 1919-24; Instructor in Home Economics; B.S. College of Industrial Arts 1917

Minor, Ora, 1924-34; Professor of Town and Country Church

Molaner, Otto William, 1916-18, 1925-26; Instructor in German 1916-18; Associate Professor of Religion 1925-26; B.D. SMU 1921

Montgomery, Clifford M., 1915-18; Instructor in Spanish; B.A. Southwestern*

Mood, Robert Gibbs, Jr., 1921-30; Assistant Professor of English; M.A. Columbia 1925

Moore, R. B., 1928-30; Instructor in Religion

Moore, Stephen H., 1919-38; Professor of Economics; M.A. Columbia 1905

Morrison, Ray, 1915-17, 1920-35; Professor of Physical Education; B.A. Vanderbilt 1912

Mouzon, Edwin Dubose, 1915-16; Dean of School of Theology; B.A. Wofford 1889

Mouzon, Edwin Dubose, Jr., 1922-66; Professor of Mathematics; Ph.D. Illinois 1929

Murley, Joseph Clyde, 1916-20; Associate Professor of Latin and Greek; M.A. Chicago 1916

Murley, Mrs. Joseph Clyde, 1917-19; Instructor in English; B.A.*

Murphey, Mary Batterton, 1920-25; Associate Professor of English 1920-25; Dean of Women 1920-22; M.A. California 1922

Myatt, Samuel Alexander, 1915-45; Professor of Spanish; M.A. Vanderbilt 1899

Myres, Samuel Dale, Jr., 1925-55; Professor of Government 1925-55; Director of Arnold School of Government 1934-55; Ph.D. Texas 1929

Nance, Gusta B., 1928-69; Professor of Comparative Literature; Ph.D. Wisconsin 1954

Neilson, Augusta, 1920-21; Instructor in Spanish; B.A. Texas*

Nethery, Ira Mae, 1939-41; Instructor in Harp

Newton, Cosette Faust, 1917-19; Assistant Professor of English 1917-19; Dean of Women 1918-19; Ph.D. Radcliffe*

Nichols, Claude Andrew, 1919-48; Professor of Education 1919-48; Director of School of Education 1925-48; Ph.D. Columbia 1930

Old, James Edward, 1926-34; Associate Professor of English; M.A. SMU 1928

Ormond, Jesse Marvin, 1921-23; Professor of Pastoral Administration; B.D. Vanderbilt 1910

Palmquist, Kenneth Siebert, 1938-43; Instructor in Mathematics; Ph.D. Kentucky 1937

Parker, Fitzgerald S., 1915-16; Professor of Christian Doctrine

Patterson, Stanley, 1919-57; Instructor in Mechanical Engineering 1940-57; Superintendent of Buildings and Grounds 1919-57

Payne, Sara, 1932-33; Instructor in Psychology; M.A. Columbia 1931

Peacock, William Levi, 1922-40; Instructor in Cello

Peak, Helen, 1926-31; Instructor in Psychology; Ph.D. Yale 1929

Pearce, Fletcher William, 1931-33; Instructor in Civil Engineering; B.S. Michigan 1924

Peebles, Mary Louise, 1931-32; Instructor in Home Economics; B.S. Iowa 1926

Pegues, Albert Shipp, 1919-21; Professor of English; Dean of College of Liberal Arts; M.A. Wofford 1895

Perkinson, Itasca Sweet, 1924-57; Professor of Education; M.A. Texas 1913

Petit, Jean, 1919-20; Assistant Professor of French; Brenet Supérieur (France) 1909

Phares, Eula, 1920-21; Instructor in Latin and English; B.A. SMU 1920

Pinckney, Pauline, 1924-32; Assistant Professor of Home Economics; M.A. Columbia 1928

Pletcher, L. J., 1916-18; Assistant Professor of Chemistry; M.S.*

Potts, Charles Shirley, 1926-49; Professor of Law; Dean of School of Law; S.J.D. Harvard 1926

Powell, Margaret, 1928-32; Instructor in Physical Education; B.A. SMU 1927

Pritchett, Henry Lucian, 1924-54; Professor of Sociology; Ph.D. New York 1928

Pritchett, Mary Montgomery, 1920-43; Associate Professor of Home Economics; M.A. Columbia 1928

Rader, Ethel, 1930-35; Instructor in Voice; Kidd-Key Conservatory 1918

Rader, Franklin K., 1926-55; Professor of Finance; B.S. SMU 1926

Ransom, Richard Bruce, 1924-26; Associate Professor of Education; M.A. SMU 1923

Ray, Roy, 1929-67; Professor of Law; S.J.D. Michigan 1930

Reddick, Walter Grady, 1919-20; Instructor in Latin and Spanish; B.A. SMU 1919

Redus, Morgan Ward, 1936-   ; Professor of Religion; Ph.D. Chicago 1935

Reed, Helen Joy, 1929-32; Assistant Professor of Psychology; Ph.D. Chicago 1929

Reedy, Frank, 1915-16; Instructor in Sunday School Organization

Reedy, John Henry, 1915-18; Professor of Chemistry; Ph.D. Yale 1915

Reinsch, Bernhard Paul, 1927-34; Professor of Mathematics; Ph.D. Illinois 1924

Renshaw, Edyth, 1924-67; Professor of Speech; Ph.D. Columbia 1950

Reudi, Oreen, 1926-30; Instructor in Sociology; M.A. Smith 1926

Rhea, William Alexander, 1925-41; Professor of Law; LL.M. Texas 1895

Rice, John Andrew, 1920-22; Professor of Old Testament; M.A. South Carolina 1887

Rickey, Harry Wynn, 1937-64; Professor of French; Docteur de l'Université de Bordeaux 1932

Riddick, John Allen, 1936-37; Instructor in Chemistry; Ph.D. Iowa 1929

Riddle, Mrs. Penn, 1937-38; Instructor in Violin; B.A. SMU 1925

Rippy, Mary Lee, 1922-23; Instructor in Biology; B.A. SMU 1922

Rix, J. Burton, 1918-19; Director of Athletics

Rockwell, Agnes, 1915-16; Instructor in English; B.A. Wellesley*

Rodabaugh, Louis Dale, 1937-38; Instructor in Mathematics; M.A. Ohio State 1933

Rodgers, Ruth Miller, 1927-28; Instructor in Sociology; M.A. Texas 1925

Rodriquez, Elias Santos, 1919-20; Instructor in Spanish

Romberg, Walter Paul, 1925-53; Professor of Violin

Root, Paul Adelbert, 1936-47; Professor of Missions and Sociology of Religion; Ph.D. Duke 1935

Ross, Crystal Ray, 1926-27; Assistant Professor of General Literature; Doctorat es Lettres, Strasbourg 1925

Ross, Floyd Hiatt, 1936-37; Instructor in Religion; Ph.D. Yale 1935

Rountree, Ralph, 1923-31; Instructor in Art

Rucker, George Foster, 1932-34; Instructor in Electrical Engineering; B.S. SMU 1931

Russell, David Riley, 1926-64; Assistant Professor of Speech; M.A. Carnegie Institute of Technology 1931

Saer, E. H., 1917-18; Instructor in Military Science

Sage, Jesse Abner, 1924-32; Professor of Voice

Sartain, Aaron Q., 1934-71; Professor of Psychology and Industrial Relations 1934-71; Dean of School of Business Administration 1963-68; Ph.D. Chicago 1939

Schuessler, Alvin Daniel, 1915-44; Professor of German; Ph.D. Michigan 1916

Scott, Donald, 1922-34; Associate Professor of Commerce; B.A. Michigan 1922

Scott, Marie, 1930-34; Instructor in Biology; M.A. Kansas 1929

Seale, Roy Q., 1922-36, 1943-63; Professor of Mathematics; Ph.D. Stanford 1935

Seay, Frank, 1915-20; Professor of New Testament; B.D. Vanderbilt 1899; M.A. Harvard 1903

Seneker, James Seehorn, 1921-57; Professor of Religious Education; B.D. Vanderbilt 1912; M.A. Columbia 1919

Sherwood, Noble Pierce, 1939-42; Instructor in Mechanical Engineering; B.S. Kansas 1934

Shuler, Ellis William, 1915-52; Professor of Geology 1915-52; Dean of Graduate School 1924-52; Ph.D. Harvard 1915

Shumaker, Clifford Harold, 1931-64; Professor of Industrial Engineering; B.S. Kansas 1930

Shurter, Edwin DuBois, 1924-25; Arnold Professor of American Statesmanship; Ph.B. Cornell 1892

Silvey, J. K. Gwynne, 1928-30; Instructor in Biology; M.A. Michigan 1928

Simmons, Virginia Carlisle, 1924-25; Instructor in Spanish; B.A. SMU 1924

Slaymaker, Robert R., 1928-38; Professor of Mechanical Engineering; M.S. Iowa State 1932

Smith, A. Frank, 1916-17; Instructor in Religious Education; B.A. Southwestern 1911

Smith, Allen Kendrick, 1932-36; Instructor in Law; LL.M. Columbia 1930

Smith, Arthur Alvin, 1939-51; Professor of Economics; Ph.D. Vanderbilt 1933

Smith, Fannie Putcamp, 1924-39; Assistant Professor of German and Latin; M.A. Wisconsin 1920

Smith, Frederick Danesbury, 1920-59; Professor of Comparative Literature 1920-59; Dean of Instruction, College of Arts and Sciences 1938-59; Ph.D. Chicago 1916

Smith, Garland Garvey, 1923-30; Assistant Professor of English; M.A. Harvard 1925

Smith, Henry Nash, 1927-41; Associate Professor of English and Comparative Literature; Ph.D. Harvard 1940

Smith, R. N., 1918-19; Instructor in Mathematics; B.A. Southwestern*

Smith, Rhea Marsh, 1928-30; Instructor in History; M.A. Princeton 1929

Soule, Flory P., 1917-18; Instructor in French; M.A.*

Spann, John Richard, 1924-27; Professor of City Church; M.A. SMU 1917; B.D. Drew 1918

Sparks, Warren M., 1936-38; Instructor in Law; LL.B. Iowa 1935

Spears, Mary Chapman, 1925-34; Associate Professor of Education; M.A. Texas 1927

Sperry, Mary, 1924-30; Assistant Professor of English; M.A. Radcliffe 1924

Spragins, Lide, 1937-57; Associate Professor of English; Dean of Women; M.A. Columbia 1927

St. Clair, James Watson, 1924-45; Professor of Physical Education; M.A. SMU 1925

Stephens, Ira Kendrick, 1920-56; Professor of Philosophy; Ph.D. Harvard 1926

Stewart, James Henry, Jr., 1925-31; Instructor in Physical Education; B.S. SMU 1924

Stokes, Melmoth Y., 1916-18; Instructor in English; B.A. Southwestern*

Strain, Milo Balch, 1919-20; Instructor in Chemistry; B.A. SMU 1919

Swindells, Minnie H., 1935-37; Associate Professor of Education; B.A. Mercer 1927

Taylor, Henry Kirby, 1922-34; Professor of Education; M.A. Kentucky Wesleyan 1891

Temple, Lura, 1921-22; Instructor in English; B.A. SMU 1920

Terry, Paul W., 1915-18; Associate Professor of Education; M.A.*

Thomas, George Finger, 1924-26; Associate Professor of Religion; B.A. Oxford 1923

Thomas, Otway, 1924-26; Instructor in Public Speaking; B.A. Rice 1921

Thompson, Sophus, 1928-67; Professor of Civil Engineering 1928-67; Dean of School of Engineering 1964-66; B.S. North Dakota State 1925

Timberlake, Rachel, 1931-36; Instructor in Religion; M.A. Columbia 1927

Tinkle, J. Lon, 1933- ; Professor of English and Comparative Literature; M.A. SMU 1932; Diplome, Institut de Phonetique, Université de Paris; Officier d'Académie

Todd, Harold Hart, 1915-49; Professor of Piano and Theory; East Prussia Conservatory School of Music 1914

Todd, Mrs. Harold Hart, 1915-57; Instructor in Piano

Todd, Mary M., 1918-19; Instructor in Home Economics; B.S. Wisconsin*

Towns, Kirk, 1915-19; Professor of Voice

Trexler, Harrison Anthony, 1929-54; Professor of History; Ph.D. Johns Hopkins 1914

Vance, Nolan R., 1936-37; Instructor in German; M.A., B.D. SMU 1935

Van Katwijk, Paul, 1918-56; Professor of Piano 1918-56; Dean of School of Music 1918-49; Royal College of Music, The Hague 1904

Van Katwijk, Viola Beck, 1923-56; Associate Professor of Piano

Vermillion, Harriet Haynes, 1933-34; Instructor in Art

Von Mickwitz, Harold, 1915-18; Professor of Piano; Dean of School of Music

Waggoner, Luther J., 1918-19; Instructor in Mathematics; B.D. SMU*

Waldrop, Arthur Gayle, 1920-21; Instructor in Journalism; M.A. Columbia 1927

Wales, William Chauncey, 1921-27; Professor of Advertising and Salesmanship; M.B.A. Harvard 1920

Walker, James Kirven, 1938-39; Instructor in Civil Engineering; B.S. SMU 1936

Wannamaker, Olin D., 1915-18; Professor of English; M.A. Harvard*

Wasson, Alfred Washington, 1926-35; Professor of Missions; Ph.D. Chicago 1931

Watson, Walter Thompson, 1929-60; Professor of Sociology; Ph.D. Chicago 1929

Webb, Ernest Clay, 1934-52; Professor of Religion; S.T.B. Yale 1911

Whaling, Horace M., Jr., 1916-32; Professor of Church History 1916-32; Vice-President 1919-32; B.D. Vanderbilt 1907

Whaling, Mrs. Horace M., Jr., 1925-37; Associate Professor of Organ

Whatley, Anita, 1920-25; Assistant Professor of Spanish; B.A. Texas 1915

White, H. E., 1915-16; Instructor in English; B.A.*

Whitsett, May Lee, 1920-42; Professor of Chemistry; Ph.D. Columbia 1930

Williams, Philip, 1938-64; Professor of Violin

Williams, Thomas S., 1939-46; Professor of Voice

Wilson, Lenoir, 1921-23; Instructor in Biology; B.A. SMU 1921

Wilson, Raymond H., Jr., 1936-37; Instructor in Mathematics; Ph.D. Pennsylvania 1935

Windhorst, Estelle Louise, 1924-25; Assistant Professor of Philosophy; M.A. Iowa 1924

Winstead, Samuel Garland, Jr., 1935-36; Instructor in Law; LL.M. Columbia 1934

Wisseman, Charles Louis, 1927-59; Assistant Professor of German 1927-31; Professor of Education 1931-59; Director of School of Education 1948-59; Ph.D. New York 1932

Withers, Alfred M., 1918-19; Associate Professor of French; M.A. Johns Hopkins*

Woodward, Comer McDonald, 1917-24; Professor of Sociology; M.A. Chicago 1916; B.D. 1917

Workman, Mims Thornburgh, 1920-25; Associate Professor of Biblical History and Literature; M.A. Emory 1919

Wright, Cecil Benjamin, 1936-39; Assistant Professor of Mathematics; Ph.D. Pittsburgh 1934

Yarborough, Joseph Ussery, 1920-57; Professor of Psychology; Ph.D. Chicago 1919

Yerion, Joe B., 1916-17; Director of Home Economics; B.S. Southeastern State Normal 1910

Zeek, Charles Franklin, 1915-37; Professor of French; Docteur de l'Université de Grenoble 1914

Zeek, Mathilde Beaullieu, 1921-34; Instructor in French; Diplomée Graduée de l'Institut Saint Louis 1883

Zumbrunnen, Albert Clay, 1926-48; Professor of Religion and Dean of Students; M.A. Missouri 1909

Notes

CHAPTER ONE

1. Frederick Eby, *The Development of Education in Texas* (New York: Macmillan Co., 1925), p. 161.

2. Ibid., pp. 162-66.

3. Ibid., pp. 195-96.

4. Rupert Norval Richardson, *Texas, The Lone Star State* (New York: Prentice-Hall, 1943), p. 409.

5. Eby, *Development of Education in Texas*, p. 312.

6. Richardson, *Texas, The Lone Star State*, p. 412.

7. The Morrill Act, passed by Congress in 1862, granted to each state 30,000 acres for each senator and representative in Congress for the purpose of endowing an agriculture college. This legislation was the keystone of higher education in the Middle West and Far West.

8. Richard Hofstadter and C. DeWitt Hardy, *The Development and Scope of Higher Education in the United States* (New York: Columbia University Press, 1952), p. 40.

9. Frederick Rudolph, *The American College and University* (New York: Random House, 1962), pp. 329-54.

10. Hofstadter and Hardy, *Higher Education in the United States*, pp. 9-18.

11. Trinity was moved again in 1942 to San Antonio, a larger and wealthier center of population.

12. Eby, *Development of Education in Texas*, pp. 282-83.

13. *Catalogue of Southwestern University, 1900-1901* (Georgetown, Texas), p. 13.

14. Claude Carr Cody, "Methodist Educational Institutions in Texas," *Bulletin of the Board of Education of the Methodist Episcopal Church, South* 3 (Nashville, 1913): 78.

15. Ray Hyer Brown, *Robert Stewart Hyer: The Man I Knew* (Salado, Texas: Anson Jones Press, 1957), p. 29.

16. *Bulletin of the Board of Education of the Methodist Episcopal Church, South* 3 (Nashville, 1913): page not numbered.

17. Hofstadter and Hardy, *Higher Education in the United States*, p. 53.

18. *Bulletin of the University of Texas, 1968* (Austin), p. 21.

19. In 1960 Rice Institute became Rice University.

20. Kenneth S. Pitzer, *Report of the President of Rice University* (Houston, 1965), pp. 6-7.

CHAPTER TWO

1. Claude Carr Cody, "Methodist Educational Institutions in Texas," *Bulletin*

of the Board of Education of the Methodist Episcopal Church, South 3 (Nashville, 1913): 80.

2. Ibid., pp. 61-76; Homer S. Thrall, *A Brief History of Methodism in Texas* (Nashville: Methodist Episcopal Church, South, 1894), pp. 265-77; Robert W. Goodloe, "Methodism in Texas, 1900-1950," Bridwell Library, SMU, 1951, pp. 36-41; John Edward Blair, "The Founding of Southern Methodist University" (M.A. thesis, SMU, 1926), pages not numbered.

3. Ben A. Matthews, "The History of Polytechnic College" (M.A. thesis, SMU, 1930), pp. 1-2.

4. *Bulletin of the Board of Education* 3 (1913): page not numbered.

5. Thrall, *Brief History of Methodism,* p. 277.

6. Donald G. Tewksbury, *The Founding of American Colleges and Universities before the Civil War* (New York: Columbia University Press, 1932), p. 103.

7. Frank Seay, "The School of Theology of Southern Methodist University," *Bulletin of the Board of Education of the Methodist Episcopal Church, South* 5 (1915): 131. Seay was a minister who taught theology at SMU from 1915 to 1920 and was regarded as a competent scholar.

8. *Texas Christian Advocate,* October 2, 1875.

9. T. R. Fehrenbach, *Lone Star: A History of Texas and the Texans* (New York: Macmillan Co., 1968), pp. 595-602; Rupert Norval Richardson, *Texas, The Lone Star State* (New York: Prentice-Hall, 1943), p. 518.

10. Blair, "The Founding of Southern Methodist University," pages not numbered; *Religious Bodies: Bureau of the Census* (Washington: U.S. Government Printing Office, 1910), pp. 439, 471.

11. Robert S. Hyer, manuscript on the founding of Southern Methodist University found after the author's death in 1929. The manuscript was written about 1915 and is in the Archives, SMU.

12. *Bulletin of the Board of Education* 3 (1913): page not numbered.

13. Hyer manuscript on the founding of SMU.

14. Robert S. Hyer, "The Founding," *SMU Ex-Students Magazine* (October, 1924): 15.

15. Hyer manuscript on the founding of SMU.

16. The Federal Reserve Act was passed by the U.S. Congress in 1913 during the first administration of Woodrow Wilson.

17. *Texas Christian Advocate,* September 22, 1910. This was the official publication of the Methodist Church in the state.

18. Robert S. Hyer to Hiram A. Boaz, Georgetown, Texas, March 15, 1910, cited in *Texas Christian Advocate,* March 24, 1910.

19. Robert S. Hyer, "Some New Measurements of Electric Waves," *Transactions of the Texas Academy of Science* 2 (1898): 57-68. This report, which Hyer read before the Texas Academy of Science, definitely indicates that he was experimenting with ether waves.

20. *Dictionary of American Biography* s.v. "Hyer, Robert Stewart." Author of this article in *DAB* is Herbert P. Gambrell, professor emeritus of history at SMU, who knew Hyer well in his last years.

21. Hyer manuscript on the founding of SMU.

22. H. A. Boaz, *Eighty-four Golden Years: An Autobiography* (Nashville: Parthenon Press, 1951), p. 77.

23. John M. Moore and John R. Nelson, eds., *Texas Methodist Educational Convention,* (n.p., 1906), p. 11.

24. Ibid., p. 69.

25. Nathan Powell, "Notes on the Founding of Southern Methodist University," Archives, SMU, 1911, pp. 4-5, 8-11.

26. Frank Reedy, bursar of Southwestern University, 1909-1911, and Southern Methodist University, 1911-1920, to Rev. E. L. Shettles, Methodist minister and book collector, May 15, 1934. Shettles tried unsuccessfully to write a history of the

founding of SMU, but did collect a valuable series of letters from those most closely associated with the project. These letters can all be found in the Shettles Letters, Archives, McFarlin Auditorium, SMU. Shettles was primarily interested in proving that Nathan Powell was responsible for founding SMU.

27. *Dallas Morning News*, February 23, 1910.

28. Reedy to H. M. Whaling, vice-president of SMU, September 4, 1929, Shettles Letters, Archives, SMU.

29. *Dallas Morning News*, February 23, 1910.

30. Edwin D. Mouzon to E. L. Shettles, December 13, 1933; J. Sam Barcus to E. L. Shettles, February 19, 1934, Shettles Letters, Archives, SMU.

31. T. F. Sessions, leading churchman from the West Texas Conference, to E. L. Shettles, January 16, 1934, Shettles Letters, Archives, SMU. John M. Barcus also believed in the dual role of Hyer. His views are quoted in a letter from J. E. Blair to Bishop H. A. Boaz, June 17, 1925, Boaz Letters, Bridwell Library, SMU.

32. Blair, "The Founding of SMU," pages not numbered.

33. H. A. Boaz to Robert S. Hyer, March 7, 1910, Boaz Letters, Bridwell Library, SMU. This exchange of letters between Hyer and Boaz was published in the *Texas Christian Advocate* between March 24 and April 21, 1910.

34. Hyer to Boaz, March 15, 1910, Boaz Letters, Bridwell Library.

35. Boaz to Hyer, n.d.

36. Boaz to Hyer, n.d.

37. Hyer to Boaz, n.d.

38. Hyer manuscript on the founding of SMU.

39. Ibid.; James Kilgore, "Removal of Southwestern University," *Texas Christian Advocate*, September 8, 1910.

40. There is no explanation of why the figure was raised $100,000. The final sum Dallas gave the new university was $300,000.

41. *Dallas Morning News*, May 18, 1910.

42. Boaz, *Eighty-four Golden Years*, p. 81.

43. *Texas Christian Advocate*, June 16, 1910.

44. *Dallas Morning News*, May 28, 1910.

45. Hyer manuscript on the founding of SMU.

46. *Georgetown Commercial*, June 13, 1910.

47. *Dallas Morning News*, June 10, 1910.

48. *Texas Christian Advocate*, June 30, 1910.

49. John M. Barcus, "Why I Oppose Accepting the Dallas Proposition," *Texas Christian Advocate*, July 14, 1910.

50. Ray Hyer Brown, *Robert Stewart Hyer: The Man I Knew* (Salado, Texas: Anson Jones Press, 1957), p. 126.

51. "Majority Report of Board of Trustees of Southwestern University," *Texas Christian Advocate*, June 30, 1910.

52. Hemphill Hosford, provost emeritus of the university, to author, April 3, 1970. Hyer made this statement to Hosford in 1929.

53. *Dallas Morning News*, July 3, 1910.

54. *Texas Christian Advocate*, September 22, 1910.

55. Ibid., August 11, 1910.

56. Ibid., September 1, 1910.

57. *Dallas Morning News*, August 7, 1910.

58. John L. Sullivan, "Let Us Rise Up and Build," *Texas Christian Advocate*, September 22, 1910.

59. Boaz, *Eighty-four Golden Years*, p. 83.

60. Minutes of the Commission of Education of the Methodist Episcopal Church, South, 1911-1914, Bridwell Library, SMU, p. 2.

61. *Georgetown Commercial*, October 21, 1910.

62. *West Texas Conference Journal* (San Antonio, 1910), p. 26.

63. *Journal of the Central Texas Conference* (Waco, 1910), p. 20.

64. *North Texas Annual Conferences* (R. G. Mood, 1910), p. 23.

65. *Journal of Northwest Texas Conference* (Amarillo, 1910), p. 28; *Journal of Texas Conference* (Pt. Bolivar, 1910), p. 24.

66. *Georgetown Commercial*, January 27, 1911.

67. C. C. Cody to Edwin D. Mouzon, March 25, 1911, Mouzon Letters, Bridwell Library, SMU.

68. Cody to Mouzon, August 30, 1911.

CHAPTER THREE

1. *Texas Christian Advocate*, January 26, 1911. Bishop Mouzon, Hyer, and Boaz met with the commission. They had a voice but no vote.

2. Minutes of the Commission of Education of the Methodist Episcopal Church, South, 1911-1914, p. 24.

3. Frank McNeny to E. L. Shettles, January 9, 1934, Shettles Letters, Archives, McFarlin Auditorium, SMU.

4. Minutes of the Commission of Education, 1911-1914, pp. 29-30.

5. *Dallas Morning News*, February 2, 1911.

6. Dr. McReynolds had been forced to make a public plea in the newspaper to get enough "machines" in which to transport the commissioners when they were in Dallas.

7. *Fort Worth Record*, February 2, 1911.

8. Ibid., February 3, 1911.

9. Ibid., February 4, 1911.

10. John O. McReynolds to William Everett, April 20, 1934; Frank McNeny to E. L. Shettles, April 20, 1934, Shettles Letters, Archives, SMU; J. W. Blanton manuscripts, 1954, Office of the President, SMU. Blanton was a member of the commission and later a faithful supporter of the university. His manuscripts contain various personal recollections about the university.

11. McNeny to Shettles, April 20, 1934; McReynolds to Everett, April 20, 1934; Everett to Shettles, March 26, 1934. In 1950 Mrs. Caruth told Hemphill Hosford, then vice-president of SMU, that McNeny had difficulty locating Caruth on short notice, but finally found him at the farmer's market selling some chickens.

12. H. A. Boaz, *Eighty-four Golden Years: An Autobiography* (Nashville: Parthenon Press, 1951), p. 85.

13. Minutes of the Commission of Education, 1911-1914, pp. 44-45; *Fort Worth Record*, February 4, 1911.

14. *Fort Worth Star-Telegram*, February 5, 1911.

15. *Dallas Morning News*, February 4, 1911.

16. McReynolds to Everett, April 20, 1934, Shettles Letters.

17. James Kilgore, member of the commission and later on the theological faculty of SMU, to Shettles, November 29, 1933, Shettles Letters, Archives, SMU; J. W. Blanton manuscripts.

18. Minutes of the Commission of Education 1911-1914, p. 25.

19. Ibid., p. 56; see also Horace Bishop manuscript on the work of the commission, April 17, 1911, Office of the President. Horace Bishop, as a member of the commission, wrote his account of these first three meetings of the commission shortly after they occurred. Later he was chairman of SMU's first Board of Trustees.

20. *Dallas Morning News*, February 5, 1911; *Fort Worth Record*, February 2, 1911.

21. Minutes of the Commission of Education, 1911-1914, p. 62.

22. Horace Bishop manuscript; see also Robert S. Hyer to H. A. Boaz, February 18, 1911, Boaz Letters, Bridwell Library, SMU.

23. Minutes of the Commission of Education, 1911-1914, p. 57.

24. Frank Reedy to H. M. Whaling, Jr., September 4, 1929, Shettles Letters, Archives, SMU.

25. Minutes of the Commission of Education, 1911-1914, p. 57; Horace Bishop manuscript.

26. Horace Bishop manuscript.

27. Minutes of the Commission of Education, 1911-1914, pp. 58-69.

28. Ibid., p. 103; Samuel Wood Geiser, *Medical Education in Dallas, 1900-1910* (Dallas: SMU Press, 1952), pp. 15-16.

29. Abraham Flexner, *Medical Education in the United States and Canada* (Boston, 1910), p. 310.

30. Charter of Southern Methodist University, April 17, 1911, Fondren Library, SMU.

31. *Bulletin of SMU*, June 1920, p. 10; Minutes of the Board of Trustees, June 4, 1912.

32. Amended Charter of Southern Methodist University, February 7, 1913, Fondren Library, SMU.

33. Edwin Mims, *A History of Vanderbilt University* (Nashville: Vanderbilt University Press, 1946), pp. 291-318.

34. Act creating the Educational Commission, adopted by the General Conference at Oklahoma City, May 20, 1914, Bridwell Library, SMU. This Commission should not be confused with the Commission of Education of the Methodist Episcopal Church, South, 1911-1914.

35. *Texas Christian Advocate*, July 23, 1914.

36. Report of the Commission of Education, 1911-1914, May 2, 1918, Bridwell Library, SMU.

37. See above, p. 14.

38. Oral interview with Paul E. Martin, July 24, 1970, Dallas, Texas. Bishop Martin was a student at SMU when it opened and later served on the Board of Trustees. After a distinguished career in the ministry, he was elected bishop in 1944. He retired in 1968.

39. Robert Goodloe, "Methodism in Texas, 1900-1950," Bridwell Library, SMU, p. 48.

40. Dorothy Amann, "Southern Methodist University—1913-1915" (1940), Archives, McFarlin Auditorium, SMU.

41. *Dallas Morning News*, April 14, 1911.

42. *Texas Christian Advocate*, June 29, 1911.

43. John S. Brubacher and Willis Rudy, *Higher Education in Transition* (New York: Harper & Bros., 1958), p. 360.

44. *Texas Christian Advocate*, June 29, 1911.

45. Ibid.

46. Ibid., September 7, 1911.

47. Ibid., May 27, 1915.

48. Ibid., November 9 and 23, 1911.

49. Hyer to Boaz, February 22, 1911.

50. *Texas Christian Advocate*, December 21, 1911. These men received able assistance from H. D. Knickerbocker, a Methodist minister, who obtained approximately 125 pledges of $1,000 or more. A plaque was erected in the rotunda of Dallas Hall in honor of the "Knickerbocker Special."

51. Boaz, *Eighty-four Golden Years*, p. 88.

52. Minutes of the Board of Trustees of Southern Methodist University, June 4, 1912.

53. Ibid., June 30, 1913.

54. Ibid., June 7, 1917.

55. Boaz, *Eighty-four Golden Years*, p. 90.

56. *Texas Christian Advocate*, July 3, 1913.

57. Minutes of the Board, June 4, 1912.

58. Ibid., February 7, 1913.

59. Ibid., June 4, 1912.

60. Minutes of the Board, April 30, 1915; see also C. C. Walsh, former board member, to Charles C. Selecman, September 10, 1933, Office of the President, SMU. Walsh gives more detailed information than the financial report does.

61. Minutes of the Board, April 30, 1915.

62. Ibid., August 31, 1916.

63. Ibid., October 12, 1916.

64. Ibid., June 13, 1921. These financial reports were interpreted with the aid of the late Wiggs Babb, former auditor of SMU.

65. *Campus*, September, 1912. This newspaper was issued monthly by Frank Reedy for promotional purposes from 1912 to 1914.

66. Minutes of the Board, June 12, 1920.

67. Report of [Financial] Commissioners SMU, August 1, 1913, to February 14, 1914, Office of the President, SMU.

68. Rupert Norval Richardson, *Texas, The Lone Star State* (New York: Prentice-Hall, 1943), p. 404.

69. Minutes of the Board, June 2, 1915.

70. *Texas Christian Advocate*, November 2, 1911, and April 18, 1912; *Southern Methodist University Bulletin*, February 1, 1912; *Campus*, June, 1912.

71. *Texas Christian Advocate*, November 12, 1914.

72. *Texas Christian Advocate*, February 11, 1915.

73. Minutes of the Commission of Education, 1911-1914, p. 25.

74. Minutes of the Board, June 30, 1913.

75. *Texas Christian Advocate*, August 17, 1911.

76. *Campus*, January, 1916.

77. *Texas Christian Advocate*, September 3, 1914.

78. *Texas Christian Advocate*, July 15, 1915.

79. Minutes of the Board, June 3, 1915.

CHAPTER FOUR

1 Robert S. Hyer, "The Purposes and Ideals of a University," *Campus*, August, 1912.

2. John S. Brubacher and Willis Rudy, *Higher Education in Transition* (New York: Harper & Bros., 1958), pp. 179-80.

3. *Bulletin of SMU*, November 1966, p. 33.

4. Ibid., April 1921, p. 95.

5. Ibid., May 1926, p. 137.

6. Ibid., p. 69.

7. Ibid., lists of students and alumni from 1915 to 1920.

8. Minutes of the Board of Trustees of Southern Methodist University, June 8, 1918.

9. Amann, "Southern Methodist University—1913-1915," Archives, SMU.

10. *Bulletin of SMU*, June 1918, p. 24; June 1929, p. 23; June 1940, p. 26.

11. Brubacher and Rudy, *Higher Education in Transition*, p. 265.

12. Ibid., p. 110.

13. SMU operated on a term or quarter basis from 1915 to 1924, when it changed to a semester system.

14. This information was taken from *Bulletin of SMU*, 1915-1940.

15. Hyer, "The Purposes and Ideals of a University."

16. All of this information on the curriculum is taken from the *Bulletin of SMU*, 1915-1944.

17. *Campus*, June 8, 1922.

18. The usual art courses of painting and drawing were taught by the same teacher in the College of Liberal Arts, which made the creation of this new college seem an unnatural division.

19. Minutes of the Commission of Education, 1911-1914, p. 67.

20. This notebook is in the Archives, SMU.

21. Herbert Gambrell, professor emeritus of history, "Notes on the Deanship of the College of Southern Methodist University," Archives, McFarlin Auditorium, SMU, 1958, p. 4.

22. Minutes of the General Faculty, October 2, 1916.

23. Gambrell, "Notes on the Deanship," p. 2.

24. Ibid., p. 4.

25. During his three years, Wannamaker wrote a poem which was adopted as Southern Methodist University's ode.

26. McGinnis and the *Review* will be discussed in chap. 6.

27. Herbert Gambrell, "John Hathaway McGinnis," *Proceedings of the Philosophical Society of Texas* 14 (Dallas, 1961): 12-14.

28. Jay B. Hubbell to Herbert Gambrell, December 8, 1960, Archives, McFarlin Auditorium, SMU.

29. Jay B. Hubbell, "*Southwest Review*, 1924-1927," *South and Southwest: Literary Essays and Reminiscences* (Durham: Duke University Press, 1965), p. 20.

30. Jay B. Hubbell, "The Makers," *Prairie Pegasus* (Dallas, 1924), p. 5; see also *Announcement of Awards, Prizes for Original Poems,* SMU, 1922-27, Archives, SMU; *Semi-Weekly Campus*, March 21, 1922, April 6, 1923, March 28, 1924, April 18, 1925.

31. Hubbell, "The Makers," *Prairie Pegasus*, p. 2; *Announcement of Awards, 1922.*

32. Herbert Gambrell, "Something about the Department of History," Archives, McFarlin Auditorium, SMU, 1954, p. 3.

33. Ibid.

34. Ibid.

35. Ibid. The Selecman-Doty incident is discussed in chap. 7.

36. In the faculty minutes, Gambrell appears as a faculty leader.

37. Harvie Branscomb to Herbert Gambrell, September 17, 1964, Archives, McFarlin Auditorium, SMU.

38. S. W. Geiser, "Edward Otto Heuse (1879-1954)," *Field & Laboratory* 22 (June 1954): 61-65.

39. Geiser, "Ellis William Shuler, Ph.D., LL.D.," *Field & Laboratory* 21 (January 1953): 5-8.

40. Geiser, "John Daniel Boon (1874-1952)," *Field & Laboratory* 20 (January 1952): 5-7.

41. Oral interview with Hemphill Hosford, provost emeritus of SMU, July 2, 1970.

42. Hosford was on the faculty of the University of Arkansas from 1929 to 1946, when he returned to SMU as dean of the university. He retired in 1962.

43. Hemphill Hosford to author, October 7, 1970.

44. Oral interview with Edwin D. Mouzon, Jr., professor emeritus of mathematics, August 17, 1970. Mouzon served on the athletic committee with McIntosh and followed him as chairman.

45. C. F. Zeek, "Early SMU: Some Reminiscences," Archives, McFarlin Auditorium, SMU, 1965.

46. Ivan Lee Holt to Herbert Gambrell, October 26, 1964, Archives, McFarlin Auditorium, SMU.

47. Edyth Renshaw, "The Show Must Go On," Archives, McFarlin Auditorium, SMU, 1964, p. 1. Renshaw was a student of McCord's and was a faculty member from 1924 to 1967.

48. Amann, "SMU—1913-1915"; Ivan Lee Holt to Herbert Gambrell, October 26, 1964, Archives, McFarlin Auditorium, SMU; "Dorothy Amann," *Dallas News*, May 2, 1963.

49. William C. Martin to Herbert Gambrell, July 10, 1965, Archives, McFarlin Auditorium, SMU. *Bulletin of SMU*, June 1916, p. 69.

50. Ivan Lee Holt, "Early Years at S.M.U.", Archives, McFarlin Auditorium, SMU.

51. Martin to Gambrell, July 10, 1965.

52. Branscomb to Gambrell, September 17, 1964.

53. Martin to Gambrell, July 10, 1965; *Texas Christian Advocate*, July 15, 1916.

54. Paul van Katwijk, "My First Year at Southern Methodist University," Archives, McFarlin Auditorium, SMU, 1964, p. 2; see also *Bulletin of SMU*, June 1916.

55. This figure was computed by averaging the ages of the arts faculty.

56. See table 3, p. 143.

57. Branscomb to Gambrell, September 17, 1964.

58. *Texas Christian Advocate*, August 26, 1915.

59. Minutes of the General Faculty, September 16, 1915.

60. Annual Report of the President to the Board, June 8, 1916.

61. Richard J. Storr, *Harper's University: The Beginnings* (Chicago: University of Chicago Press, 1966), p. 257.

62. Annual Report of the President to the Board, June 8, 1916.

63. Minutes of the General Faculty, December 4, 1918, p. 88.

64. Hemphill Hosford, "Southern Methodist University, World War I, 1917-18," Archives, McFarlin Auditorium, SMU, 1954.

65. Report of the President to the Board of Trustees, June 8, 1918.

66. Minutes of the Board, June 7, 1917, and June 9, 1918.

67. *Campus*, April 13, 1917.

68. Report of the President to the Board, June 7, 1917.

69. *Campus*, April 6, 1917.

70. Minutes of the General Faculty, May 1, 1917.

71. Report of the President to the Board, June 7, 1917.

72. Ibid.

73. Hosford, "SMU and World War I," pp. 5-6.

74. Minutes of the General Faculty, May 8, 1918.

75. *Campus*, October 1, 1918.

76. Ibid., October 23, 1918.

77. Report of the President to the Board, June 8, 1918.

78. Minutes of the Board, April 25, 1917; *Campus*, April 27, 1917.

79. *House Rules, Women's Building, 1925*, Archives, SMU. Similar rules were in effect during the early years.

80. Flora Lowrey, on her student days, Archives, McFarlin Auditorium, SMU, 1964.

81. Minutes of the Board, October 12, 1916; Ray Hyer Brown, *Robert Stewart Hyer: The Man I Knew* (Salado, Texas: Anson Jones Press, 1957), pp. 161-62.

82. Brubacher and Rudy, *Higher Education in Transition*, p. 122.

83. Goldie Capers Smith, "A Part of All That I Have Met," Archives, McFarlin Auditorium, SMU, 1964, p. 4.

84. *Bulletin of SMU*, June 1917, p. 33.

85. Minutes of the Board, June 8, 1916. Smith later was elected bishop and served as chairman of the board.

86. *Bulletin of SMU*, June 1916; June 1917, p. 33.

87. Minutes of the General Faculty, November 16 and November 30, 1915.

88. Brubacher and Rudy, *Higher Education in Transition*, p. 119.

89. Ibid., pp. 120-21.

90. *Bulletin of SMU*, June 1918, p. 15.

91. Ibid., p. 19.

92. These conclusions were reached by reading the Minutes of the General Faculty.

93. Minutes of the General Faculty, September 28, 1915.

94. Charles W. Ferguson, "How the Honor Council Worked," *Mustang* 2 (June 1938): 7-9.

95. Year	Percent of Students 100 Miles or Less	Percent of Students 100 Miles or More
1915-16	68	32
1917-18	70	30
1919-20	70	30
1925-26	79	21

96. Branscomb to Gambrell, September 7, 1964.

97. Ibid.

98. Flora Lowrey, on her student days, p. 7.

99. Van Katwijk, "My First Year at SMU," p. 1.

100. Herbert Gambrell, "The Way I Remember It," *Mustang* (May 1951), p. 18.

CHAPTER FIVE

1. H. A. Boaz, *Eighty-four Golden Years* (Nashville: Parthenon Press, 1951), p. 91.

2. Minutes of the Board of Trustees of Southern Methodist University, June 3, 1919.

3. *Bulletin of SMU*, June 1917, p. 13, and June 1920, p. 15.

4. Minutes of the Board, June 3, 1915.

5. Ibid., August 31, 1916.

6. Ibid., May 2, 1922.

7. Ibid., February 20, 1920.

8. Ibid., June 9, 1919.

9. Ibid., July 9, 1918.

10. J. W. Blanton, "Southern Methodist University Faces a Crisis," Blanton Papers, Office of the President, SMU, 1954. Blanton was one of the twenty businessmen, as well as having been a member of the Commission of Education, 1911-1914, that founded the university.

11. Edwin D. Mouzon to John M. Moore, April 18, 1919; Moore to Mouzon, April 21, 1919, Mouzon Letters, Bridwell Library, SMU.

12. F. N. Duncan, R. A. Hearon, J. S. McIntosh, O. D. Wannamaker, J. P. Comer, A. D. Schuessler, C. F. Zeek, John H. McGinnis, S. A. Myatt, E. O. Heuse, and E. H. Jones to Edwin D. Mouzon, chairman of the Board of Trustees of Southern Methodist University, June 4, 1919, Mouzon Letters, Bridwell Library, SMU.

13. Boaz, *Eighty-four Golden Years*, p. 100.

14. Edwin D. Mouzon to H. A. Boaz, December 10, 1919, Mouzon Letters, Bridwell Library, SMU.

15. Boaz, *Eighty-four Golden Years*, p. 101.

16. J. E. Cockrell to H. A. Boaz, February 13, 1920, Boaz Letters, Bridwell Library, SMU; Boaz, *Eighty-four Golden Years*, pp. 101-2.

17. Ray Hyer Brown, *Robert Stewart Hyer: The Man I Knew* (Salado, Texas: Anson Jones Press, 1957), p. 162.

18. Minutes of the Board, February 20, 1920.

19. Ibid., June 10, 1919.

20. Edwin D. Mouzon to W. D. Bradfield, November 14, 1919, Mouzon Letters, Bridwell Library, SMU.

21. Minutes of the Board, February 20, 1920.

22. Brown, *Robert Stewart Hyer*, pp. 166-67; John M. Moore, *Life and I* (Nashville: Parthenon Press, 1948), p. 211; Minutes of the Board, June 12, 1920. Hyer and Buttrick had first met fifteen years earlier when Hyer was trying to secure money for Southwestern.

23. Annual Report of the President, Minutes of the Board, June 4, 1920.

24. Minutes of the Board, February 20, 1920.

25. Ibid., June 12, 1920; Boaz, *Eighty-four Golden Years*, p. 105.

26. Annual Report of the President, Minutes of the Board, May 2, 1922.

27. Boaz, *Eighty-four Golden Years*, p. 107; Annual Report of the President, Minutes of the Board, May 2, 1922.

28. Minutes of the Board, May 2, 1922.

29. Ibid., June 12, 1920.

30. See pp. 39-40.

31. Thorkelson's report, Minutes of the Board, May 2, 1922.

32. Annual Report of the President, Minutes of the Board, June 9, 1924.

33. Ibid.

34. Ibid.

35. Rupert Norval Richardson, *Texas, The Lone Star State* (New York: Prentice-Hall, 1943), pp. 440-43.

36. Annual Report of the President, Minutes of the Board, June 13, 1921.

37. Minutes of the Board, June 9, 1924. Using the figures listed, 71.5 percent of the dollars and 83.6 percent of the donors came from Dallas.

38. *Bulletin of SMU*, June 1925, Tables of Enrollments.

39. Annual Report of the President, Minutes of the Board, June 9, 1924.

40. Minutes of the Board, July 21, 1922.

41. Annual Report of the President, Minutes of the Board, June 13, 1921.

42. Minutes of the Board, December 31, 1923.

43. Annual Report of the President, Minutes of the Board, June 24, 1919.

44. Minutes of the Board, June 13, 1921.

45. Boaz, *Eighty-four Golden Years*, p. 109.

46. Minutes of the Board, June 13, 1921.

47. James Atkins to Mrs. H. A. Boaz, July 11, 1922, in which the bishop gives Boaz credit for saving the university. This letter is in the personal possession of Ruth Boaz Penniman, Dallas, Texas.

48. Minutes of the Board, May 2, 1922.

49. Cullom H. Booth to Edwin D. Mouzon, September 6, 1922, Mouzon Letters, Bridwell Library, SMU.

50. Ibid.

51. Minutes of the Board, October 11, 1922.

52. *Campus*, October 14, 1922.

53. Ibid.

54. Ibid., October 20, 1922.

55. Minutes of the Board, October 11, 1922; *Campus*, October 14, 1922.

56. Minutes of the Board, October 11, 1922.

57. Ivan Lee Holt, "Early Years at S.M.U.," Archives, McFarlin Auditorium, SMU, p. 5.

58. *Dallas Morning News*, March 22, 1923; Minutes of the Board, March 21, 1923.

59. *Campus*, March 31, 1923.

60. Harold V. Ratliff, *The Power and the Glory: The Story of Southwest Conference Football* (Lubbock, Texas: Texas Tech Press, 1957), p. 123.

61. Boaz, *Eighty-four Golden Years*, p. 111.

62. In nearly every issue of the *Campus*, 1921-22, there was a reference to the future Mustangs.

63. Boaz, *Eighty-four Golden Years*, pp. 111-12.

64. This paper was published only on April 1, and its name came from the streetcar that ran between the end of the Dallas streetcar line and the campus.

65. *Dinkey*, April 1, 1922, Office of the President, SMU; *Campus*, April 20, 1922; Minutes of the Board, April 14, 1922.

66. *Campus*, May 11, 1922.

67. These facts were established in the subsequent investigation.

68. *Rotunda*, 1921 and 1922.

69. *Campus*, December 8, 1922; *Dallas Morning News*, December 8, 1922. Those favoring suspension were the University of Texas, Texas A&M, Rice, and the University of Arkansas; those opposed were Oklahoma A&M, Baylor, and SMU.

70. *Campus*, December 8, 1922.

71. James Kilgore, E. D. Jennings, Paul B. Kern, and R. A. Hearon to Charles Selecman, February 19, 1923, Office of the President, SMU.

72. Minutes of the Board, January 13, 1923.

73. Majority Report of the Athletic Committee, February 10, 1923, Office of the President, SMU; *Semi-Weekly Campus*, February 17, 1923.

74. Minutes of the General Faculty, February 15, 1923.

75. Majority Report of the Athletic Committee, February 10, 1923; *Semi-Weekly Campus*, February 17, 1923; *Dallas Morning News*, February 16, 1923.

76. J. E. Cockrell to E. H. Jones, January 11, 1923; Minutes of the Board, January 13, 1923.

77. Minutes of the Board, February 8, 1923.

78. *Semi-Weekly Campus*, February 10, 1923.

79. Edwin D. Mouzon to Cullom H. Booth, September 14, 1922, Mouzon Letters, Bridwell Library, SMU.

80. Minutes of the Board, July 21 and October 11, 1922.

81. Edwin D. Mouzon to Charles Selecman, March 31, 1923, Mouzon Letters, Bridwell Library, SMU.

82. J. E. Cockrell to James Kilgore, Paul B. Kern, E. D. Jennings, and R. A. Hearon, February 23, 1923, Office of the President, SMU.

83. *Semi-Weekly Campus*, February 17, 1923.

84. J. E. Cockrell, *A Review of the Athletic Situation and the Case of Huff and Smith* (n.p., n.d.).

85. Minutes of the Board, February 8, 1923.

86. Oral interview with Garland Smith, April 3, 1969, Atlanta, Georgia. Smith was on the faculty of SMU in 1923 and followed these events with interest. He feels confident that Whaling, not Cockrell, did most of the work on the book.

87. Minutes of the Board, March 31, 1923.

88. Ibid.

89. Kenneth K. Bailey, *Southern White Protestantism in the Twentieth Century* (New York: Harper & Row, 1964), pp. 70-71.

90. Katherine Balderston to Herbert Gambrell, February 5, 1965, Archives, McFarlin Auditorium, SMU.

91. Ibid.

92. Katherine Balderston later received the Ph.D. from Yale University and pursued a distinguished teaching career at Wellesley College.

93. *Campus*, September 22, 1920.

94. Ibid., December 8, 1920.

95. John A. Rice, *The Old Testament in the Life of Today* (New York: Macmillan Co., 1920), pp. vii-viii.

96. John A. Rice, letter to the *Texas Christian Advocate*, September 22, 1921.

97. S. A. Steel, "From the Pelican Pines," *Texas Christian Advocate*, April 14, 1921.

98. C. B. Meador, letter to the *Texas Christian Advocate*, September 8, 1921.

99. Edwin D. Mouzon, "Dr. John Rice and His Book 'The Old Testament in the Life of Today,'" *Texas Christian Advocate*, July 28, 1921.

100. Ibid.

101. Norman F. Furniss, *The Fundamentalist Controversy, 1918-1931* (New Haven: Yale University Press, 1954), pp. 86-87.

102. Ibid., pp. 121-22.

103. Boaz, *Eighty-four Golden Years*, p. 110.

104. *Campus*, June 1, 1922.

105. Minutes of the Board, October 3, 1921.

106. Ibid., October 4, 1921.

107. Ibid., October 11, 1921.

108. Boaz, *Eighty-four Golden Years*, pp. 110-11.

109. Minutes of the Board, November 25. 1921.

110. Walter N. Vernon, *Methodism Moves across North Texas* (Dallas: Historical Society of North Texas Conference, 1967), p. 281.

111. John A. Rice to Edwin D. Mouzon, October 23, 1922; Mouzon to Rice, November 6, 1922, Mouzon Letters, Bridwell Library, SMU.

112. *Campus*, November 8, 1921.

113. Ibid., January 11, 1922.

114. Ibid., June 1, 1922.

115. Upton Sinclair, *The Goose-Step* (published by the author, Pasadena, California, 1922), pp. 352-53.

116. *Campus*, September 22, 1920.

117. Furniss, *The Fundamentalist Controversy, 1918-1931*, pp. 52-53.

118. *Campus*, May 5, 1923. The student's parents were missionaries to China.

119. Forest E. Dudley to Walter N. Vernon, July 18, 1966, cited in Vernon, *Methodism Moves across North Texas*, p. 283. Dudley was a student assistant to Workman in 1922-23. Later he became a prominent Methodist minister serving the First Methodist Church in Dallas before his retirement.

120. *Campus*, May 5, 1923.

121. *Dallas Times Herald*, May 7, 1925.

122. Ibid.

123. Ibid., May 8, 1925.

124. Ibid., May 7, 1925.

125. Herbert Gambrell to author, March 24, 1971.

126. *Rotunda*, 1925, p. 50.

127. Program for Senior Vespers, May 31, 1925, Archival Boxes, Fondren Library, SMU.

128. *Campus*, May 6, 1925; *Dallas Times Herald*, May 5 and May 8, 1925. See also "Principle or Expediency? an open letter to Dr. Charles C. Selecman from George M. Gibson, Jr., touching the case of Mims Thornburg Workman, May 26, 1925," Archival Boxes, Fondren Library, SMU.

129. Bryan Hall to Herbert Gambrell, March 15, 1965, Archives, McFarlin Auditorium, SMU. Hall was one of the students who appeared before the board. See also Minutes of the Board, June 1, 1925.

130. Minutes of the Board, June 1, 1925.

131. Gambrell to author, March 24, 1971. Selecman always stressed "cooperation" and "internal harmony" in his annual reports to the board. He often claimed such a situation existed when, indeed, the facts show otherwise.

132. Gambrell to author, March 24 and April 13, 1971. Gambrell was a close friend of Workman's in 1925.

133. Mims Thornburg Workman to Herbert Gambrell, November 10, 1964, Archives, McFarlin Auditorium, SMU.

134. *Who's Who in Methodism*, 1952, p. 764.

135. Gambrell to author, April 13, 1971.

136. Minutes of the General Faculty, May 29, 1925. See also *Dallas Morning News*, May 30, 1925.

137. Herbert Gambrell to author, March 13, 1971.

138. *Dallas Morning News*, May 30, 1925.

139. Ibid., June 1, 1925.

140. Harvie Branscomb to author, April 7, 1971. Selecman's exact words were, "I have just read your gratuitous letter in the morning *News* and want to say to you that the sooner you leave this campus the better."

141. The minutes do not contain Branscomb's statement, only a sentence that he submitted his resignation. See also *Dallas Morning News*, June 3, 1925.

142. Branscomb became dean of the Duke divinity school in 1945 and served as chancellor of Vanderbilt, 1946-1963. In 1961 SMU awarded him an honorary doctorate. By his actions in this matter Selecman may have harmed his chances to be elected bishop in 1930, because the Branscombs were a strong Methodist family in Alabama and the Workmans equally influential in Arkansas. Harvie Branscomb's father headed the Alabama delegates and refused to support Selecman, according to Herbert Gambrell.

143. Daniel B. Stevick, *Beyond Fundamentalism* (Richmond, Va.: John Knox Press, 1964), p. 22.

144. Moore, *Life and I*, pp. 150-51.

145. *Nashville Christian Advocate*, March 15, 1929.

146. There are twenty-four letters in the Moore collection, Bridwell Library, SMU, which praise the bishop's stand.

147. Edwin D. Mouzon, *So-Called Fundamentalism* (Nashville, 1923), p. 4.

CHAPTER SIX

1. Minutes of the Board of Trustees of Southern Methodist University, June 13, 1921, and June 1, 1925.

2. Ibid., June 1, 1925.

3. *Campus*, March 31, 1923.

4. Minutes of the Board, June 12, 1923.

5. Ibid., June 1, 1925.

6. Ibid. This money was borrowed and was part of the debt during the 1930s.

7. *Campus*, February 9, 1924.

8. Minutes of the Board, June 9, 1924.

9. *Campus*, March 3, 1926.

10. Minutes of the Board, June 12, 1923.

11. Ibid., June 9, 1924.

12. Ibid., June 4, 1928. The discrepancy in the figures probably occurs because of interest charges.

13. Ibid.

14. Ibid., June 6, 1931.

15. Ibid., March 23-24, 1926.

16. Ibid., June 4, 1928. The discrepancy in the figures probably occurs because of interest charges.

17. *Campus*, January 15, 1926.

18. Minutes of the Board, June 7, 1938.

19. *Campus*, February 8, 1939.

20. Ibid., February 13, 1926; *Dallas Morning News*, February 13, 1926.

21. Minutes of the Board, June 4, 1926.

22. Ibid., March 23-24, 1926.

23. Oral interviews with Jay Osborne, then business manager, August 11, 1970, and with Layton Bailey, retired business manager, August 12, 1970.

24. Minutes of the Board, March 23-24, 1926.

25. Ibid., June 1, 1931. Evidently the total amount pledged was never collected.

26. *Campus*, September 10, 1926. Atkins Hall has since undergone another name change. In 1965 it was completely remodeled with money from the Clements family and is now a classroom building known as Clements Hall.

27. Wilbur Evans and Bill Mouzon, eds., *The Official Southwest Athletic Conference Football Roster and Record Book, 1970* (Dallas: Southwest Athletic Conference, 1970), p. 198.

28. Minutes of the Board, June 6, 1923.

29. *Campus*, October 2, 1926.

30. Minutes of the Board, March 23-24, 1926.

31. Ibid., June 4, 1926.

32. *Campus*, October 2, 1926.

33. Minutes of the Board, June 7, 1927. This was a tentative figure; when the fiscal year closed, athletics showed a deficit of $5,840.

34. Ibid., June 1, 1931. See list of summary figures on athletic expenses in Minutes of the Board, June 7, 1932.

35. Minutes of the Board, June 4, 1926, June 7, 1927, June 4, 1928, and June 3, 1929.

36. Ibid., March 22, 1928.

37. Ibid., January 18, 1938.

38. Hemphill Hosford to author, March 4, 1971. Mrs. Fondren told Hosford of the incident in 1954.

39. Minutes of the Board, June 4, 1940. Fondren died in 1939 and Mrs. Fondren was selected to fill his place on the board. She has continued her interest in SMU and is a powerful force on the board.

40. Ibid., June 6, 1939.

41. *Campus*, September 1, 1939.

42. The main approach to the university from Dallas is up Bishop Boulevard, which was named for Horace Bishop, who served on the educational commission that founded SMU and was also the first chairman of the Board of Trustees.

43. See map, opposite p. 52.

44. James F. White, *Architecture at SMU: 50 Years and 50 Buildings* (Dallas: SMU Press, 1966), p. 3.

45. Minutes of the Board, March 22, 1928.

46. A building had been built in 1928 at a cost of $22,000.

47. By 1929 the university was recognized by the Association of Colleges and Secondary Schools of the Southern States, the Association of American Universities, and the American Association of University Women. In 1935 it became a member of the Southern University Conference.

48. Report of the Board of Trustees of Southern Methodist University to the Methodist Episcopal Church, South, May 7, 1930, p. 19; *Bulletin of SMU*, October 1930, p. 223.

49. Minutes of the Board, February 10, 1925.

50. Ibid., February 11, 1925.

51. Report of the Board to the M.E. Church, South, May 7, 1930, p. 19.

52. *Bulletin of SMU*, October 1940, p. 208.

53. *Campus*, March 11, 1925.

54. Report of the Board to the M.E. Church, South, May 7, 1930, p. 20.

55. Originally architecture was included in the areas of specialization, but it was dropped after the first year.

56. Minutes of the Board, March 23, 1926; the report of the dean of the engineering school, Earl Flath, which was included in the minutes, was far more realistic about the cost.

57. Oral interview with Hemphill Hosford, January 1, 1971.

58. Annual Report of the Registrar to the President, 1939-40, Office of the President, SMU.

59. *Bulletin of SMU*, April 1926, p. 203; April 1930, p. 222.

60. Minutes of the Board, June 6, 1933; Report of the Dean of the College of Arts and Sciences to the President, 1932-33.

61. Minutes of the Board, June 4, 1935.

62. Ibid., June 6, 1939.

63. Ibid., February 6, 1940.

64. Ibid., February 10, 1925.

65. *Campus*, February 21, 1925.

66. *Bulletin of SMU*, October 1940, pp. 236-41.

67. Annual Report of the Registrar 1939-40, Office of the President, SMU.

68. *Bulletin of SMU*, June 1930, p. 246.

69. The first two members of the law faculty were William Alexander Rhea

(LL.B., Texas, 1894) and Robert Bourland Holland (LL.B., Texas, 1925). Peter J. Hamilton, a once able lawyer and judge in Puerto Rico, was elected dean in 1926. But he arrived much broken in health and was relieved of his duties after one month.

70. Oral interview with Hemphill Hosford, January 1, 1971.

71. Minutes of the Board, June 7, 1938, June 6, 1939; *Bulletin of SMU*, October 1940, p. 236.

72. Minutes of the Board, June 7, 1938.

73. Annual Report of the Registrar, 1939-40; in 1938-39 there were 80 day and 165 evening students; in 1939-40 there were 86 day and 155 evening students.

74. Minutes of the Board, June 4, 1940.

75. Annual Report of the Registrar, 1946-47.

76. Ibid., 1939-40.

77. Ibid.

78. See p. 60.

79. Minutes of the Board, February 11, 1925, March 23, 1926. On these two occasions the chairman of the department, C. A. Nichols, gave a lengthy report to the board.

80. These figures were compiled from the *SMU Bulletin* of 1920, 1925, 1935, and 1940. A further analysis of the courses shows:

1920	*1925*	*1930*	*1935*
3 elementary	7 elementary	7 elementary	4 elementary
1 intermediate	12 intermediate	21 intermediate	19 intermediate
10 advanced	27 advanced	26 advanced	35 advanced
14 total	46 total	54 total	58 total

81. Minutes of the Board, March 23, 1926.

82. See table 2, p. 121.

83. Minutes of the Board, February 11, 1925 and March 23, 1926.

84. Ibid., May 2, 1922; Annual Report of the Registrar to the President, 1921-22.

85. These facts were compiled from the *Bulletin of SMU* for the respective years.

86. See table 1, p. 121.

87. Minutes of the Board, February 6, 1941.

88. These figures were compiled from the Annual Report of the Registrar to the President, 1922-1940.

YEARS	B.A. AND B.S. DEGREES IN ACADEMIC SUBJECTS		B.S. DEGREES IN COMMERCE, EDUCATION, PHYSICAL EDUCATION, JOURNALISM, AND HOME ECONOMICS	
	Number	Percent	Number	Percent
1922-26	487	84	93	16
1927-31	690	72	273	28
1932-36	674	65	358	35
1937-40	488	55	400	45

89. Richard Hofstadter and Wilson Smith, eds., *American Higher Education: A Documentary History* (Chicago: University of Chicago Press, 1961), 2:894.

90. Abraham Flexner, *Universities: American, English, and German* (New York: Oxford University Press, 1930), pp. 41-42, 74-77.

91. Robert M. Hutchins, *The Higher Learning in America* (New Haven: Yale University Press, 1936), pp. 29-38, 85-87.

92. Harry D. Gideonse, *The Higher Learning in a Democracy* (New York: Holt, Rinehart, & Winston, 1936), pp. 38-39, 30-34.

93. John Dewey, "President Hutchins' Proposals to Remake Higher Education," *Social Frontier* 3 (January 1937): 103-4.

94. Minutes of the College Council, March 28, 1934.

95. Report of the College Curriculum Committee, SMU, April 15, 1940, Fondren Library, SMU. This report was begun in 1934, but was not completed and compiled until 1940 after Umphrey Lee was elected president.

96. Ibid.

97. See biographical material on Linus Glanville, p. 137, and on I. K. Stephens, p. 134.

98. Herbert Gambrell, Tentative Plan for Handling Social Science 1 and 2, February 9, 1935, Gambrell's personal files, Dallas; Gambrell to author, February 13, 1971.

99. *Bulletin of SMU*, October 1935, p. 111.

100. Gambrell to author, February 13, 1971. Gambrell also suggests in a letter to the dean of the college, August 31, 1962, that the divisional major was devised to keep the one- or two-man departments from being abolished during the depression. This letter is in Gambrell's personal files.

101. Gambrell to author, February 13, 1971.

102. *Bulletin of SMU*, January 1942, p. 25.

103. Minutes of the Board, June 6, 1939.

104. Report of the College Curriculum Committee, April 15, 1940.

105. Ibid., part 3, General Suggestions and Recommendations, pp. 1-5.

106. Minutes of the Board, June 4, 1940.

107. *Bulletin of SMU*, 1950-53.

CHAPTER SEVEN

1. Oral interview with Samuel Wood Geiser, professor emeritus of biology, December 31, 1970. Selecman made this request of Geiser during the late twenties when Geiser was doing writing in his office in the evening.

2. Statement made by John H. McGinnis to Samuel Wood Geiser, quoted in biographical article on Edward Otto Heuse, *Field & Laboratory* 22 (June 1954): 63.

3. Jay B. Hubbell, "Southwest Review, 1924-1927," *Southwest Review* 50 (Winter 1965): 4.

4. Ibid., pp. 7-11.

5. Henry Nash Smith, "McGinnis and the *Southwest Review*: A Reminiscence," *Southwest Review* 40 (Autumn 1955): 301.

6. Ibid., pp. 302-3.

7. Ibid., p. 303.

8. Charles W. Ferguson, "McGinnis: Portrait of an Individual," *Southwest Review* 45 (Summer 1960): 198. This article was published at the time of McGinnis's death. Ferguson himself had gone on to a writing career as an editor of the *Reader's Digest* and author of several books.

9. Minutes of the Board of Trustees of Southern Methodist University, June 7, 1927.

10. Ibid., June 6, 1933.

11. Smith, "McGinnis and the *Southwest Review*," pp. 306-7. See also Mary Maud Trippet, *A History of the "Southwest Review"* (Ann Arbor: University microfilms, published on demand).

12. J. Frank Dobie, "As the Moving Finger Writ," *Southwest Review* 40 (Autumn 1955): 293.

13. Smith, "McGinnis and the *Southwest Review*," p. 301.

14. Samuel Wood Geiser, *Naturalists of the Frontier* (Dallas: University Press in Dallas, 1937), pp. 11-12.

15. Minutes of the Board, January 26, 1936. The Schoellkopf family donated the money because they were the descendants of Jacob Boll, one of the naturalists in Geiser's book.

16. Allen Maxwell, "The First One Hundred Books: A Brief History of Southern

Methodist University Press, 1937-1964," *Journal of the Graduate Research Center* 33 (August 1964): 55-56.

17. Ibid., pp. 56-57.

18. Herbert Gambrell, "James Stephen Hogg: Statesman or Demagogue?" *Southwest Review* 13 (April 1928): 338-66; "Anson Jones," Ibid. 18 (January 1933): 139-68. See biographical material on Gambrell, chap. 4, above.

19. H. A. Trexler, "Episode in Border History," *Southwest Review* 16 (January 1931): 236-50; "The Causes of Confederate Defeat," Ibid. 18 (October 1932): 87-95; "The Confederate Navy Department and the Fall of New Orleans," Ibid. 19 (October 1933): 88-102.

20. Herbert Gambrell, "Something about the Department of History," Archives, McFarlin Auditorium, SMU, 1954, p. 3.

21. Jerry Bywaters, "With Southwestern Artists," *Southwest Review* 16 (October 1930): 137-39; "More about Southwestern Architecture," Ibid. 18 (April 1933): 234-64; "Dallas Allied Arts Show," Ibid. 20 (April 1935): 319-20; "The New Texas Painters," Ibid. 21 (April 1936): 330-42.

22. Ernest E. Leisy, "The Novel in America: Notes for a Survey," *Southwest Review* 22 (October 1936): 88-99.

23. I. K. Stephens, "Edmund Montgomery: The Hermit Philosopher of Liendo Plantation," *Southwest Review* 16 (January 1931): 200-235.

24. Hemphill Hosford to author, January 20, 1971.

25. There were really only four departments, because geology and geography were not divided.

26. Oral interview with Samuel Wood Geiser, December 31, 1970.

27. *Field & Laboratory* 1 (November 1932): 31.

28. These figures were compiled by Samuel Wood Geiser, December, 1970.

29. S. W. Geiser, "John Daniel Boon (1874-1952)," *Field & Laboratory* 20 (January 1952): 7.

30. See earlier reference, chap. 4, p. 56.

31. Minutes of the Board, June 9, 1924.

32. *Bulletin of SMU*, June 1929, pp. 112-14.

33. The Arnold School of Government had always operated somewhat independently of the university since Mrs. Arnold retained partial control over the endowment funds. By 1932 Mrs. Arnold was dissatisfied with "her" foundation and desired to give it further identity of its own. At her request Myres proposed a series of scholarly studies and annual conferences devoted to topics of current interest. Myres was then made director and the program launched. Guice was given a teaching assignment in the School of Commerce. Myres wrote a brief account of the Arnold Foundation in a letter to Herbert Gambrell dated May 28, 1971, which is in the Archives.

34. S. D. Myres, Jr., ed., Proceedings of the Institute of Public Affairs (Dallas: Arnold Foundation, 1934-39), Fondren Library, SMU.

35. S. D. Myres, Jr., *Party Bolting: American Foreign Policy—An Interpretation*; *Politics in the South*; *Governmental Reform in Texas*. These are a sample of the titles published by the Arnold Foundation during the 1930s.

36. Glanville's articles were "Revisionism or the Status Quo," "Forces Which Disturb World Peace," and "Fascism and International Peace."

37. Morton B. King and Bruce M. Pringle, "Walter Thompson Watson, 1895-1967," *American Sociologist* 4 (November 1969): 343. Both King and Pringle are currently members of the Department of Sociology at SMU and worked with Watson.

38. E. L. Hooker, "Urban Tourist Camps," Studies in Sociology 1 (Summer 1936): 2-7; "The Greeks and the Independents," Ibid. 3 (Summer 1938): 2-8.

39. Minutes of the Board, June 1, 1939.

40. In 1920 there were seventy-one faculty members in the College of Arts and Sciences, in 1925 sixty-three, and in 1940 sixty-six. These figures come from the *Bulletin of SMU*, June 1930, 1935, and 1940.

41. Winifred T. Weiss and Charles S. Proctor, *Umphrey Lee: A Biography* (Nashville: Abingdon Press, 1971), p. 180.

42. Dobie, "As the Moving Finger Writ," p. 294.

43. John O. Beaty to E. Gordon Perry, member of the Board of Trustees, November 28, 1932, Office of the President, SMU.

44. Charles Selecman to Henry Nash Smith, August 6, 1932, Office of the President, SMU.

45. Dobie, "As the Moving Finger Writ," p. 294.

46. Edwin D. Mouzon, Jr., to Julia Spann, his sister, n.d., personal possession of Mouzon, Dallas, Texas. From the internal evidence the letter was written about the first of October, 1932.

47. Ibid.

48. Henry Nash Smith to Charles Selecman, October 3, 1932, Office of the President, SMU.

49. F. D. Smith had a Ph.D. from the University of Chicago (1916) and had taught Latin and Greek at various midwestern colleges before coming to Dallas.

50. Oral interview with Lon Tinkle, January 21, 1970, Dallas, Texas; Henry Nash Smith to Charles Selecman, November 12, 1932, Office of the President, SMU.

51. Smith used his time during the fall semester of 1932 when his case was being debated to work full time for the *Southwest Review.*

52. Beaty to Perry, November 28, 1932.

53. John O. Beaty to all Methodist ministers in Texas and Oklahoma, December 1, 1932, Moore Letters, Bridwell Library, SMU.

54. Dobie, "As the Moving Finger Writ," p. 294.

55. General Faculty to Charles Selecman, December 9, 1932, Office of the President, SMU.

56. Ivan Lee Holt to John O. Beaty, December 5, 1932, Moore Letters, Bridwell Library, SMU.

57. Minutes of the Board, January 24-25, 1933.

58. Ibid.

59. J. J. Perkins to Charles Selecman, January 27, 1933, Office of the President, SMU.

60. Winifred T. Weiss and Charles S. Proctor, *Umphrey Lee,* p. 182.

61. Charles Selecman to John M. Moore, December 8, 1932, Moore Letters, Bridwell Library, SMU.

62. Minutes of the Board, June 4, 1940.

63. See table 3, p. 143.

64. Ibid.

65. A total of eighty-four graduates of SMU served on the faculty during the twenties and thirties. Those who stayed until retirement or death in addition to the ones mentioned elsewhere were Margaret Harrison in history; Gusta Nance in comparative literature; Roy Seale in mathematics; Edyth Renshaw and David Russell in speech; Aaron Sartain in psychology; Charles Wisseman in education; A. W. Foscue and Frank Rader in business; Dorothy McCommas and Leona Holt in Spanish; William F. Foster and James St. Clair in physical education; Viola Beck van Katwijk and Dora Poteet Barclay in music; Stanley Patterson in engineering; and Robert Goodloe in theology. Dudley W. Curry is still an active faculty member in business administration, as is Nannie M. Fitzhugh in English.

CHAPTER EIGHT

1. See chap. 5, pp. 83-85.

2. Charles W. Ferguson, *Pigskin* (New York: Doubleday, Doran, 1929), p. 57. Ferguson, who was a student at SMU 1919-1923 and editor of the *Campus,* wrote this novel of Martha Sumner University located in Oil City and presided over by Chancellor Horace Ethelmore Dickey. Ferguson uses as prototypes faculty and students from the entire decade, but they are thinly veiled and not difficult to identify.

3. President's Report to the Board of Trustees, June 4, 1928. See also Ferguson, *Pigskin*, pp. 54, 93-96.

4. Ferguson, *Pigskin*, pp. 20, 49-50.

5. Oral interview with Hemphill Hosford, January 7, 1970; Herbert Gambrell to author, March 3, 1971.

6. *Rotunda*, 1927, p. 309.

7. Edwin Lindsey and W. C. Miller to Charles Selecman, June 5, 1927, Office of the President, SMU.

8. A. C. Zumbrunnen, J. W. St. Clair, and E. D. Jennings to Charles Selecman, September 28, 1927, Office of the President, SMU.

9. Minutes of the Board of Trustees of Southern Methodist University, June 7, 1927; Herbert Gambrell, "Something about the Department of History," Archives, McFarlin Auditorium, SMU.

10. See chap. 6, pp. 114-23.

11. Ferguson, *Pigskin*, pp. 196-215. Herein is a vivid description of a homecoming at Martha Sumner University. The young newspaper editor remarks that they might as well close down the university during football season.

12. See chap. 6, pp. 109-10.

13. Ferguson, *Pigskin*, p. 309.

14. Herbert Gambrell to author, March 3, 1971; oral interview with Edwin D. Mouzon, Jr., August 18, 1970; oral interview with Hemphill Hosford, January 6, 1971.

15. *Dallas Morning News*, May 1, 1930.

16. Ibid., May 21 and May 22, 1930.

17. Gambrell to author, March 3, 1971; W. D. Bradfield, "An Interior View of Our Troubles at Southern Methodist University," Office of the President, SMU, 1931. Bradfield was on both the theological faculty and the Board of Trustees.

18. Minutes of the Board, May 29, 1930.

19. *Dallas Morning News*, May 5, 1938.

20. Minutes of the Board, February 4, 1931.

21. R. N. Blackwell to Charles Selecman, February 18, 1931, Office of the President, SMU.

22. Bradfield, "An Interior View," p. 12.

23. Ibid., p. 13.

24. Ibid., p. 14.

25. *Dallas Morning News*, May 15, 1931.

26. Bradfield, "An Interior View," pp. 16-17.

27. Oral interview with Mouzon, August 18, 1970.

28. Minutes of the Board, February 4, 1932.

29. Bradfield, "An Interior View," p. 20.

30. Minutes of the Board, June 1, 1931.

31. Oral interview with Mouzon, August 18, 1970. Mouzon was one of the faculty members who tried to oust Selecman.

32. Minutes of the Board, June 2, 1930.

33. Report of the Dean of the College of Arts and Sciences to the President, May 15, 1930, Fondren Library, SMU.

34. Minutes of the Board, June 2, 1930.

35. Charles Selecman to all the members of the faculty and staff, November 24, 1930, Office of the President, SMU.

36. Bradfield, "An Interior View," p. 7.

37. Oral interview with Mouzon, August 18, 1970; see also *Dallas Times Herald*, May 14, 1931.

38. Bradfield, "An Interior View," pp. 20-22.

39. See chap. 5, p. 90.

40. Bradfield, "An Interior View," p. 28.

41. Minutes of the Board, April 10, 1931.

42. This petition is in Gambrell's personal files. See also *Dallas Times Herald*, May 14, 1931.

43. Ibid.

44. *Bulletin of SMU*, June 1931.

45. Gambrell to author, March 3, 1971.

46. Minutes of the Board, June 1, 1931; *Dallas Morning News*, June 2, 1931.

47. Gambrell to author, March 3, 1971.

48. *Minutes of the North Texas Annual Conference, 1932* (R. G. Mood, publisher, n.p.,n.d.), p. 39. These were the charges leveled against Shuttles at the North Texas Conference in 1931.

49. Oddly enough it was not considered inappropriate for faculty members to serve on the board. There were three such cases, Selecman from the North Texas Conference, James Kilgore from the Texas Conference, and W. D. Bradfield, elected at large.

50. *Minutes of the North Texas Annual Conference, 1931*, p. 41. See also *Dallas Times Herald*, October 30, 1931.

51. *Minutes of the North Texas Annual Conference, 1932*, p. 39.

52. Ibid.; see also Walter N. Vernon, *Methodism Moves across North Texas* (Dallas: Historical Society of North Texas Conference, 1967), pp. 271-72.

53. Minutes of the General Faculty, February 15, 1933.

54. Report of the Committee on Faculty Reorganization, 1932-33, Fondren Library, SMU, p. 3.

55. These groups were (1) English and arts, (2) foreign languages, (3) social sciences, (4) science and mathematics, (5) education, and (6) commerce.

56. Report of the Committee on Faculty Reorganization, pp. 3-4.

57. See chap. 8, n. 55.

58. Faculty Minutes of College of Arts and Sciences, September 28, 1919, September 30, 1920, October 3, 1922.

59. Report of the Committee on Faculty Reorganization, p. 6; Minutes of the Faculty of the College of Arts and Sciences, September 19, 1933.

60. The names of the members of the College Council are printed in the annual *Bulletin*. In only three instances were the appointees of President Selecman elected to the council.

61. Gambrell to author, March 3, 1971; oral interview with Mouzon, August 18, 1970. Mouzon was a member of the Boon committee and did most of the writing of the report.

62. Oral interview with Hemphill Hosford, January 20, 1971.

63. Report of the Committee on Better Teaching, 1935, personal possession of Mrs. Bowyer, Dallas, Texas.

64. Ibid.

65. Minutes of the Board, June 1, 1931.

66. Ibid.

67. Ibid.

68. Ibid., June 1, 1931 and June 7, 1932.

69. See chap. 6, p. 116.

70. Minutes of the Board, June 6, 1933.

71. Oral interview with Gilbert Jordan, professor emeritus of German, August 12, 1970, Dallas, Texas.

72. Minutes of the Board, January 18, 1937.

73. See chap. 6, p. 110.

74. John M. Moore, *Life and I* (Nashville: Parthenon Press, 1948), p. 210.

75. Minutes of the Board, February 4, 1936, and June 1, 1936.

76. Ibid., June 4, 1934.

77. Ibid., January 18, 1938.

78. Ibid.

79. Ibid., June 1, 1937, June 7, 1938, June 2, 1943.

80. Annual Report of the Registrar to the President, 1931-40, Office of the President, SMU.

81. Ibid.; the enrollment figures for every five years are as follows:

YEAR	NUMBER	YEAR	NUMBER
1915	706	1930	3,110
1920	1,118	1935	3,112
1925	2,530	1940	3,921

82. Minutes of the Board, January 31, 1934.

83. Ibid., June 4, 1934.

84. Annual Report of the Registrar, 1939-40.

85. The registrar's reports show the following figures:

YEAR	PERCENTAGE DALLAS STUDENTS
1929-30	56
1934-35	64
1939-40	61

86. Minutes of the Board, June 6, 1933, and June 1, 1937.

87. Ibid., June 2, 1930, June 1, 1931, June 7, 1932.

88. Report of the College Curriculum Committee, April 15, 1940. Upper class neighborhoods were University Park, Highland Park, Lakewood (52%) and East Dallas, Oak Lawn (25%). Lower class sections were Oak Cliff, downtown Dallas (16%) and South Dallas (7%).

89. Ibid.; see also the reports of the registrar.

90. Elbert L. Hooker, "The Greeks and the Independents: A Study of the Fraternity System at Southern Methodist University," Studies in Sociology 3 (Summer 1938): 5-7.

91. Ibid., p. 10.

92. Ibid., p. 25. These conclusions were reached as a result of interviews with both fraternity and nonfraternity students.

93. Ibid., p. 35. The averages of grade points for both groups for 1937 were: fraternity men, 2.12; nonfraternity men, 2.21; sorority women, 2.47; nonsorority women, 2.70. These figures are based upon a grade point system of "A" equaling four points.

94. The *Campus* listed these activities in the social pages all during the 1930s.

95. Hooker, "The Greeks and the Independents," p. 15. This conclusion was reached by interviews with fraternity students.

96. Report of the Committee for the Study of Social Life on the Campus, January 25, 1935, Office of the President, SMU.

97. Faculty Committee on Student Activities and Organizations to Charles Selecman, January 26, 1935; A. C. Zumbrunnen, dean of students, and Mrs. L. S. Holt, dean of women to Charles Selecman, January 26, 1935; petition from the Student Association of SMU to Charles Selecman, January 26, 1935, all found in the Office of the President, SMU.

98. Minutes of the Board, January 29, 1935.

99. *Campus*, February 8, 1936.

100. Minutes of the Board, June 1, 1936.

101. *Journal of the Uniting Conferences of the Methodist Episcopal Church,* April 26–May 10, 1939 (Nashville: Methodist Publishing House, 1939).

102. Minutes of the Board, June 6, 1939.

103. Ibid., June 1, 1936, June 1, 1937, June 7, 1938.

104. *Campus*, 1932-1939.

105. As a conservative estimate, there were around 30 parties a week, or 120 a month, which, if divided by the 25 fraternities and sororities, would equal 4 to 5 parties a month, or a little more than 1 a week.

106. Oral interview with Lon Tinkle, professor emeritus of literature, January 21, 1970. The author, who was a student at SMU, 1946-48, corroborates this opinion of Tinkle's.

107. Ibid.

108. *Campus*, September 20, 1935.

109. Ibid., September 25, 1937.

110. Minutes of the Board, January 24, 1933.

111. General Report on Southern Methodist University, Presented for Consideration by the Committee on Qualifications of the United Chapters of Phi Beta Kappa, February 27, 1948, Office of the Secretary of Phi Beta Kappa. A charter was granted in 1949.

112. Minutes of the Board, June 1938.

113. Oral interview with Gilbert Jordan, August 17, 1970.

114. The minutes of the board listed the final six candidates as John N. Andrews, W. K. Greene, Guy Snaveley, W. W. Parker, J. N. R. Score, and Umphrey Lee; the *Dallas Times Herald,* May 4, 1938, suggested Umphrey Lee, Eugene B. Hawk, J. N. R. Score, and Paul Quillian as major candidates; Winifred Weiss and Charles S. Proctor, *Umphrey Lee: A Biography* (Nashville: Abingdon Press, 1971) lists J. N. R. Score, Paul Quillian, W. M. Alexander, Eugene B. Hawk, John T. Anderson, and Umphrey Lee. Evidently both Hawk and Quillian asked that their names not be considered.

115. Weiss and Proctor, *Umphrey Lee*, p. 231.

116. John W. Bowyer, "Lee Elected President," *Mustang* (December 1938), p. 5.

117. Weiss and Proctor, *Umphrey Lee*, p. 9.

118. Speech by Umphrey Lee, *Dallas Morning News*, March 15, 1939.

119. Minutes of the Board, June 6, 1939.

120. Lon Tinkle, a review of *Umphrey Lee, Dallas Morning News*, January 17, 1971.

Bibliography

DESPITE THE FACT that Southern Methodist University is more than half a century old, little has been written about the history of the institution. After the death of Robert S. Hyer in 1929, President Selecman and the Board of Trustees became aware that the history of the university was going to be lost unless it was recorded. A. F. Henning, professor of journalism, was asked to write a history of the founding and first fifteen years of the life of the university. In 1930 he produced a two-volume manuscript, "The Story of Southern Methodist University, 1910-1920," which is not a true history but rather a collection of copies of documents with a thin narrative holding them all together. This manuscript is extremely valuable to the researcher, but it offers little insight into the how and why of events. Though volume 2 contains histories of all the departments written by the current chairmen, these histories proved disappointing because they are vague and general.

Henning relied heavily upon a master's thesis written at SMU in 1926 by John Edward Blair, "The Founding of Southern Methodist University." This thesis concerns the agonizing decision about whether or not Southwestern should be moved; it is a chronological narrative, based on copies of letters and newspaper articles. Two other M.A. theses have been written: Joan Dunning Craig's "SMU under the Leadership of Dr. C. C. Selecman" (1965) and Judith Lynn Petit's "The Founding of Southern Methodist University, 1910-1916" (1965).

Two additional master's theses were useful: Ben Matthew's "History of Polytechnic College" (1931) and Sue Wheatley Kean's "A Study of the Class of 1936 at SMU" (1939). Mary Maud Trippet wrote a Ph.D. dissertation at the University of Illinois (1966) on *A History of the "Southwest Review": Toward an Understanding of Regionalism* (Ann Arbor: University Microfilms, published on demand), which was well done.

The best source for basic information is the minutes of the Board of Trustees, located in the office of the secretary to the board. The annual, and later semiannual, reports of the president to the board, as well as the annual reports of the deans, give a good summary of the events of the previous six months or year and include also a financial report. While these minutes are a good starting place, on many occasions important events are covered in a sentence or two, or their importance is disguised by means of seemingly innocuous statements, so that the minutes have to be used with care. The minutes of the General Faculty, the Arts and Sciences Faculty, the College Council, and the University Council, all kept in the Archives in McFarlin Auditorium, provide the basic information about the actions of the faculty but fail to give much insight into why events occurred. Facts and figures about both faculty and students were best obtained from the Annual Reports of the Dean of the College of Arts and Sciences and the Annual Reports of the Registrar, which are located in the respective offices.

The single most valuable source for the rules and regulations governing the university—entrance requirements, graduation requirements, and the curriculum—was the *Annual Bulletins of Southern Methodist University*, Fondren Library. These volumes also contain lists of students and graduates, with their home towns, which supplemented the reports of the registrar. Lists of faculty, with the names and dates of their degrees, were also invaluable.

The most useful sources which give insight into why and how certain events occurred are personal letters, official correspondence, unpublished manuscripts, and personal reminiscences. Several letter collections, all located in Bridwell Library of the Perkins School of Theology, are available to the researcher. The largest of these consists of 18,449 letters which Bishop Edwin D. Mouzon wrote between 1908 and 1937, and which are numbered and cataloged after a fashion. There is a wealth of material in his letters concerning the planning, founding, and early years of the institution. A much smaller collection of letters written by Bishop John M. Moore is available; these letters offer information especially about the period when Bishop Moore was chairman of the Board of Trustees. There are 2,500 of these, covering the period between 1893 and 1948. Bishop Moore also wrote an autobiography, *Life and I* (Nashville: Parthenon Press, 1948) which includes a small section on SMU. Only about 200 letters written by Bishop H. A. Boaz have been preserved; some of these pertain to the university. Bishop Boaz also wrote an autobiography, *Eighty-four Golden Years* (Nashville: Parthenon Press, 1951), which has several useful chapters about his role in establishing the university and his brief presidency.

E. L. Shettles assembled an interesting collection of letters, now located in the Archives, pertaining to the founding of the university. These letters are not contemporaneous with the events but were written in the mid-1930s. Shettles was a Methodist minister who was trying to prove that

Nathan Powell was responsible for founding Southern Methodist University. He wrote a series of letters asking those who were active at the time of founding what role Powell played. The replies were illuminating, not about Powell, whose role was slight, but about the motives and actions of Hyer.

Few letters of Hyer's are still in existence, but several of his speeches and manuscripts are available in the Archives. Most of these were written after he retired as president and one, written in 1915, and recalling the founding of the university, proved especially valuable because it showed the large role he himself played.

Other manuscripts include an article by Horace Bishop, written on April 17, 1911, immediately after the decision was made to establish a university in Dallas, which gives the most accurate account of that event. Nathan Powell's "Notes on the Founding of Southern Methodist University" was written sometime after 1911 and is an attempt by Powell to claim the honor of having founded the university. His argument is unconvincing, but he throws some light on the subject. Both the Bishop and Powell manuscripts are in the Archives. J. W. Blanton, also a member of the commission that founded the university, wrote of these events as well as some others in 1954 documents, which are in the office of the president; but Blanton's account does not coincide with other sources. Robert Goodloe, professor in the Perkins School of Theology, wrote a history of "Methodism in Texas, 1900-1950" (1951), which contains some useful information on the establishment of the university; this is located in Bridwell Library.

Several faculty members have recorded their recollections of earlier days and have produced reliable accounts. In 1940 Dorothy Amann wrote "Southern Methodist University—1913-1915," which recalled the hectic days before the university opened. She also made a tape recording, in answer to questions, in 1953; but unfortunately the questions were not good ones and she simply told a group of meaningless little stories. Herbert Gambrell prepared two manuscripts which were extremely perceptive. "Something about the Department of History" (1954) analyzes all the members of that department, and "Notes on the Deanship of the College of Southern Methodist University" (1958) provides a brief history of that office. Hemphill Hosford wrote "Southern Methodist University, World War I, 1917-18" (1954), which describes the effect of the war on the infant institution. All of these sources are located in the Archives.

An indispensable manuscript was W. D. Bradfield's "An Interior View of Our Troubles at Southern Methodist University" (1931), which is in the office of the president. Bradfield prepared this manuscript as a defense of President Selecman, but in doing so illustrated also his lack of knowledge about the feelings of the faculty toward Selecman. A revised version of this manuscript was given by Bradfield as a speech at the North Texas Annual

Conference in 1932 and later was printed as a pamphlet, *A Reply to Mr. R. H. Shuttles' Attack upon the President of Southern Methodist University.* It can be found in both Fondren and Bridwell libraries.

In anticipation of the assembling of a history of the university for its fiftieth anniversary, reminiscences were collected from past faculty members and students. The history never materialized; these papers are now preserved in the Archives. The more useful ones came from Harvie Branscomb, Bishop Ivan Lee Holt, Jay B. Hubbell, Goldie Capers Smith, Bishop William C. Martin, Flora Lowrey, C. Franklin Zeek, Edyth Renshaw, Ray Morrison, Mims Thornburg Workman, and Paul van Katwijk. Most were brief letters recounting humorous anecdotes, which have limited value.

A satirical novel, *Pigskin* (New York: Doubleday, Doran, 1929), was written about Southern Methodist University by Charles W. Ferguson. Ferguson was a student in the early twenties. His novel satirized Selecman, but the faculty members portrayed are those of Ferguson's college days. The characters are easy to identify, and even Ferguson himself appears in the novel as the editor of the student newspaper, a role he played in real life. Ferguson was able to capture the spirit and atmosphere of the early Selecman years better than the writer of any letter or manuscript discovered.

The various publications of the university itself provide excellent sources. The most frequently used one was the student newspaper, the *Campus* (1915-   ). Other publications are the yearbook, the *Rotunda* (1915-   ); the SMU *Ex-Students Magazine* (1922-1927); the *Mustang* 1920, 1936-1940, 1946-   ), a publication for alumni; the *Southwest Review* (1924-   ); *Field & Laboratory* (1932-1952), continued as *Journal of the Graduate Research Center* (1952-1970); Studies in Sociology (1936-1940); Arnold Foundation Studies in Public Affairs (1932-1943); and Proceedings of the Institute of Public Affairs (1934-1939). These are all in Fondren Library.

Newspapers were a valuable source. The *Texas Christian Advocate*, the official publication of the Methodist church, a file of which is located in Bridwell Library, was most useful on the founding period, 1905-1915. The *Dallas Morning News* and the *Dallas Times Herald* covered the university closely. Occasional use was made of the *Fort Worth Record*, the *Fort Worth Star-Telegram,* and the *Georgetown Commercial.* Files of all of these are located in Fondren Library.

Wide use was made of the records of the Methodist church. These included articles from the *Bulletin of the Board of Education of the Methodist Episcopal Church, South,* and the Records of Annual Conferences in Texas. The minutes of the Educational Commission that founded Southern Methodist University were highly significant. The reports of the Board of Trustees to the General Conference were often good summaries of developments at the university. All of these church records are in Bridwell Library.

The Fondren Library staff, ever since the days of Dorothy Amann, have consistently collected various mementos, programs, newspaper clippings, pamphlets, etc., in archival boxes, from 1915 to the present. The substantial yield from this source was, however, small.

Oral interviews and letters from students and faculty members were invaluable in gaining insights into events. The following people were generous with their time and observations: Herbert Gambrell, Hemphill Hosford, Edwin D. Mouzon, Jr., Samuel W. Geiser, Lon Tinkle, Morton King, Bishop Paul E. Martin, Layton W. Bailey, Wiggs N. Babb, Charles W. Ferguson, Harvie Branscomb, and Gilbert Jordan.

The university did not use the system of committees and report writing extensively, but there were a few notable reports: Report of the Committee on Faculty Reorganization (1932-33), Report of the Committee on Better Teaching (1935), Report of the Committee for Study of Social Life on the Campus (1935), Report of the College Curriculum Committee (1940), and General Report on Southern Methodist University, Presented for Consideration by Committee on Qualifications of the United Chapters of Phi Beta Kappa (1948). All of these are located in Fondren Library except the last one, which is in the office of the secretary of Phi Beta Kappa.

There are published biographies of two of the presidents. Ray Hyer Brown wrote a biography of her father, *Robert Stewart Hyer: The Man I Knew* (Salado, Texas: Anson Jones Press, 1957). It is written mostly from memory. The book is notable because the author fails to mention H. A. Boaz, despite the close association between Boaz and Hyer. The omission reflects the bitterness and tension between the two men dating from the days when Boaz wanted to move Southwestern to Fort Worth. Winifred Weiss and Charles S. Proctor are the authors of *Umphrey Lee: A Biography* (Nashville: Abingdon Press, 1971), which is a chatty, informal account of the fourth president based largely on his speeches.

Walter N. Vernon's *Methodism Moves across North Texas* (Dallas: Historical Society of North Texas Conference, 1967), provides a clear account of the church in that area and contains several chapters on SMU. *The History of Texas Methodism 1900-1960*, Olin W. Nail, ed. (Austin: Capital Printing Co., 1961) is a collection of articles on various aspects of the church in Texas which only marginally pertain to SMU.

The history of the early Methodist colleges in Texas is covered by Homer S. Thrall in *A Brief History of Methodism in Texas* (Nashville: Methodist Episcopal Church, South, 1894) and Frederick B. Eby in *The Development of Education in Texas* (New York: Macmillan Co., 1925). Eby was for years the leading authority in his field, and his book still shows great understanding of the problems of education.

Education in the South as a whole is covered by Charles William Dabney,

Universal Education in the South (New York: Doubleday, Page & Co., 1926); Edgar W. Knight, *Public Education in the South* (Boston: Ginn & Co., 1922); and Thomas D. Clark and Albert D. Kirwan, *The South since Appomattox* (New York: Oxford University Press, 1967).

General references on Texas history include Rupert Norval Richardson, *Texas, The Lone Star State* (New York: Prentice-Hall, 1943); T. R. Fehrenbach, *Lone Star: A History of Texas and the Texans* (New York: Macmillan Co., 1968); Ralph W. Steen, *Twentieth Century Texas* (Austin: Steck Co., 1942), and John William Rogers, *The Lusty Texans of Dallas* New York: Dutton, 1960). Two excellent general accounts of the dispute over fundamentalism are Norman Furniss, *The Fundamentalist Controversy, 1918-1931* (New Haven: Yale University Press, 1954) and Kenneth K. Bailey, *Southern White Protestantism in the Twentieth Century* (New York: Harper & Row, 1964). Upton Sinclair in *The Goose-Step* (published by the author, Pasadena, California, 1922) criticizes American education, especially its tendency to conform to the doctrines of the fundamentalists. Bishop Edwin D. Mouzon refutes the extreme fundamentalist position in a small book, *So-Called Fundamentalism* (Nashville, 1923).

Useful references on the history of higher education include Donald G. Tewksbury, *The Founding of American Colleges and Universities before the Civil War* (New York: Columbia University Press, 1932); Freeman Butts, *The College Charts Its Course* (New York: McGraw-Hill, 1939); Richard Hofstadter and C. DeWitt Hardy, *The Development and Scope of Higher Education in the United States* (New York: Columbia University Press, 1952); Richard Hofstadter and Wilson Smith, eds., *American Higher Education: A Documentary History* (Chicago: University of Chicago Press, 1961); Frederick Rudolph, *The American College and University* (New York: Random House, 1962); John S. Brubacher and Willis Rudy, *Higher Education in Transition* (New York: Harper & Bros., 1958); Edwin Mims, *A History of Vanderbilt University* (Nashville: Vanderbilt University Press, 1946); Richard J. Storr, *Harper's University: The Beginnings* (Chicago: University of Chicago Press, 1966); and Harold V. Ratliff, *The Power and the Glory: The Story of Southwest Conference Football* (Lubbock, Texas: Texas Tech Press, 1957).

Index